D1601081

NEW PERSPECTIVES ON FAMILY

NCFR   Published in cooperation with National Council on Familiy Relations

Series Editor: **Maximiliane Szinovacz**
University of Illinois, Urbana—Champaign

Series Editor-Elect: **Linda Thompson**
Virginia Polytechnic Institute & State University

Books appearing in New Perspectives on Family are either single- or multiple-authored volumes or concisely edited books of original articles on focused topics within the broad field of marriage and family. Books can be reports of significant research, innovations in methodology, treatises on family theory, or syntheses of current knowledge in a subfield of the discipline. Each volume meets the highest academic standards and makes a substantial contribution to our knowledge of marriage and family.

SINGLES: Myths and Realities, *Leonard Cargan and Matthew Melko*

THE CHILDBEARING DECISION: Fertility Attitudes and Behavior,
   Greer Litton Fox, ed.

AT HOME AND AT WORK: The Family's Allocation of Labor,
   Michael Geerken and Walter R. Gove

PREVENTION IN FAMILY SERVICES: Approaches to Family Wellness,
   David R. Mace, ed.

WORKING WIVES/WORKING HUSBANDS, *Joseph H. Pleck*

THE WARMTH DIMENSION: Foundations of Parental Acceptance-Rejection Theory,
   Ronald P. Rohner

FAMILIES AND SOCIAL NETWORKS, *Robert M. Milardo, ed.*

FAMILIES AND ECONOMIC DISTRESS: Coping Strategies and Social Policy,
   Patricia Voydanoff and Linda C. Majka, eds.

Other volumes currently available from Sage and sponsored by NCFR:

THE SOCIAL WORLD OF OLD WOMEN: Management of Self-Identity,
   Sarah H. Matthews

ASSESSING MARRIAGE: New Behavioral Approaches,
   Erik E. Filsinger and Robert A. Louis, ed.

THE VIOLENT HOME, Updated Edition, *Richard J. Gelles*

SEX AND PREGNANCY IN ADOLESCENCE, *Melvin Zelnik, John F.
   Kantner, and Kathleen Ford*

FAMILIES AND ECONOMIC DISTRESS

Coping Strategies and Social Policy

EDITED BY

Patricia Voydanoff
Linda C. Majka

Published in cooperation with
the National Council on Family Relations

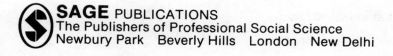
SAGE PUBLICATIONS
The Publishers of Professional Social Science
Newbury Park   Beverly Hills   London   New Delhi

For information address:

SAGE Publications, Inc.
2111 West Hillcrest Drive
Newbury Park, California 91320

SAGE Publications Inc.
275 South Beverly Drive
Beverly Hills
California 90212

SAGE Publications Ltd.
28 Banner Street
London EC1Y 8QE
England

SAGE PUBLICATIONS India Pvt. Ltd.
M-32 Market
Greater Kailash I
New Delhi 110 048 India

Printed in the United States of America

Library of Congress Cataloging-in-Publication Data

Families and economic distress : coping strategies and social policy /
 [edited by] Patricia Voydanoff, Linda C. Majka.
  p. cm. — (New perspectives on family)
  Proceedings of a symposium held at the University of Dayton, Oct.
24-25, 1985.
  Bibliography: p.
  ISBN 0-8039-2999-4 :   ISBN 0-8039-3000-3 (pbk.) :
  1. Family—Economic aspects—United States—Congresses.
2. Unemployment—United States—Congresses. 3. United States—
Economic conditions—1971-81—Congresses. 4. United States—
Economic conditions—1981- —Congresses. 5. Family policy—United
States—Congresses. I. Voydanoff, Patricia. II. Majka, Linda C.
III. Series.
HQ536.F3334 1985
330.973'092—dc19   87-34674
                                                         CIP

FIRST PRINTING 1988

Contents

This book is gratefully dedicated to
William and **Erma Bombeck,**
benefactors of the Center for the Study
of Family Development

Series Editor's Foreword

Hardship brought about by large-scale economic change penetrates to the heart of family life. For families, depressions or recessions mean more than not being able to pay the bills. They mean enhanced marital tensions or closeness, upheaval, or reversal of family roles, impaired life chances and reorientation in values. The psychological and interpersonal consequences of economic hardship have been noted in research on the unemployed and the poor. In his foreword to the 1971 American edition of Marienthal, the study of an Austrian community hit severely during the Great Depression, Paul Lazarsfeld points out "that prolonged unemployment leads to a state of apathy in which the victims do not utilize any longer even the few opportunities left to them" (Jahoda et al., 1971, chap. VII) and emphasizes the similarities between this finding and Michael Harrington's (1963) description of the psychological implications of poverty: "To be poor is not simply to be deprived of the material things of this world. It is to enter a fatal, futile universe. . . ." At its worst, such resignation expresses itself in parents' despair—"I couldn't care less now. . . . If I could hand the children over to the welfare people I would gladly do so" says one of the Marienthal mothers (Jahoda et al., 1971, p. 61)—and in the crushed hopes of children: "The (Christmas) presents the children of Marienthal wanted cost only about one-third as much as the presents the other children (from less depressed areas) hoped to get. And the children barely dared openly to state even these modest wishes. . . . A nine-year-old elementary schoolboy said: 'I would have loved to get a picture album. I did not get anything because my parents are unemployed'" (Jahoda et al., 1971, p. 58). While investigations into the long-term effects of the Great Depression on individuals and families are still underway, the recent recession led to a new wave of studies exploring the immediate and more persistent impact of unemployment. Chapters presented in this volume depict the economic, psychological, and familial consequences of unemployment, review political responses to economic hardship, and provide policy recommendations. Given the divergent approaches and perspectives taken by the chapter authors, the book offers a multifaceted

9

yet well integrated discussion of what unemployment means for families and how policies could alleviate the hardships these families experience. Through its reliance on sophisticated methodologies, through its incorporation of recent theoretical developments (such as family stress theory), and through its in-depth policy analyses and recommendations the volume goes well beyond earlier work. Yet by showing "the pain in family relationships that results from economic instability, uncertainty and deprivation" (Preface) and by combining empirical analyses with sociopolitical critique the book follows in the tradition well worth sponsorthip by the National Council on Family Relations.

—*Maximiliane Szinovacz*

Preface

This book addresses the impact of economic distress on family life. The U.S. economy is undergoing significant and long-term structural changes. Employment in manufacturing industries is declining for white-collar as well as blue-collar workers. Many of those displaced by shrinking manufacturing industries do not have appropriate skills for jobs in the growing sectors of the economy or find it difficult to take lower-paying service jobs. Deindustrialization, job displacement, changes in family structure, and other factors are resulting in increasing numbers of families and children living in poverty.

Economic changes are creating high levels of distress for individuals and families. Distress is reflected in mental and physical health problems for adults and children and family tensions and instability. In addition, local economic problems and federal cutbacks are placing an extreme burden on budgets for human services in the public and private sectors at the same time as needs for social services are increasing. There is a critical need to know more about the types of coping strategies and programs that most effectively prevent or reduce individual and family problems resulting from economic distress.

This book presents the work of an interdisciplinary group of scholars who examine issues dealing with family life and economic distress related to structural economic change. It documents the pain in family relationships that results from economic instability, uncertainty, and deprivation. The studies reported here demonstrate "chain reaction" effects within families and communities as family resources fail to protect members from economic distress, and as the local economy and community institutions—including public, private, and charitable organizations—undergo a declining ability to respond to hardships.

This book is also about the social consequences of economic policies. Many of the chapters reveal how social inequality is aggravated by unemployment and underemployment. The authors assume greater equality is possible especially if social benefits are a direct goal rather than merely a possible byproduct of economic policies. Alternative approaches to existing social policies are explored in relation to empirical studies and analysis of underlying principles and assumptions. Especially important are economic strategies that guarantee adequate employment levels, wages and benefits, and better use of productive skills. Information about these social issues is essential as our society makes choices about the distribution of social and economic resources among different groups and between public and private purposes.

There is a special relationship between the studies in this book and the research on unemployment by sociologists during the 1930s. Much has been learned from the monographs and articles of the Depression that examined the effects of unemployment on individuals and families. However, the original research and scholarship in this collection is more comprehensive in its approach to varieties of economic distress and the range of coping strategies and policy options. Developments in quantitative methods permit studies of large samples, specification of the role of different variables, testing for interactions, and other statistical techniques for documenting family impacts.

The policy analysis is also different in important ways from Depression-era research and much current work. Diverse methodological approaches esesand orientations are brought to focus on families and economic distress, not so much with the idea of reaching consensus, but to open discussion on a broader base of information than most policy analysis starts with. Researchers in sociology, psychology, and economics evaluate existing policies in light of the implications of their data and propose new directions for policy debate.

We wish to express our appreciation to those who contributed to the development and preparation of this volume. The chapters were presented first at a symposium held at the University of Dayton on October 24-25, 1985. We received considerable assistance from the administration and faculty of the University of Dayton. Brother Raymond L. Fitz, S.M., President, and Francis M. Lazarus, Dean of the College of Arts and Sciences, provided support throughout the planning and execution of the symposium. Professors Brenda W. Donnelly and Sandra K. Moore served with us on the symposium planning committee.

The following faculty reviewed and commented on individual contributions: Rita Bowen, Mark Fine, Dean Lovelace, Theo J. Majka, Robert Marotto, Martha May, Sandra K. Moore, Frances G. Pestello, Mary Ruffolo, and Stanley L. Saxton. We also acknowledge the skilled assistance of Lora J. Durham in preparing the manuscript and compiling the references.

We would also like to thank the sociology majors who discussed and evaluated earlier drafts of the manuscript and contributed valuable suggestions for improvements: Hector Cordero, Rachel Hammer, Steve Mitchell, Kathy Oakar, Cheryl Stackhouse, and Missy Wildenhaus.

Generous financial support for the symposium was provided by the William and Erma Bombeck Endowment; the Marianists; Project Extend, Cincinnati Province, Marianists; and the New York Marianist Sharing Fund.

The suggestions of the Sage series editor, Maximiliane Szinovacz, and anonymous reviewers have enhanced the organization, coherence, and content of the book. Our greatest debt is to the contributors to the volume, whose intellectual contributions form the substance of the book.

—Patricia Voydanoff
—Linda C. Majka

PART I

Effects of Economic Dislocation

During the past fifteen years, the U.S. economy has experienced successive recessions and extensive restructuring of major manufacturing industries that produce automobiles, steel, and other durable goods. Since factors contributing to this economic dislocation, for example, increased foreign competition, still operate, we can expect a continuation of current trends during the next several years.

Economic dislocation results in several types of economic distress among individuals and families. These include employment instability and uncertainty and economic deprivation and strain. The chapters in this section document these consequences among blue-collar workers who have experienced layoffs or plant closings. They focus on patterns of unemployment and reemployment, wage changes, and income loss.

Buss and Redburn point out the role of alternative sources of comparable employment in the community and a national recession in determining the level and type of reemployment experienced by workers after a steel mill closing. Their findings indicate that most workers had become reemployed, a majority in manufacturing jobs, or had retired in the eight years following the closing. However, a sizable minority experienced episodic or continuous unemployment or earned lower wages.

Gordus and Yamakawa compare the effects of major layoffs in the automobile industry on female and male workers. Their analysis documents the significance of women's lower seniority, which results from their recent entry into automobile manufacturing, for the different outcomes experienced by women and men. More men had become reemployed and more of the reemployed men had been recalled by the automobile company. Women also encountered economic disadvantages relative to men—they earned a lower percentage of their previous wage if they were reemployed outside the automobile industry and they reported a greater loss of household income following the layoff.

Perrucci and Targ's analysis of the effects of a plant closing on the family life of male and female workers indicates that nine months after the closing a slight majority of workers were reemployed; however, their average hourly pay was substantially lower and almost three-fourths of the respondents were experiencing economic strain. The reported similarity in employment and economic effects found for men and women may be due to the fact that the loss of employment was less tied to seniority than in the Gordus and Yamakawa study of laid-off automobile workers.

Perrucci and Targ also provide a context for the rest of the volume by mapping out some general consequences of economic dislocation for family life. Their findings show that the plant closing had little effect on marital stability; however, marital happiness, family cohesion, and family adaptability were somewhat lower nine months after the closing. These declines, which were similar for women and men, were more strongly related to economic strain than to reemployment status.

This section also provides information that is needed for the formulation and evaluation of political and policy responses to economic dislocation and its effects on families. Buss and Redburn report that retraining and moving outside the area to find employment are relatively ineffective approaches to dealing with economic distress among their sample of steel workers. Gordus and Yamakawa point to the need for women's living and child-care costs to be covered while they obtain additional education and train for alternative employment. This recommendation differs from that Buss and Redburn; however, the women workers were less entrenched in the automobile industry and may have had fewer transferable skills than the Youngstown steel workers. Perrucci and Targ stress the value of advance notification and severance pay as well as the role of internal and external coping strategies in preventing and alleviating the negative effects of plant closings on family life.

1

Reemployment After a Shutdown: The Youngstown Steel Mill Closing, 1977 to 1985

Terry F. Buss
F. Stevens Redburn

Mass unemployment on a scale unprecedented since the Great Depression of the 1930s has renewed interest in studying the impacts of plant closings on workers and their families (Jahoda, 1979). During and immediately following the 1930s, researchers conducted many studies that were, at the time, applications of state-of-the-art social science research methodology. Jahoda, Lazarsfeld, and Zeisel's (1971) study of Marienthal, along with Bakke's (1940) study of unemployed men are best known. During the 1960s, several classic studies of plant shutdowns were undertaken, but there was no broad effort by social scientists to examine such events (see Foltman, 1968; Aiken, Ferman, and Sheppard, 1966; Slote, 1969; Wilcock and Franke, 1963;

AUTHORS' NOTE: This research was supported by the Ohio Department of Mental Health (ODMH), the National Institute of Mental Health (NIMH), and Youngstown State University as part of the Ohio Board of Regents Urban University Demonstration Program. The authors thank Dee Roth, ODMH, for her support and encouragement. The authors assume sole responsibility for the views, interpretations, and conclusions contained in this chapter.

Schultz and Weber, 1966). In contrast to earlier periods, the study of plant closings since the late 1970s has seen the application of modern social science and psychometric techniques to virtually every aspect of mass unemployment and its impacts, at both individual and community levels. Cobb and Kasl (1977), Mick (1975), Hansen et al. (1980), Weeks and Drengacz (1982), Strange (1977), Sadler (1984), Hudson and Sadler (1985), and many others (see Buss and Redburn, 1983a, 1983b; Fisher, 1983, for reviews) have examined various aspects of the plant closing phenomenon.

Given that the impact of plant closings has been studied on and off for some fifty years, it is ironic that the long-term effects of mass unemployment have not been rigorously examined (Jahoda, 1982). At best, most studies have based their findings on one- or two-year panel studies (e.g., Cobb and Kasl, 1977; Cohn, 1978; Buss and Redburn, 1983b). This absence probably has more to do with biases toward short-term work inherent in the system of funding and rewards for social science research in general than with the perceived importance of the research question. Indeed, there is reason to think that the longer-term effects of mass unemployment may be substantial (see Buss and Redburn, 1983a, chap. 9). To be sure, researchers have studied the effects of long-term unemployment from data gathered in national longitudinal panel surveys of the general public (e.g., Flaim and Sehgal, 1985; Bendick and Buss, n.d.; Hill and Corcoran, 1979; Department of Health and Social Security, 1985), but these studies do not provide the local plant closing focus that is so important to understanding individual, family, and community-level impacts.

In this chapter, we report the preliminary results of our long-term study of workers whose jobs were initially terminated in September 1977 with the closing of the Campbell Works of the former Youngstown Sheet and Tube Company—at the time one of the nation's largest steel mills, employing nearly 4,100 workers. The initial studies were conducted on nearly 300 workers during the summers of 1978 and 1979, one and two years following the shutdown. A follow-up study of 155 workers was completed in the summer of 1985, eight years later. Although our study concerns the multidimensional impacts of the closing, attention in this chapter has been focused on the employment status of workers, past and present, and on their prospects for the future. The complete analysis will be presented in a book-length report.

SOME EXPECTATIONS

Our prior research, and the literature on plant closings, generally, had led us to the following expectations about worker behavior eight years after a shutdown.

(1) Few workers will be unemployed; most will be either retired or reemployed.

Retirement should be a reasonably attractive option for many workers. Steelworkers tend to be older than workers in other manufacturing trades, in part because of the nature and quality of their work life: The previous long- term stability of employment, a tradition of generations of family employment in the mills, the attraction of the highest industrial blue-collar wage, and excellent fringe benefit packages all had led to a stable senior work force. At the time of layoff, many were eligible for and took early retirement; in the subsequent years, others have reached retirement age (see Bould, 1980).

For those unable or unwilling to retire, reemployment prospects appeared good. Many former steelworkers are highly skilled in trades that should be transferable to other industries: carpenters, bricklayers, iron-workers, plumbers, welders, and so on. Other workers who did not possess skills transferable to other industries had good work records and other characteristics that would make them good candidates for retraining. From a business perspective, therefore, this group of laid-off workers represented a pool of readily available, high-quality labor.

The reemployment of an experienced skilled work force obviously is facilitated by the presence of other expanding industries. Many distressed communities do create jobs (Vaughan, Pollard, and Dyer, 1985); and in the Youngstown area in the 1978-1980 period, there were many jobs available due to turnover caused by retirements and other terminations and to growth in autos and services. This reinforced our expectation that, after several years, most nonretired, laid-off workers would be employed. In fact, this was the experience of most in the first year or two following the closing (Buss and Redburn, 1983a).

(2) Whether employed or unemployed, workers will have experienced episodic unemployment spells.

The closing of Youngstown Sheet and Tube in 1977 was the beginning of a particularly volatile economic period for the region. Severe industrial restructuring saw many of the remaining steel mills in the region shut down or drastically curtail operations. In the local auto industry, employment initially grew but was retarded when Japanese imports of automobiles in the United States gained a substantial market share. Two back-to-back recessions during the period were accompanied by sharp drops in employment across all those industries affected by the business cycle (Liu and Stocks, 1983). Because this was a period of economic upheaval and because the reemployed steelworkers would have little seniority in their new jobs, it seems likely that many would experience repeated spells of unemployment (Buss and Redburn, 1983b).

(3) Most workers will seek and find jobs after Unemployment Insurance benefits are exhausted.

Unemployment Insurance (UI) benefits are intended to support jobless workers financially during temporary periods of involuntary unemployment. Receipt of UI benefits reduces the cost of unemployment, thereby encouraging workers to look longer for jobs that better suit their needs and skills. It is hypothesized that most workers will exhaust or nearly exhaust their UI benefits in order to help them secure the best possible job (Young, 1979; Katz and Hight, 1977).

(4) Workers who have found replacement jobs will be working primarily in manufacturing.

Ferman and Gordus (1979, p. 195) hypothesize that layoffs produce a chain of job changes involving many workers not initially affected: "The displacement and replacement of some workers by others (bumping) and the taking of jobs that provide less status, offer less income or fewer fringe benefits, or less protection from arbitrary work practices (skidding)." However, the lack of transferable skills may set limits on the range of jobs into which steelworkers can "bump" or "skid."

Most steelworkers will not take jobs in the service sector, either because they are unqualified (for instance, for many jobs requiring computers, as is the case with accounting, finance, or other business services) or because they view service jobs (such as those in fast-food restaurants and department stores) as undesirable. If manufacturing jobs are to be had anywhere, it is likely that steelworkers will seek these out in preference to others (Bendick and Buss, n.d.).

(5) Most workers will not seek retraining opportunities and, when they do, retraining will not be associated with higher-skilled, higher-paying jobs.

Retraining is expected to play a minor role in creating job opportunities for steelworkers. First, most publicly subsidized training programs provide only entry-level skills. Most highly skilled workers resist these programs (Bendick, 1983). Second, laid-off workers, until recently, were not eligible for many subsidized programs (Beauregard, Van Horn, and Ford, 1983). Therefore, many opted not to expend their own scarce resources on what they perceived as a risky, low pay-off venture (Foltman, 1968; Schultz and Weber, 1966). This avoidance of retraining investment with personal resources is made worse because federal and state tax laws do not permit workers to deduct the cost of training (Buss and Redburn, 1983a). Third, jobs in the local economy, although perhaps not preferable to those lost, were available to many workers who sought them out (see Bagshaw and Schnorbus, 1980).

(6) Few workers will have left the area to search for greener pastures in other communities.

By all accounts, the steelworkers are deeply rooted in their community, so much so that they are unlikely to leave in search of jobs elsewhere. Several reasons may be cited for this lack of mobility. First, many steelworkers have lived their entire lives in tightly knit ethnic communities. This makes moving not merely an economic choice but the abandonment of a familiar web of social relationships and commitments for a potentially strange, hostile, lonely environment. Second, during the years following the closing, many other places in the United States also experienced major job losses. Workers, probably correctly, calculated that their chances for security were better at home than elsewhere. Third, moving without promise of a job or traveling in search of a job is very expensive, even with possible assistance from government. Most workers, therefore, were expected to stay home (Ferman, 1971; Samuelson, 1980).

(7) Most of those who are employed will hold jobs that are lower paying than jobs they held as steelworkers.

Over the past few decades, steelworkers have been (although they may not, because of wage concessions and new labor contracts, continue to be) among the highest paid industrial workers. In the Youngstown area, the only jobs approaching this pay range are those in the auto industry; and these levels are often reached only with extensive overtime work and seniority jobs. Jobs taken by most laid-off steel workers will necessarily be at lower wages (Ohio Legislature, 1980).

(8) Because workers will have lower-paying jobs than previously, it is likely that many spouses will also be working. If a worker is unemployed, the spouse is likely to be working.

Because steelworkers were so well paid in the past, most had achieved a comfortable standard of living that they sought to maintain at lower wages, with financial help from a working spouse. If the worker is unemployed, a working spouse will be necessary, in most cases, just to make ends meet.

Mediating Factors

The general expectations summarized above may be mediated by a number of factors (see King, 1982) as follows:

(9) Marital status will not be associated, in any straightforward way, with successful reemployment.

Married workers generally can rely on their families to support them during times of crisis. This support ranges from the social/psychological—offering an understanding ear or encouragement—to financial support—providing enough income to allow the unemployed worker to search longer for a suitable job. Marriage can be burdensome, however, when one or both spouses are unemployed. Mutual support in the family may dwindle the longer a worker remains unemployed. Eventually, lack of support can lead to major family crisis: divorce, child abuse, spouse abuse, or alcohol and drug problems. This is especially the case when no family members are working. Divorce or separation may be one indication that a worker was unable to cope with the stresses of job loss. Previously single workers, in contrast to others, may lack the social support offered by the family, but escape the burden of family responsibilities. As the foregoing statements suggest, marriage and coping are likely to be associated in complex ways that defy generalization.

(10) Minority workers may have more difficulty than others in finding new jobs.

Racial discrimination, past and present, affects the employment chances of minority workers. Minorities are often "last hired and first fired" under conditions of fluctuating labor demand. When a local economy declines, therefore, minority workers can be expected to experience greater difficulty than others of equal circumstances in securing jobs (Sinfield, 1981).

(11) The older a worker becomes, the lower the probability the worker will find a new job.

On balance, the U.S. labor market appears biased against older workers. Companies often are reluctant to hire those with few productive years left to work. Some older workers, especially those in the steel industry, have health problems that preclude employment in many jobs. Others, who entered the labor force when education was not as important as it is today, may find that younger, educated workers are replacing them in the labor force. Older displaced workers, therefore, are expected to be less employable than others (Sheppard, Ferman, and Faber, 1959).

(12) The higher the laid-off worker's level of education, the greater the chances for successful reemployment.

The more formal education a worker has, the wider the range of jobs for which he or she is qualified. A grade school education is insufficient even for widely available entry-level service jobs. A worker with at least some college-level courses is employable in a variety of white-collar positions. Education, then, is likely to be associated with success in obtaining a replacement job (see Lipsky, 1970).

THE CLOSING OF
YOUNGSTOWN SHEET AND TUBE

On September 19, 1977, the Lykes Corporation announced that it would close the Campbell Works of its giant subsidiary, Youngstown Sheet and Tube Company. Nearly 4,100 workers lost their jobs, some immediately and most others by the end of that year (see Redburn and Buss, 1984, for an overview). This closing was the first of many shutdowns in the local steel industry. Over the next eight years, Jones and Laughlin, U.S. Steel, Republic Steel, Wean United, Pollock, and many other firms either permanently shut down major Youngstown area mills or greatly curtailed operations through retrenchment. Of the 30,100 area jobs in basic steel-making in 1973, only 7,300 remain. Most of those remaining are in jeopardy of termination. In the face of such massive losses, workers whose experience and skills would ordinarily have allowed them to find other steel jobs saw such possibilities disappearing wherever they turned.

Although the community over this period tried to develop an effective response to this wave of closings, most efforts either failed to address the needs of workers or were ineffective in reaching the large numbers in need (see Buss and Redburn, 1983a, 1983b, 1980). Most workers were largely on their own in dealing with unemployment.

Government efforts at alternative job creation were almost totally unsuccessful. And aside from a temporary rise in automobile industry employment, the marketplace failed to produce new jobs. All manufacturing jobs in the area declined from 93,000 in 1973 to about 53,000 in 1985. Today, government, hospitals, schools, and grocery stores constitute the region's largest employers.

ABOUT THE STUDY

Detailed personal interviews with the Youngstown Sheet and Tube workers were conducted approximately 8 months (summer 1978) and 18 months (summer 1979) after layoffs began. Respondents were selected so as to be statistically representative of the work force at the end of 1977. The workers were union members, hourly employees, and engaged in steel production or administration, but were not considered management. In total, 273 were interviewed in the first year and 150 in the second year of the study. A more complete description of the sample is given in Buss and Redburn (1983a, 1983b).

Workers from the initial 273 interviewed in 1978 were contacted again in the summer of 1985, in an effort to reinterview them or, failing that, to discover what happened to them since the closing.

Of the original 273 interviewed, 155 (56.8%) were reinterviewed. Another 61 workers (22.3%) were located and minimal information about their employment status was obtained from one or more informants. In total, 57 (20.9%) were, for a variety of reasons, unaccounted for. [1]

Sample Characteristics

Table 1.1 summarizes the characteristics of displaced workers in the study sample in 1985. Nearly all (98.7%) of the workers interviewed are males, reflecting the character of that male-dominated industry. Whites account for about four-fifths of those interviewed. The steelworkers, as noted earlier, were on average much older (51.3 years) than those in the Youngstown area labor force (38.4 years). Most workers (about 98% of the sample) are, or were at one time, married. In total, 70% are high school graduates. [2]

FINDINGS

Labor Force Status
Eight Years Later

Our initial expectations about the status of displaced workers eight years following the shutdown were somewhat optimistic (see Table 1.2). In 1985, two-thirds of those laid off eight years earlier were either reemployed (32.4%) or retired (34.3%). The remaining one-third (33.3%) were now unemployed (14.4%), had left the area (13.4%), or were deceased (4.6%).

The magnitude of the closing's impact is more apparent when the percentages above are converted into numbers of workers affected. Applying the percentages to the 4,100 originally laid off: 1,328 are now employed, 1,406 are retired, 590 are jobless, 549 have moved away, and 189 are deceased.

Comparison with other studies. The labor force status of those affected by a single plant shutdown is difficult to interpret without baseline data. Fortunately, in this instance, two recent studies permit such comparisons. In January 1984, the Bureau of Labor Statistics conducted a nationwide survey of workers who had been permanently laid off in plant closings after January 1979 (see Flaim and Sehgal, 1985). This study was replicated in the Youngstown/Warren area in June 1984 (Buss, 1984, 1986).

In all three studies, displaced steelworkers had about the same level of employment: BLS at 45.7%, Youngstown at 40.8%, and Sheet and Tube at 40.8%. Where the studies differ is in terms of unemployment and retirement (including those not in the labor force): the BLS (38.7%) and Youngstown (35.7%) labor market studies show that nearly two-fifths of all workers dislocated from the steel industry, between 1979 and 1984,

TABLE 1.1
Demographics of Displaced Workers in 1985

Demographic	N	%
Sex		
Male	147	98.7
Female	2	1.3
Race		
White	117	81.8
Black	22	15.4
Hispanic	3	2.0
Age		
65+	27	18.5
55 to 64	41	28.1
44 to 54	32	21.9
33 to 43	34	23.3
28 to 32	12	8.2
Marital Status		
Married	136	91.9
Single	3	2.0
Widowed	3	2.0
Divorced	4	2.7
Separated	2	1.4
Education		
Grade School	16	10.9
Some High School	28	19.0
High School/Voc. Tech.	63	42.9
Some College	32	21.8
College	7	4.8
Grad School/Prof.	1	0.7

were unemployed and looking for work as of January 1984 and June 1984, respectively, compared to only 16.9% of the former Sheet and Tube workers; on the other hand, nearly twice as many Sheet and Tube workers (42.2%) had dropped out of the labor force when compared with their counterparts nationwide (15.6%) and locally (23.5%). [3] In other words, seven to eight years after the layoffs, many of the Sheet and Tube workers had abandoned the search for new jobs.

Demographics. Not all demographic characteristics of displaced workers are related to current employment status as expected (see Table 1.3). As expected, minorities (blacks, Hispanics, and others) are

TABLE 1.2
Employment Status of Displaced Workers
Eight Years Following the Closing

Current Employment Status	Interviewed		Other[a]		Total[b]	
	N	%	N	%	N	%
Employed	63	40.8	7	11.5	70	32.4
Unemployed	26	16.9	5	8.2	31	14.4
Retired	65	42.2	8	13.1	74	34.3
Deceased	NA	NA	10	16.4	10	4.6
Moved	NA	NA	29	47.5	29	13.4
Unknown	NA	NA	2	3.3	2	0.9
Total	155	99.9	61	100.0	216	100.0

a. Interviews were not conducted with respondent, but reliable information about employment status was obtained from another person.
b. Total of those interviewed and others.

much more likely to be unemployed in 1985 than whites. Age proved to be a good predictor of employment status, but not as hypothesized: Rather than employment prospects decreasing with age, quite the opposite has been the case here. Marital status is not associated with current employment. Education, surprisingly, also is not associated with current employment status: Those with less education are just as likely to be employed as those with more education.

Unemployment rates compared. It is instructive to compare the current unemployment rate (defined as the number of unemployed divided by the sum of the unemployed and employed) among the displaced Sheet and Tube steelworkers with that, as of June 1984, for the entire Youngstown area labor force (Buss, 1986).

Although only 16.9% of those laid off from the Sheet and Tube closing are unemployed, when this rate is converted to an unemployment rate comparable to the standard labor force statistic, those remaining in the labor force have a rate of unemployment nearly twice that of the labor force generally (26.8% versus 16.9%). In other words, these ex-steelworkers are more likely to be unemployed than others in the labor force, despite the fact that many were able to retire and eight years had passed since the initial shock of the mill closing.

This startling and wide difference in unemployment rates is also apparent when comparing workers of the same race or level of education. White displaced steelworkers had a rate about twice (26.0%) that of

TABLE 1.3
Demographics and Employment Status, in 1985,
of Displaced Workers[a]

Demographic	Mean[d]	N	F-Ratio	Significance
Race				
White	1.26	73	3.799	.055
All minorities[b]	1.55	11		
Age				
65+	1.08	12	2.798	.031
55 to 64	1.23	35		
44 to 54	1.38	24		
33 to 43	1.57	14		
28 to 32	1.00	3		
Marital Status				
Married	1.27	81	0.770	.383
No spouse	1.43	7		
Education				
Grade School	1.67	6	1.508	.219
Some High School	1.30	10		
High School/Voc. Tech.	1.29	41		
Some College[c]	1.23	30		

a. Retired respondents are not included.
b. Includes blacks, Hispanics, and other minorities.
c. Includes some college, college degree, and advanced degree.
d. 1 = employed, 2 = unemployed.

the entire labor force (15.0%); while the differential for blacks was slightly less, at rates of 54.5 and 37.2%, respectively. Those laid-off steelworkers with at least a high school education (26.8%) and those with less (43.7%) also had approximately twice the rates as their counterparts in the labor force generally (14.4% and 27.0%, respectively). Among those in their prime working years—age 33 to 64—the former Sheet and Tube workers had at least twice the rate of unemployment as their counterparts in the entire area labor force.

Change in Employment Status

Our all-too-optimistic expectations about employment and retirement may be accounted for in part by looking at labor force status one, two, and eight years following the closing. Unemployment in the first two years after the layoffs lessened from 41.1% in 1978 to 27.3% in 1979. Some of those initially forced to retire early returned to the labor force in that year—that is 24.7% were retired in 1978 but only 19.7% in 1979. Projecting this trend, we expected that within a few years nearly all of the laid-off steelworkers would either find new jobs or retire; but this was not the case.

Episodic employment. The Sheet and Tube workers' current employment status reveals only part of the pain produced by job loss in the long term. For some workers, spells of unemployment have been frequent. Well over one-half (57.2%) of those employed and nearly one-fourth (23.1%) of those now unemployed held at least two jobs after the shutdown. Among those remaining in the labor force (i.e., those employed or unemployed), 47.2% have experienced episodic unemployment. Episodic employment did not affect some groups more than others.

Unemployment duration. The crisis of job loss is presumed to be less for those who are reemployed quickly or at least before Unemployment Insurance has been exhausted. Of the workers remaining in the labor force eight years after the closing, some 28.1% obtained a job before UI benefits were exhausted—that is, within six months. Of these, 24.0% are now unemployed (see Table 1.4). Others obtained jobs only after six months or more. Nearly one-half (49.4%) of these found alternative employment. Of those who took longer to find new jobs, 13.6% are now unemployed. In other words, workers who took longer to find or accept a job are now more likely to be employed than those who took much less time.

Not to be overlooked is the fact that about one-half (53.8%) of the currently unemployed had failed to find any job following the closing. Translating this into possible numbers affected, as many as 450 workers in the original 4,100 work force have remained in the labor force but have been unable to get a job at any time since the closing. Again, duration of unemployment was unrelated to demographic distinctions.

Jobs in Manufacturing

Of 155 interviewed, 69 workers in 1985 had obtained jobs *at some time* following the shutdown. As hypothesized, most (71.0%) obtained jobs in a manufacturing industry. Of these, only 2 obtained jobs in nondurable goods manufacturing, while the remainder found jobs in durable goods production. Nearly all of the durable goods manufacturing jobs were in metal-forming industries. Those not obtaining jobs in

TABLE 1.4

Episodic Employment and Timing for Reemployment

Current Employment Status/Spells and Timing	N	%
Employed		
Single job obtained	21	33.3
Within 6 months	8	12.7
After 6 months	13	20.6
Several jobs obtained	36	57.2
Within 6 months	11	17.5
After 6 months	25	39.7
Never terminated (LTV acquisition)	6	9.5
Total	63	100.0
Unemployed		
Unable to obtain a job	15	57.7
Single job obtained	5	19.2
Within 6 months	2	7.7
After 6 months	3	11.5
Several jobs obtained	6	23.1
Within 6 months	2	7.7
After 6 months	4	15.4
Total	26	100.0

manufacturing were employed in public utilities (n = 2), retail (n = 3), finance (n = 3), repair service (n = 3), personal services (n = 1), government (n = 1), and professional services (n = 7) (e.g., accounting).

This finding helps explain the episodic unemployment of workers observed above. Most terminated Sheet and Tube workers, either because of preference or limited alternatives, took jobs in basic manufacturing industries. These industries, like steel, have experienced major job retrenchments after 1979.

Retraining opportunities. Retraining played a minor role in worker strategies for securing replacement jobs, and the benefits of the programs attended were not especially great. About one-fifth (n = 14) of those who obtained jobs (n = 69) following the closing took advantage of retraining programs offered in the area. Of the 14 enrolling, 9 reported that the retraining helped them secure a replacement job. In only one case—a worker who became a boilermaker—was the replacement job comparable in wage level to that lost at Youngstown Sheet and Tube.

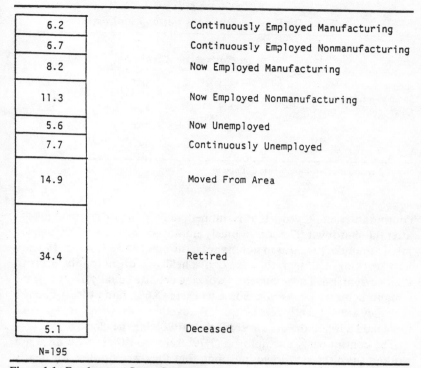

6.2	Continuously Employed Manufacturing
6.7	Continuously Employed Nonmanufacturing
8.2	Now Employed Manufacturing
11.3	Now Employed Nonmanufacturing
5.6	Now Unemployed
7.7	Continuously Unemployed
14.9	Moved From Area
34.4	Retired
5.1	Deceased

N=195

Figure 1.1 Employment Status Summary

Of the 21 workers who were unemployed eight years later, only 4 had enrolled in retraining programs; and none of these was successful in obtaining a job.

The rate of participation in training and retraining programs by displaced steelworkers differed little from that for the labor force in the Youngstown/Warren area generally (Buss, 1984). In June 1984, 16.3% of the area labor force reported participation in such a program within the last two years. In total, 17% of the employed and 14% of the unemployed participated in such programs.

Interim Summary

Findings above may be tied together to present an overview of the past and present status of laid-off steelworkers from Sheet and Tube (see Figure 1.1). Only 12.9% of the original work force remained

TABLE 1.5
Wages for Replacement Jobs Versus Jobs Lost

Wages	Initial Job After Closing	Second Job	Third Job
Higher than job lost	16.4	38.5	61.1
Same as job lost	20.9	17.9	16.7
Lower than job lost	62.7	43.6	22.2
Total	100.0	100.0	100.0
(N)	(67)	(39)	(18)

NOTE: In current, not constant, dollars.

continuously employed—that is, immediately found or retained jobs—
after the shutdown. The continuously employed are just as likely to have
jobs in manufacturing as in nonmanufacturing sectors. Another 19% are
now working, although they may have held one or more jobs prior to
their current job. Those currently working are also equally likely to have
a manufacturing job as not. Some workers (5.6%) had at least one job
that they subsequently lost or quit. Altogether, two-fifths of the work
force held a job in the area at some time following the closing.

The continuously unemployed, 7.7%, represent those who have not
worked since the shutdown, meaning that they were jobless for nearly
eight years. Adding these workers to those above, a little less than one-
half (45.7%) of the laid-off work force remained in the labor market.

Out-migrants constituted about 14.9% of the work force. Although
we have only anecdotal evidence, there is reason to believe that many in
this group have or eventually will return to the area. Those returning
home do so either to accept local job openings or to recover from a failure to secure satisfactory employment outside the area.

The retired are by far the largest contingent in the work force once
at Sheet and Tube. Nearly all of these workers indicated that they were
unlikely to return to the labor market, although some reported that they
would accept jobs.

About 1 in every 20 who worked at Sheet and Tube in 1977 is now
deceased. In a work force where workers are not only older and more
likely to have severe health problems than the average worker, it is not
surprising that this is true eight years following the closing.

Family Finances

For most workers, the closing has meant a substantial loss of income, relative to what they would have earned had they remained steadily employed in the steel industry.

Wages after the shutdown. Over one-third (37.3%) of the laid-off workers who found new jobs initially maintained (20.9%) or increased (16.4%) their wage levels relative to wages earned at Youngstown Sheet and Tube. Nearly two-thirds (62.7%), however, initially earned less than they had at the steel mills.

To the extent that they represent voluntary moves, job changes appeared to lead to a net improvement in employment status for a minority of laid-off workers. Of those who changed jobs after the closing, or who quit their initial job and found a replacement, most were able to improve their wages. Over one-half (56.4%) of those who took a second replacement job either equaled or bettered their previous pay at Youngstown Sheet and Tube. Of those who obtained a third job, 61.1% reported higher wages than from the second job, and another 16.7% reported wages about the same as from the second job.

Working spouse. Many of those still in the labor force—that is, the employed and unemployed—depend on their spouses to contribute to the family's income. About one-half report that their wives are working for pay. Employed workers are slightly more likely (54.2%) than unemployed workers (47.8%) to have a working spouse.

Of all married males in the Youngstown labor force in June 1984, two-fifths (40.7%) had a working wife. However, in the entire labor force, working males were much more likely to have a working wife (42.8%) than were the unemployed (23.7%).

Findings suggest that many families with an unemployed male head of household are additionally penalized in the labor market by not having a working spouse. Apparently, there is a multiplier effect of unemployment in families already hit by unemployment.

Family income. Income levels are another important measure of how severely the closing of the mills has affected the displaced workers over the long term. Workers were asked about their total family income before taxes for the year 1984 (see Table 1.6). Based on their responses, the average laid-off steelworker's family earned about $17,500 in 1984, an amount only slightly less than the Youngstown/Warren labor force average ($17,556) (Buss, 1984). In other words, former steelworkers

TABLE 1.6
Family Income in 1984, Before Taxes, by Selected Demographics

Demographic	Mean	N	F-Ratio	Significance
Total	17,500	148	NA	NA
Race				
Whites	19,500	118	6.709	.011
Minorities	13,250	26		
Age				
28-32	18,500	12	3.629	.008
33-43	17,250	35		
44-54	18,750	31		
55-64	14,750	41		
65+	13,000	29		
Marital Status				
Married	16,750	135	8.761	.004
Others	11,000	14		
Education				
Grade School	16,500	16	3.575	.016
Some High School	16,000	28		
High School/Voc. Tech.	17,500	64		
Some College	18,750	40		
Employment Status				
Employed	19,000	60	8.898	.000
Unemployed	15,000	25		
Retired	12,500	65		

appear to have fared no better or worse than the average worker. However, when working at Sheet and Tube, they were among the highest paid blue-collar workers anywhere.

Although the former steelworkers' wages have averaged about the same as those of other workers in the labor force, important differences are apparent. For those workers in our sample, income levels vary in predictable ways.

(1) Whites have higher incomes, on average, than blacks.
(2) Married couples typically have higher incomes than those who are single, widowed, divorced, or separated.
(3) Educated workers earn more, on average, than those with less education.
(4) Workers in their prime work years (ages 28 to 54) have higher incomes than older workers.

(5) Employed workers earn more than either the unemployed or retired; but surprisingly, unemployed workers have about the same level of income as the retired.

CONCLUSION

The conventional wisdom about the long-term effects of plant closings, developed primarily from anecdotal evidence or extrapolated from longitudinal studies of the unemployed generally, is only partly consistent with the preliminary findings reported here on the long-term impacts of the Youngstown closing. These results suggest that the long-term effects of plant closings are more substantial than might have been expected, given the relatively rapid reemployment of most nonretired workers after their first layoffs.

We had assumed that the rapidly expanding economy of the mid-1980s along with the option of many workers to seek early retirement or eventually to become eligible for retirement, would have permitted nearly all of the displaced steelworkers who desired new jobs to obtain them. Within the first two years following the layoffs, those who were most employable—that is, skilled, educated, nonminority workers—were quickly absorbed into the labor force. These early layoffs immediately preceded a period (1978-1980) during which durable goods manufacturing expanded in the Youngstown area. Although reemployment and retirement did reduce joblessness, the displaced work force was still unemployed in mid-1985 at a rate well above that of the labor force as a whole.

Undoubtedly, this results partly from recessions experienced by regional and world economies after 1980, which cut deeply into demand for steel. Having taken jobs in basic manufacturing, either because of preference or for lack of other opportunities, many steelworkers who initially found replacement jobs found those jobs being eliminated in a new wave of closings and reorganization. Those who found no jobs initially were unable to reenter the labor force. Prolonged difficulty in finding new work locally may also have increased the proportion who eventually left the region in search of jobs.

Both initial and later reemployment of the laid-off workers in manufacturing and higher-level service sector jobs casts doubt on Ferman and Gardner's "bumping and skidding" hypothesis. Rather than displacing or replacing workers competing for entry-level or lower-status jobs, laid-off steelworkers, at least in this closing, either were jobless, were retired, or held jobs not open to workers competing at a lower level. It is essential that public policy initiatives continue to address the needs of displaced workers through time. Otherwise, the core of the labor force may begin to slip into a labor reserve, only weakly attached to work. Once in the reserve, it is unlikely, we suspect, that displaced workers can be restored to productive employment easily or quickly.

Unemployment Insurance, job search assistance, retraining, and other components of the standard package of public benefits for displaced workers have been of limited value under these conditions. This is not surprising in light of previous research suggesting the limited utility of such measures, even in better economic circumstances (Beauregard, Van Horn, and Ford, 1983).

Perhaps more important for purposes of policy development is the finding that so many experienced, and, in many cases, skilled workers were either unable or unwilling to move into alternative employment. Other research, at the national level, has indicated that most displaced workers make a fairly rapid adjustment (see Bendick, 1983). Apparently, this is not the case where a series of layoffs in one industry is combined with the near absence of alternatives to which the skills of affected workers are transferable.

Given the pattern of industrial layoffs and plant closings in the United States over the past decade, there soon may be many more communities where large pools of skilled, experienced labor sit idle. The costs of this situation must be measured not only in terms of the accumulating income loss and hardship experienced by the workers and their families and the additional transfer payments and payouts from Social Security and retirement funds this requires, but also in terms of waste of skilled labor at a time when the nation's industrial productivity is lagging and the future of its manufacturing industries is in doubt.

NOTES

1. Those for whom information was unavailable were not residents of the address at which they were last interviewed and were not listed in area telephone books. It was impossible to determine if lack of a telephone listing meant that they had moved from the area, had an unlisted number, had a telephone that was listed in another name, or were deceased.

2. The comparison excludes those in the Sheet and Tube sample who no longer live in the Youngstown area.

3. In our original research design for the 1978 and 1979 study, our sample included 146 workers who were laid off and 138 who were still employed. Those laid off—4,100 jobs were terminated—came from the Campbell Works of Sheet and Tube. Those employed came

from departments remaining open in the Campbell Works and those in the Brier Hill Works—about 1,400 were employed—also of Sheet and Tube. By early 1980, nearly all workers at both Works were laid off. In reporting our figures for 1978 and 1979, we have provided only the employment status for those in the Campbell Works. In 1985, however, we have included all workers from the Campbell and Brier Hill Works. Because workers were similar in both Works, results do not change substantially when groups are separated. The only exception is that those from Brier Hill have a shorter duration (1 or 2 years) of unemployment and slightly less episodic unemployment than their counterparts in the Campbell Works.

2

Incomparable Losses: Economic and Labor Market Outcomes for Unemployed Female Versus Male Autoworkers

Jeanne Prial Gordus
Karen Yamakawa

There are at least two broad categories of studies of the impact of unemployment on individuals and families. One group of studies emphasizes the noneconomic aspects of unemployment, including the negative impact of job loss on physical and mental health, coping and adaptation to the job loss, and a variety of other social and psychological changes associated with unemployment. There are several recent reviews of this (Gordus and McAlinden, 1984; Acosta et al., 1985) that summarize the majority of current research in the area and lay out future research agendas.

AUTHORS' NOTE: We wish to acknowledge the contributions made to this study by Sean McAlinden who developed the coding system, assisted with the questionnaire and performed many analyses. We also acknowledge the assistance of Robert K. Holloway who

The second area of research is concerned with economic and labor market phenomena and most often involves evaluation of programs developed to reduce the duration of unemployment, programs that may indeed have significant psychological effects as well. It has been demonstrated that reemployment has a significant positive effect on mental health measures. A subset of the labor market literature is concerned with permanent job loss for industrial workers. In the two broad categories, but especially in the literature concerned with permanent job loss, women are conspicuous by their absence. When women and unemployment are linked, it is by virtue of their roles as wives of job losers (Buss and Redburn, 1983; Liem and Rayman, 1982). Relatively little work has been done on families, although anecdotal evidence from a variety of social service agencies provides a rich source for hypothesis generation.

A particularly critical issue not addressed in any rigorous fashion is the impact of unemployment on families where the unemployed individual is a woman. Perhaps the most significant feature of the American labor market since World War II has been the rapidly increasing rate at which women have entered the labor force. In the past two or three decades, the rapidly increasing number of households headed by women makes the impact of female unemployment upon families an important policy issue.

For those who hypothesize a relationship between economic deprivation and/or relative economic deprivation and negative social, psychological, and physical effects of unemployment (Ferman and Gardner, 1979), it is obviously important to ascertain the differences between men and women job losers in terms of duration of unemployment, levels of benefits, program participation, program impacts, and final labor market status.

This chapter aims to outline the labor market and economic impacts of unemployment upon women who have had "good jobs" in the auto industry, to ascertain their posttermination level of economic distress

supervised our phone interview staff. The research on which this chapter is based was supported in part by the Office of Automotive Affairs of the U.S. Department of Commerce through the Transportation Systems Center of the U.S. Department of Transportation. We appreciate the support and assistance of then Deputy Undersecretary of Commerce for Automotive Affairs, Michael Driggs, Director of the Office of Automotive Affairs, Russell Smith, and particularly the Director of Economic and Policy Analysis, Albert Warner. Other support for part of this study was drawn from funds made available for a job-search intervention program for displaced workers funded by the U.S. Department of Education's Fund for the Improvement of Postsecondary Education. We appreciate the support of Lynn DeMeester, our program officer, during our work with laid-off autoworkers.

and their program participation, as a backdrop to a discussion of the different types of noneconomic impacts that are likely to affect the different types of families in which these women function. The chapter discusses the findings that indefinite layoff from manufacturing jobs means very different things to women compared to men. In a time when pressures mount for comparable pay for comparable work for women, we find that unemployment related losses to women autoworkers exceed the losses suffered by their male coworkers.

SURVEY DESCRIPTION
AND SAMPLING PROCEDURES

In January 1980, approximately 143,700 hourly workers from the three largest U.S. auto manufacturers were on indefinite layoff. By January 1982, the number of layoffs had risen to 262,254—an increase of 82.5%. In April 1983, a list of those on indefinite layoff from one auto manufacturer, covering four union locals and 33 plant locations, totaling 10,839 individuals was provided to us. This population constituted approximately 5% of all auto worker layoffs in the United States. Besides providing the names and addresses of the population members, the company also provided a number of useful background characteristics corresponding to population members, including local membership, original firm hiring date, last layoff date, firm job classification, and the last firm location from which the population member was laid off. Three of the four union locals, Locals 1, 2, and 4 represented single-firm locations (facilities or plants) and were grouped together in a single semirural county about 40 miles from a large, intensive automobile-manufacturing Midwestern Standard Metropolitan Statistical Area (SMSA). Local 3, in contrast, represented layoffs from 30 firm locations primarily located immediately south of the central city of the automotive SMSA. Together, the four union locals represented laid-off autoworkers from a wide variety of firm locations whose production activities include almost every manufacturing activity directly involved in the automobile-manufacturing process, including final assembly, parts assembly, glass and steel production, modeling activities, and parts distribution.

The population membership, based on provided addresses, could also be broken down by member's place of residence. Over 100 municipalities (cities, towns, and townships) were represented in the population, and were grouped into six basic labor market regions based on significantly different average unemployment rates. Regions 1, 3, 4, and 5 were all located in the automotive SMSA itself, with Region 1 being the central city itself. Region 2 was the semirural county where three of the union locals were located, and Region 6 was a catch-all category for outstate and out-of-state member residences. Layoffs from all four locals were included in all six of the regions.

Using firm hiring and last layoff date records, it was possible to determine both the company seniority and time since layoff of the population membership, as of April 3, 1983. The average company seniority of the laid-off population was 74.5 months at the firm (SD of 44.1) and the average time since layoff was 20.8 months (SD of 17.3). Of special interest was the proportion of the population with 12 or fewer months since layoff, the approximate maximum coverage of unemployment compensation benefits with extensions, and the proportion of the population with more than 12 months since layoff.

With regard to sampling procedures, our primary concern was to choose a sample size large enough both to minimize sampling error on certain basic estimates and not to exceed the expected capacity of our research team. The method of proportionate stratified random sampling of the population was used in order to make the most efficient use of the known population characteristics in order to lower sampling error. A sample of 740 members of the population was thus drawn at a sampling percentage of 6.8%.

Four basic coded population background characteristics were used to divide the population into substrata. They included union local membership, involvement in a plant closing, whether the member was laid off more than 12 months or not, and labor market region residence. Three primary criteria were used in selecting these characteristics for use in sample stratification:

(1) Whether this characteristic was thought to affect the variance of the probability of reemployment of the laid-off population member, based both on results shown in the literature and on the survey research team's experience.
(2) Whether this characteristic was thought to affect the variance of the population member's perception of his or her chances of recall, based on both results already shown in the literature or in the survey team's experience.
(3) Whether this characteristic was known for the population and could be coded into a limited number of significant categories, in order to prevent the creation of too many substrata.

TABLE 2.1
Background Characteristics of Survey Population,
Sample, and Respondents

Characteristics	Population (Total N = 10,839)		Sample (Total N = 740)		Respondents (Total N = 379)	
	N	%	N	%	N	%
Union Local						
Local 1	1,384	12.77	93	12.57	49	12.93
Local 2	941	8.68	65	8.78	36	9.50
Local 3	8,217	75.81	562	75.95	282	74.41
Local 4	297	2.74	20	2.70	12	3.16
Plant Closing Layoff Status						
Laid Off from Plant Closing	2,117	19.53	145	19.59	61	16.09
Not Laid Off from Plant Closing	8,722	80.47	595	80.41	318	83.91
Labor Market Region Residence						
Region 1	3,805	35.10	260	35.14	105	27.70
Region 2	2,132	19.67	145	19.59	87	22.96
Region 3	1,067	9.84	73	9.86	44	11.61
Region 4	3,251	29.99	224	30.27	120	31.66
Region 5	409	3.77	27	3.65	18	4.75
Region 6	175	1.61	11	1,49	5	1.32
Layoff Period (Layoff Date to April 3, 1983)						
0–12 Months Since Layoff	4,193	38.68	286	38.65	158	41.69
More than 12 Months Since Layoff	6,646	61.32	454	61.35	221	58.31

Breakdowns of the population, the sample, and respondents by these four background characteristics are given in Table 2.1.

The survey instrument was designed to measure current labor market status, complete employment and earnings histories from the date of last layoff, and the types and amounts of compensation received. Other variables measured included job search and retraining program participation, work history prior to auto employment, as well as personal characteristics and financial circumstances. From these data, three major areas, current labor market status, net income loss and labor market experience from the period 1980-1982, and household income status for

TABLE 2.2
Current Labor Market Status by Gender as of
January 1984 (in percentages)

	Total *N = 379*	*Working,* *not at* *Auto Firm*	*Not Working,* *Looking* *for Work*	*Not Working,* *not Looking* *for Work*[a]	*Recalled to* *Auto Firm*
Total Sample	100.0	24.8	36.1	9.5	29.6
Column					
Male	78.9	78.7	75.9	63.9	87.5
Female	21.1	21.3	24.1	36.1	12.5
Row					
Male		24.7	34.8	7.7	32.8
Female		25.0	41.3	16.3	17.5

a. Data refer to persons who were not working and not looking for work during a 4-week period prior to survey.

one year, 1982, were explored (Gordus, McAlinden, and Yamakawa, 1984).

SURVEY RESULTS

From November 1983 to January 1984, a total of 379 members of the sample responded to our questionnaire. The percentage of women among respondents was 21.1 compared with men who were 78.9% of the respondents. Women have less seniority than men on average. Consequently, the percentage of women among the laid off is higher while the percentage in the active auto work force is lower as the younger workers with lower seniority are placed on indefinite layoff.

Labor Market Status

At the time of the survey, there were marked differences in labor market status between men and women. In this study, four possible situations were identified for laid-off auto workers: working in nonauto, not working but looking for work, not working and not looking (discouraged workers), or recalled to auto firm. In Table 2.2, data on respondents' labor market status is shown. The proportion of reemployed respondents was 57.5% for men and 42.5% for women. The majority (59%) of women who were reemployed were working outside the auto industry while the majority (57%) of reemployed men had returned to the auto employer. Seniority is the predictor of recall to auto employment, and the outcome of such reemployment is generally a higher wage rate.

Labor Market Experience

In Table 2.3, data are presented on male and female status among autoworkers on indefinite layoff, length of layoff, posttermination employment status, and history, layoff wage, current nonauto wage rate, and the wage difference between auto and nonauto wage rates. These data are tabulated for the entire population, and then broken out by post-termination status.

That women had a longer duration (about 25 weeks) of layoff to the time of interview than men could be explained by the fact that women had lower seniority (4.7 years) compared to 6.2 years for men. We have recently observed a similar age gap between women and men in a study of autoworkers currently employed. In many cases, women had problems entering the industry and they are relative latecomers compared with men. In other cases, women joined the automotive work force having lost some time to family activities. Women were also found to be slightly older than men in every group except for those not working and not looking for work. Particularly significant is the comparative length of layoff of those women who were recalled to the auto firm compared with men. Women who were recalled, that is, those highest on the recall queue, had experienced 35.8 more weeks of unemployment than men who had been recalled and women had two fewer weeks of work at the auto firm after recall than men.

As Table 2.3 shows, there are some significant differences across the groups with different labor force status. Those with the lowest seniority, men and women were working at the time of the survey in nonauto jobs. Those with the highest seniority were also working, recalled to the auto firm. The two groups who were not working differed in seniority. Those who were not looking, with 6.5 average years of seniority had some expectation of recall.

In terms of net weeks on layoff, there are some striking differences. Those who were working outside the auto industry, had an average of 141 weeks on layoff, 25 weeks longer than the two groups who were not working. Those not working and not looking and those not working but looking had 116 weeks on layoff, 25 weeks fewer than those who had successfully sought some sort of reemployment. Those who had been recalled had a much lower number of layoff weeks on average, 72.

TABLE 2.3
Labor Market Status by Duration of Unemployment and Reemployment, Wage Rates, Age, and Seniority

	Total Sample N = 379 100.0%			Working, not at Auto Firm 24.8%			Not Working, Looking for Work 36.1%			Not Working, not Looking for Work 9.5%			Recalled to Auto Firm 29.6%		
	Total	M	F	Total	M	F	Total	M	F	Total	M	F	Total	M	F
Weeks from Layoff to Interview Date	114.4	109.0	134.0	141.2	139.5	147.2	116.4	113.0	127.9	116.6	101.5	143.4	88.3	83.9	119.0
Weeks since Recall	–	–	–	–	–	–	–	–	–	–	–	–	15.6	15.9	13.2
Net Layoff Weeks	109.9	103.9	131.6	141.2	139.5	147.2	116.4	113.0	127.9	116.6	101.5	143.4	72.1	67.3	104.8
Total Weeks[a] Worked during Layoff	29.0	28.8	29.8	78.9	79.1	78.1	13.5	14.4	10.2	10.4	6.8	16.8	13.3	13.1	15.0
Weeks on Current[a] Non-Auto Job	–	–	–	57.8	56.5	61.8	–	–	–	–	–	–	–	–	–
Weeks Not Worked during Layoff	81.2	75.6	101.9	64.0	62.4	69.5	103.3	99.0	117.6	106.3	94.7	126.6	58.5	54.0	89.8
% of Net Layoff Not Worked (average % over respondents)	79.6%	79.6%	79.8%	49.5%	49.5%	49.6%	91.5%	90.9%	93.4%	91.7%	95.1%	85.7%	85.5%	85.2%	87.3%
Age (in years)	34.2	33.8	35.5	32.4	31.8	34.5	33.4	32.6	35.9	35.4	37.0	32.7	36.3	36.0	38.4
Seniority (in years)	5.9	6.2	4.7	4.4	4.4	4.3	5.0	5.4	4.0	6.5	7.2	5.2	7.9	8.1	6.5
Layoff Company Hourly Wage	$11.15	$11.33	$10.47	$10.71	$10.96	$9.80	$11.09	$11.19	$10.80	$10.97	$11.27	$10.45	$11.63	$11.80	$10.70
Current Non-Auto Hourly Wage	–	–	–	$7.42	$7.89	$5.67	–	–	–	–	–	–	–	–	–
Wage Difference	–	–	–	$3.30	$3.06	$4.08	–	–	–	–	–	–	–	–	–

NOTE: All figures are average *weekly* figures, except where otherwise noted.

a. Weeks worked at non-auto job are not corrected for temporary layoff periods within starting and leaving dates for those jobs. Net Layoff Weeks: Number of weeks since last layoff date that fell in the 1980-1982 period (Net Layoff Period). % of Net Layoff = Weeks not Worked/Net Layoff Weeks. Wage Difference = Layoff Company Hourly Wage–Current Non-Auto Hourly Wage.

There is not a great difference in the net number of layoff weeks between men and women working outside the auto industry, a group that was 25% of the respondents. This group had the lowest seniority and had also worked more weeks than other groups during the layoff period. Among the remaining 75% of the population, including those not working and looking, those not working and not looking, and those recalled, women had significantly greater numbers of weeks without work than men. Several possible explanations can be suggested for these differences. In a traditional household with a working male, relatively high wage rates are required to attract women, a wage in excess of their household product; and an employed spouse would permit waiting for a higher wage job. However, the area in which this survey was conducted was characterized during the layoff period by extremely high rates of unemployment. Jobs of any kind were scarce and high wages for skilled job openings were virtually nonexistent. Moreover, when the weeks not worked during layoff for both men and women is compared with the percentage of net layoff time not worked, it is clear that women simply had a longer layoff period and worked during that layoff period in the same rough proportion as men did. Women were without work for 79.8% of a 131.6 week layoff period compared to 79.6% of a 103.9 week period for men.

The last three tabulations in this table deal with wage rates. The wage at the auto firm at time of layoff differs for men and women. Since wage rates are relatively flat across many job categories in this industry, the lower wage rates for women reflect the fact that their layoffs occurred a year or more before men's layoffs when the wage rates for all were pegged lower. Some of the difference is attributable to different job classes but the time factor weighs much more heavily. Those recalled, both men and women, have the highest wage rates at the time of layoff reflecting their late layoff and high position on the recall queue. Most significant of all is the reemployment wage rates in new, nonauto jobs acquired by men and women. While men reemployed outside the auto industry were paid roughly 72% of their auto wage rate, women received only 58% of their former wage rate.

Male and Female
Household Income, 1982

In the survey, the research team was able to collect complete data to construct the sources, types, and amounts of household income for a year that was the trough of the recession. In Table 2.4, we show the

TABLE 2.4
1982 Household Income Status by Income Source

Income Source	Average Amount						% of Potential[1] Household Income					
	Total		Male		Female		Total		Male		Female	
	Amount	N	Amount	N	Amount	N	%	N	%	N	%	N
(1) Earnings by Respondent	$9,431.9	310	10,641.0	241	9,963.0	69	33.0	243	36.6	193	17.4	50
(2) Earnings by Family Members	5,838.2	281	5,216.3	220	7,475.4	61	13.6	250	12.7	199	17.0	51
(3) UI & TRA by Respondent	2,065.5	336	2,157.3	263	1,734.7	73	7.5	250	7.9	199	6.2	51
(4) SUB by Respondent	252.9	336	300.5	263	81.4	73	1.0	250	1.1	199	0.4	51
(5) UI by Family Members	156.5	336	171.4	263	103.0	73	0.5	250	0.6	199	0.4	51
(6) Other Compensations[2] by Respondent	552.9	321	508.9	251	710.4	70	2.7	238	2.5	189	3.6	49
(7) Other Compensations[2] by Family Members	172.1	325	131.4	254	318.0	71	0.6	247	0.4	196	1.2	51
(8) Private Contributions	77.8	317	70.5	248	97.1	69	0.2	243	0.2	193	0.5	50
(9) Interest or Dividends	126.8	298	169.9	232	11.2	66	0.4	250	0.4	199	–	51
(10) Total Income	20,065.0	207	20,986.0	166	16,340.0	41	64.0	207	67.8	166	48.6	41
(11) Net Income Loss	9,329.9	207	8,358.9	166	13,261.0	41	36.0	207	32.2	166	51.4	41

NOTE: Average amounts are line estimates based on the maximum number of complete responses for that particular statistic.

1. Potential Household Income: respondent's auto wage loss[3] + earnings by family members + UI and other compensation by family members + business income + interest and/or dividends.

2. Other Compensations:
- Social Security
- veterans' compensation or pension
- workmen's compensation
- aid to the blind or the permanently or totally disabled
- public assistance or welfare payments
- pensions from local, state or federal government
- other compensation type not listed

3. Respondent's Auto Wage Loss: (auto hourly wage + COLA) × 40 hours × 52 weeks.

average household income by source for respondents to this survey. The sources include earnings by respondent, earnings by other household members, and various types of compensation. The average net income loss was 36% for the entire group. These data enable us to estimate hardship during that year.

The contrast between men and women autoworkers in this analysis of posttermination household income is particularly striking, since it reveals the impact in economic terms of the last hired, first laid-off phenomenon. By this stage of the recession, most laid-off autoworkers had either exhausted or come close to exhaustion of Unemployment Insurance (UI) benefits, but women had less benefits left or had been without benefits longer than men since, on average, they had been laid off earlier. Further, although there is not much difference, women collected less Supplemental Unemployment Benefits (SUB), partly because on average they had lower seniority than men, and therefore a lower probability of complete SUB payments. Only those with over 10 years seniority receive full SUB pay (95% of the weekly average wage including UI benefits minus $12) while those with less than 10 years receive different levels of payment depending on the condition of the SUB fund that may be very low in the trough of a recession due to heavy utilization.

The majority of the income replacement for both men and women were earnings by the respondent and by family members. Men who were reemployed replaced more than twice the money that women did. In households headed by male respondents, a lower fraction of the earnings replacement was accounted for by family members, reflecting, no doubt, the probability that married women respondents with working husbands were economically better off than those who were sole supports of families.

But the most important finding about comparative household income is that while men suffered an income loss of $8,358.90 on average (32.2%) women's loss was much higher at $13,261.00 for an average income loss of 51.4%.

The economic impact of the loss of a job in the automobile industry for women is obviously very serious. The detailed data available from this study about earnings replacement shows that, contrary to generalizations about women's position as secondary wage earner, the household income of women autoworkers depends heavily on that job. Real hardship results for those on indefinite layoff.

As shown in Table 2.5, women fared significantly worse than men in terms of household income. First, women received less compensation than men. Over one-half received no compensation at all. Some of this lack of unemployment-related compensation, such as Supplementary Unemployment Benefits, was offset by other forms of need-based compensation, such as AFDC and Food Stamps, but still over one-half the women received no compensation. These differences can be attributed to low seniority and long layoff, two variables that are closely associated with each other. In general, women had exhausted all compensation eligibility by 1982. The fact that their private earnings were well below those earned by men, despite the longer layoff period in which to gain reemployment, accounts for the greater income loss and the larger incidence of poverty.

Finally, as shown in Table 2.6, unmarried women were more likely to fall below the poverty level. Almost 35% of single women experienced poverty in 1982 compared to 28% for single men and 23.6% for all married workers.

DISCUSSION

There has been considerable discussion of segmented labor markets. Initially, the labor market was conceptually divided into two segments. One with relatively high wages, good benefits and opportunities for advancement, called the primary labor market is often characterized by stability. The other segment, the secondary labor market, has relatively low wages, few if any benefits, and no opportunity for advancement, and is often associated with instability. Women and minorities are disproportionately represented in the secondary labor market. This school of analysis (Doeringer and Piore, 1971) has recently undergone a revision (Piore, 1975; Schervish, 1981) and an intermediate segment, primary subordinate, was identified that features high wages and benefits but less stability, a situation similar to that encountered by women and to some degree minority workers in the auto industry. As our data indicate, women in the auto industry—an industry with primary labor market jobs—have a more tenuous foothold in that industry and that labor market. They are, because of their late entry and lower seniority, at higher risk for unemployment, longer durations of unemployment when laid off, lower levels of negotiated SUB benefits, and therefore greater financial hardship.

There is a rather significant body of research, notably the work of Louis Ferman and others in the sociological tradition, that makes a strong case for economic deprivation, relative economic deprivation, and

TABLE 2.5
1982 Household Income Status by Gender

Row %	Male 78.3%	Female 21.7%
Potential Household Income (Gross Loss)		
Average	$28,810.0	$29,347.0
Median	$24,586.0	$23,774.0
Total Household Income		
Average	$20,986.0	$16,340.0
Median	$18,500.0	$12,000.0
% of Gross Loss		
Average	67.8	48.6
Median	68.4	49.0
Private Earnings		
Average	$16,900.0	$12,522.0
Median	$15,100.0	$8,000.0
% of Gross Loss		
Average	53.3	35.5
Median	57.2	34.2
UI, TRA, & SUB		
Average	$2,629.1	$1,919.1
Median	$1,514.0	$0.0
% of Gross Loss		
Average	9.6	7.0
Median	5.2	0.0
Other Compensation		
Average	$659.7	$1,063.4
Median	$0.0	$0.0
% of Gross Loss		
Average	2.9	4.9
Total Compensation		
Average	$3,408.1	$3,069.6
Median	$2,430.0	$1,700.0
% of Gross Loss		
Average	11.8	13.4
Median	8.5	7.8

(continued)

duration of unemployment as major predictors of higher noneconomic costs of unemployment. Obviously, women auto workers encounter economic deprivation; they also, compared with their male coworkers,

TABLE 2.5 Continued

Row %	Male 78.3%	Female 21.7%
Income Loss before Compensation		
Average	$12,097.0	$16,573.0
Median	$12,586.0	$17,861.0
Net Income Loss With Compensation		
Average	$8,358.9	$13,261.0
Median	$9,486.4	$14,395.0
% of Gross Loss		
Average	32.2	51.4
Median	30.8	51.0
% Household Below Poverty Level Before Compensation		
Average	38.1	37.2
% Household Below Poverty Level With Compensation		
Average	25.3	29.3

NOTE: Medians are 50% quantile medians. Poverty is defined as falling below the threshold based on a U.S. Department of Agriculture study of the consumption requirements of family by size for 1982.

encounter greater economic deprivation. And, equally clearly, their low seniority means longer durations of unemployment, and a lower probability of being recalled to the auto industry. Unemployment-related stress and physical and mental health risks for women should therefore be higher than they are for male autoworkers.

DECREASING WOMEN'S VULNERABILITY: POLICY IMPLICATIONS AND RECOMMENDATIONS

That there are demonstrable correlations between unemployed status and economic deprivation, and that there are equally demonstrable correlations between deprivation and negative physical health, mental health and social outcomes are accepted in the research

TABLE 2.6

1982 Household Earnings as a Percentage of Potential
Household Income by Marital Status and Gender

		Respondent Earnings	Family Member Earnings	UI & TRA	% Below Poverty Level	
					Before Total Compensation	With Total Compensation
Total Sample (100%)		32.6	13.6	7.5	37.9	26.1
Marital Status						
Married	(62.2%)	34.7	16.9	7.7	33.8	23.6
Male	(52.3%)	38.6	13.9	8.0	34.7	23.9
Female	(9.9%)	9.2	35.2	5.8	27.8	22.2
Unmarried	(37.8%)	29.2	8.4	7.3	44.2	30.0
Male	(25.9%)	32.2	10.2	7.7	44.3	28.0
Female	(11.9%)	22.8	4.3	6.5	44.0	34.8
Gender						
Male	(78.3%)	36.5	12.7	7.9	38.1	25.3
Female	(21.7%)	17.3	17.0	6.2	37.2	29.3

NOTE: Poverty is defined as falling below the threshold based on a U.S. Department of Agriculture study of the consumption requirements of family by size for 1982.

community. Moreover, the casualty in an unemployed family may very well not be the unemployed individual; instead another family member, vulnerable to physical, emotional, or behavioral problems, may exhibit the first difficulties (Gordus and McAlinden, 1984; Buss and Redburn, 1980). However, as we have noted above, little research has been done that establishes connections between high-risk status for unemployment, high-risk status for descent into the secondary labor market, and the associated risk status for negative noneconomic outcomes for women and families. Still, strong inferences based on a series of studies of different types can reasonably be drawn, and from these inferences, policy implications are quite clear.

Proposition: Women in the primary labor market, even those protected by strong unions, are at higher risk for unemployment than their male counterparts.

Proposition: Women displaced from primary labor market jobs are less likely than their male counterparts to secure primary labor market jobs without significant assistance.

Proposition: Women displaced from primary labor market jobs and who are also heads of household are at elevated risk for the rapid onset of serious financial problems that will promote rapid job search and early acceptance of "survival" jobs.

Proposition: Such doubly disadvantaged women are subject to greater risks of enduring relative economic deprivation and downward mobility and thus at higher risk for negative outcomes of noneconomic kinds as well.

Proposition: Families of such doubly disadvantaged women will experience not only the problem of working poverty but of downward mobility, experiences with significant lifelong residues for these children (Elder, 1974).

It is clear that intervention is required for women who have lost a "good job" but who have few if any transferable skills. The benefit of such an intervention, especially for single heads of household, is that it not only returns a breadwinner to productive employment but it is a significant preventive measure for unemployment-related health and mental health problems for laid-off women and their children. However, even autoworkers, who gained access to an excellent array of training programs, may require retraining of a duration that exceeds the period of unemployment insurance. Single women, especially those with dependents, will find the opportunity costs of such training excessive. Still, as other research we have recently completed (Gordus et al., 1986) shows, it is women, even more than men, whose postprogram wage rates are most positively influenced by education.

The policy recommendation that emerges from this research is relatively modest and simple. It is that stipends be made available for living costs for women without other means of support. We propose that these stipends be federally funded, to be used in association with joint labor-management program funds or with Job Training Partnership Act (JTPA) funds and that the stipends be available only while the student remains in good academic standing. We propose that similar formulas as those applied for student scholarships be used, and that such items as child care and transportation costs be included. We further propose that these funds be distributed through the training vendor or postsecondary institution and that any contracts let to these institutions be performance based. This will ensure a serious effort to develop appropriate training for the local labor market, and will also ensure that good job development and placement efforts are made on behalf of these women.

The mechanism proposed here is deliberately set up so as to link stipends and support services to academic performance and should not be considered an income maintenance program. If unemployment compensation payments are not exhausted, their amount should be deducted from the training stipend.

While equity clearly requires that such programs be made available to men as well, the multiple disadvantages suffered by women breadwinners, as well as women's demonstrated eagerness to participate in education and the extent of economic payoff of this participation, makes the availability of such a program for women an important priority.

Women encounter extraordinarily high costs as the economy restructures as the case of women autoworkers shows, and this relatively modest program has the potential for reducing incalculable economic and personal costs to these women and their families in the future.

3

Effects of a Plant Closing on Marriage and Family Life

Carolyn C. Perrucci

Dena B. Targ

Plant closings have unfortunately become a common occurrence in contemporary America (Bluestone and Harrison, 1982), leaving individuals, families, and communities to try to cope with the aftermath. Diverse social science literatures address varied questions on the effects of job loss and other negative life events on individuals and families. However, plant closings, in particular, have received relatively little attention in the context of familial coping with adversity. In addition, most research on the effect of unemployment (from whatever cause) concentrates on the individual male worker and his family.

The present study places job loss within the context of negative life event research and examines the stress process with respect to changes in marriage and family relationships for a sample of blue-collar women and men who were displaced by a midwestern plant closing. Our model of the stress process includes as stressors the families' experience of negative life events, in addition to the shutdown, and level of economic strain perceived by the displaced workers. We expect that all families are not equally vulnerable to negative life events because of moderating variables

AUTHORS' NOTE: The research reported here is part of a larger project conducted by the Labor Studies Research Group, which includes Robert Perrucci and Harry R. Targ in addition to the authors.

and include in our model the variables of perceived social support and use of family coping strategies. Our dependent variables are changes in marital stability and happiness and changes in family cohesiveness and adaptability over a nine-month period subsequent to the plant closure. We begin with a discussion of the literature related to each of the variables utilized in this study. Second, in a methodology section, we briefly describe the shutdown, the demographic characteristics of our sample, and the indices of our independent and dependent variables. Third, in a results section, we characterize the displaced workers in terms of each of the variables under study and account for change in marriage and family-life by means of a series of multiple-regression equations. Finally, we close with a summary and conclusions section.

RATIONALE

Job Loss and
Life Events Research

Unlike studies of general unemployment, our research concerns unanticipated, involuntary job loss for all subjects, because of a plant closing. Job loss thus characterized qualifies as a major negative life event (Thoits, 1983a). The economic hardship that unemployment entails may be particularly stressful for displaced workers (Pearlin, 1983) and their families (Voydanoff, 1983). To the extent that unemployment because of plant closure entails stress, then, we expect marriage and family relationships of displaced workers to deteriorate measurably.

Also, unlike general unemployment, job loss from a plant closing cannot be caused by other life crises or preexisting individual conditions, for example, poor mental health (Cronkite and Moos, 1984). Nevertheless, in addition to the plant closure, displaced workers and/or members of their social networks may have recently experienced various other negative life events (Kessler and McLeod, 1984). In our research a count is taken of such additional life events and entered into analyses since stress from these could influence negatively workers' marriages and family lives.

Gender and Plant Closings

Most sociological research on job loss, including plant closing studies, ignores the possible impact on displaced women *workers'* families (with notable exceptions of Nowak and Snyder, 1984; Perrucci et al., 1985; Rayman, 1982; Rosen, 1983; Schlozman, 1979). It focuses instead on male workers' unemployment and, occasionally, on impacts on women as wives of the displaced men (see Buss and Redburn, 1983; Larson, 1984). In actuality, an increasing percentage of wives and mothers are employed outside the home. For example, the labor force participation rate of mothers with children under 18 years of age rose from 8.6% in 1940 to nearly 60.0% by the fourth quarter of 1985 (Bureau of National Affairs, 1986). Moreover, for many blue-collar marriages, the two spouses' incomes are often necessary to keep the family above the official poverty line. The poverty-reducing effects of the increased earnings of wives grew from 1967 to 1984 so that by 1984 poverty was 35% lower than it would have been without wives' earnings (Danziger and Gottschalk, 1986).

The present research systematically examines the impact of the plant closure on the families of both women and men who were displaced. Since important, objective conditions of each gender's work were similar (i.e., same industry, firm, and union representation) as were the subjective meanings that they attached to their employment, [1] we expect to find their reactions to the shutdown to be similar (Marshall, 1984).

Clearly not everyone or every family experiences potentially stressful events in the same way. We expect that variations in social support and family coping strategies are factors that affect not only the vulnerability of the individual but also his or her family (Gore, 1978; Pearlin et al., 1981).

Social Support

Cognizant of the multidimensionality of the support concept, we choose to examine it from the viewpoint of the displaced workers themselves. Our assessment in terms of workers' perceptions of being supported by others has the advantage of being operationally distinct from stress as measured by our count of life events (Turner, 1983). Moreover, following research to date we examine the effect of emotional support from the spouse (House, 1981).

Coping Strategies

Recent studies of plant closings and blue-collar unemployment have emphasized the impact of job loss on individuals and families rather than the coping skills that might be used to ameliorate the stress (for exceptions, see Root, 1984; Voydanoff and Donnelly, this volume).

Sociological studies of coping behavior in response to disruptive life events or life strains have either not focused on unemployment (Pearlin and Schooler, 1978) or been concerned only with coping through redefinition of the situation and with individual depression rather than family effects (Pearlin et al., 1981). Research on family stress does not focus on unemployment as a life event (McCubbin et al., 1980).

In addition, until recently, studies of individual and family coping have concentrated on intraindividual or intrafamily coping. The subject of active coping, the use of social and community resources as well as collective action to solve social problems that are experienced as individual or family troubles, has just begun to receive theoretical and empirical attention (McCubbin, 1979; McCubbin et al., 1980; Pearlin and Schooler, 1978).

In this study we consider several coping mechanisms that families could use to improve their situation, including reframing or redefinition of the event in more positive terms, acquiring social support from a variety of sources, and utilization of community resources, including collective action.

Stability and Quality of Marriage and Family Relationships

Our dependent variables include both quality of marriage and family relationships and marital stability. Regarding quality of relationships, our approach takes spouses' perceptions of their marital and familial conditions as the basis for assessment. The dimension of marital-quality of interest here is level of marital happiness (Spanier, 1976). To the extent that the plant closing experience resulted in decreased economic adequacy of workers' marriages (economic strain), we expect lowered quality in terms of less marital happiness (Lewis and Spanier, 1979).

Marital quality, in turn, is thought to be the main determinant of marital stability, controlling for contingencies of alternative attractions outside of marriage and external pressures to remain married (Lewis and Spanier, 1979). To the extent that the plant shutdown resulted in perceived economic strain, we expect an increase in marital instability.

Studies of families during the Great Depression (Angell, 1936; Bakke, 1940; Cavan and Ranck, 1938) and more recent studies of general family-functioning have focused on family cohesion (integration or organization) and adaptability as important variables (Olson, Sprenkle, and Russell, 1979). [2]

We expect that family cohesion and adaptability will decrease over the time period of this study. Although we expect initial levels of cohesion and adaptability to be strong predictors of later levels of each, we also posit that other factors such as coping strategies will affect the family's ability to retain its cohesiveness and adaptability.

METHODOLOGY

Shutdown Setting

This chapter is part of a larger longitudinal study of the impact of a plant closing on displaced workers and their families. On November 4, 1983, a candy-producing plant that had been in operation in a midwestern community for twenty-five years (since 1958) closed, leaving about 240 workers without jobs.

From the president of the plant's union, Local 1976 of the Retail Wholesale Department Store Union AFL-CIO, we obtained a list of workers displaced by the closing. In early December 1983—one month after the shutdown—we distributed a lengthy (sixteen-page) mail questionnaire to a sample of 200 of these individuals. We received 93 usable returns (46%). In April 1984—four months after the shutdown—we mailed a briefer (six-page) questionnaire to the 93 respondents to the initial questionnaire. With the aid of follow-up telephone calls, we received 86 usable returns (92%). Finally, at the end of July 1984—almost nine months after the closing—we distributed another brief (nine-page) questionnaire to the 87 respondents to the second questionnaire. Probably aided by the $5 bill enclosed as a token of our appreciation, we received 75 usable questionnaires (87%). [3]

The Displaced Workers

Our sample of 75 displaced workers was composed of 54 women (72%) and 21 men (28%). Almost 70% (69.3%) were married, while 30.7% were single, including those who were separated, divorced, or widowed. Average household size was three persons. Workers were 41 years old and long-term residents of Clinton County (32 years), on the average. Our respondents had a high school education (11.7 years of schooling) and relatively stable work careers (laid off 1.5 times for one month or longer in the past ten years). Length of work experience with the factory that closed averaged 16.5 years. Hourly wages at the time of the closing ranged from $6.00 to $8.50, with $7.35 being the average.

Indices of Variables

Measures of independent variables are discussed first, followed by dependent variables.

INDEPENDENT VARIABLES

The life events scale score, measured in Wave 1, is an unweighted summation of the number of nine undesirable and ambiguous family-related events that workers or their close social network members experienced in the year preceding our study (Holmes and Rahe, 1967; Kessler and McLeod, 1984; Tausig, 1982).

Gender is a dichotomous variable with male coded "0."

Reemployment status refers to workers' self-reports at Wave 3 as to whether they were still unemployed, coded "1"; reemployed on a part-time basis, coded "2"; or reemployed on a full-time basis, coded "3."

Economic strain is the sum of eight items that ask whether workers have difficulty acquiring both necessary and more optional consumer items (Pearlin et al., 1981).

Social support is perceived emotional support from the spouse measured at Wave 1 (Schaefer, Coyne, and Lazarus, 1981). Response categories were "not at all," coded "1"; "a little," coded "2"; and "extremely," coded "3."

Both internal and external family coping strategies were measured during the second wave of the study. Internal family coping, through redefining or reframing the situation (eight items), and external family coping, through the acquisition of social support (nine items), were measured using subscales of F-COPES (McCubbin, Larsen, and Olson, 1982). Both subscales were scored 1-5, with higher scores indicating more coping efforts. Cronbach's alphas are .881 and .823, respectively.

External coping through engaging in union, company, or community activities was measured with a twelve-item scale developed for this research. For each type of activity participated in, the respondent received a score of "1."

DEPENDENT VARIABLES

Marital happiness was measured by a single item with response categories ranging from "Extremely Unhappy," coded "0" to "Perfect," coded "6" (dyadic satisfaction subscale of Dyadic Adjustment Scale developed by Spanier, 1976). Marital stability refers to relative constancy of marital status—whether single, separated or divorced, widowed, or married—from the first wave of our study to the third wave.

Three subgroups of items, Emotional Bonding, Time, and Decision Making, from the Family Adaptability and Cohesion Evaluation Scales or FACES II (Olson et al., 1982) were used to measure cohesion in the first and third waves. Two subgroups, Assertiveness and Roles, from the Family Adaptability and Cohesion Evaluation Scales or FACES II (Olson et al., 1982) were used to measure family adaptability in the first and third waves. For each subgroup of items, respondents were asked to evaluate their families, using a five-point scale, the higher scores indicating greater family cohesion or adaptability. For cohesion Cronbach's alphas are .884 for Wave 1 and .869 for Wave 3; for adaptability, alphas are .710 and .763.

RESULTS

In this section we first describe the displaced workers in terms of each independent and dependent variable in the study. We then examine change in marital and family relationships through multiple-regression analyses.

Life Events

While all our respondents had experienced job loss because of the plant closing, 57.2% had also experienced one or more other undesirable life events in the past year. The average (mean) number of such life event experiences were similar for women versus men (0.7 versus 0.9), most often the death of an extended family member.

Economic Resources

Despite receipt of advance notification of the plant closing, only 19.4% of the displaced workers reported being reemployed within one month of the shutdown. There were no differences by gender of workers in employment status, at any time. The vast majority of workers, however, had access to one or more sources of income at this early time. Most notably, workers received severance pay for a length of time dependent upon their years of service with the company. Women were as likely as men to be receiving severance pay.

In addition, some workers indicated one month following the closing that they had (or could have) income from alternative sources such as their spouse's job, 51.4%; savings, 50.0%; family or friends from whom they could borrow money if necessary, 37.5%; life insurance, 31.9%; house mortgages, 26.4%; their own unemployment compensation, 19.4%; and pensions, 18.1%.

Economic Strain

Recalling their economic status *before* they had heard about the impending plant closing (i.e., seven months prior to receipt of our initial questionnaire), about one-third (35.6%) of all our respondents reported that they had had economic strain in the sense of not being able to afford some selected consumer items for themselves and/or their families (see Table 3.1). In contrast, when we recontacted them five months *after* the closing, which was after severance pay had ended for most, but reemployment had begun for only 34.6%, 80.8% perceived that they were experiencing some economic strain.

Nine months after the closing, when 56.0% of all the workers were reemployed, 71.6% reported that they were experiencing some economic strain. Of the reemployed, 44% worked on a full-time basis and 12% on a part-time basis. Hourly pay on the new jobs ranged from $3.35 to $9.98, with the mean being $5.73 per hour. This compared unfavorably with preshutdown pay (and severance pay) of $7.35 per hour for full-time jobs. Thus it is understandable that as many as 71.6% of the sample reported that they were still experiencing some economic strain. Interestingly, the families of married women workers experienced similar amounts and kinds of economic strain as the families of married men.

Social Support and
Coping Strategies

Regarding emotional support, 80% of respondents said their spouse cared extremely much about them.

The level of internal coping of the families of the displaced workers was high. With 40 as a maximum possible score, 68.3% were at or above 32. Most workers reported that their families were able to put their situation into a positive perspective and to see themselves as able to solve their problems.

In terms of external coping, the level of help sought by families from social contacts outside of the nuclear family—extended family, friends, and neighbors—was not as consistently high. With a possible range of 9 to 45, actual scores ranged from 12 to 43, with a mean of 27 and a median

TABLE 3.1
Percentage of Displaced Workers Saying They Cannot
Afford Items for Selves/Families (N = 75)

	Wave 1[a]	*Wave 2*[b]	*Wave 3*[c]
Suitable home	4.1	13.3	16.2
Furniture/equipment	11.0	61.3	44.6
Car	8.2	47.3	41.9
Food	5.5	24.0	17.6
Clothing	4.1	38.7	28.4
Desired leisure	19.2	67.6	64.9
Difficulty paying bills	8.2	36.5	29.7
No money left over at end of month	20.5	66.2	50.0

a. The Wave 1 questionnaire was administered one month after the shutdown but asked respondents to recall their economic stress six months prior to the closing.
b. The Wave 2 questionnaire was administered four months after the closing.
c. The Wave 3 questionnaire was administered nine months after the closing.

of 28. There was no difference within marital status between the families of male and female respondents in the use of this method.

External coping through engaging in at least one union, company, or community activity characterized 46% of the respondents. Almost one-fourth (24.4%) engaged in two or more activities. There was no difference between the women and men workers as to the use of external resources.

Marriage Stability and Change Following the Closing

At the beginning of the study, one month subsequent to the shutdown, over two-thirds of all the workers (69.3%) were married, nearly one-fifth (18.7%) were divorced, 4% were widowed, and 8% were single. Marital status was comparable for women and men. By the end of our study period eight months later, workers' marital status had changed hardly at all; one person who had been single initially had gotten married.

Among the married workers, perceived quality of relationships with spouses was also relatively stable, although some change did occur, according to two separate indices. First, in response to our second ques-

tionnaire five months after the closing, 71% of married workers reported that unemployment had not affected their relationships with their
spouses. On the other hand, 18% indicated that their marital relationships had worsened, and 12% said that theirs had changed for the better.

Displaced workers presented a similar picture when we compared
their assessments of the degree of their marital happiness at one month
and then at nine months following the shutdown. In general, workers'
marriages were relatively happy, at both times. Over the eight-month
period, 51.1% indicated that no change occurred in the quality of their
marriages. On the other hand, 33.3% felt that their marriages became less
happy and 15.6% reported increased happiness.

Our approach to measuring change in marital happiness (and in
cohesiveness and adaptability of families discussed below) is to use
regression analysis to predict the Time 2 scores based on a knowledge of
Time 1 scores. [4] Deviations of each person's observed Time 2 score from
his or her predicted Time 2 score (e.g., the residual variation not accounted for by the Time 1 marital happiness scores) is the "change" score.
Thus the Time 1 marital happiness score is always entered first in equations, followed by a block of variables that we expect to account for a
portion of the regressed change (Menaghan, 1983; Thoits, 1983b).

Because *change* in marital and familial relationships is the major
dependent variable in this section of the chapter, analysis is restricted to
people married at both time points. Since the relatively small number of
married workers (N = 52) put constraints on the number of independent
variables we could use, we computed a series of multiple-regression equations, each with varying combinations of independent variables (see
Table 3.2).

The first set of equations assessed the effects of gender, number of
negative life event experiences (in addition to the shutdown), economic
status in terms of whether reemployed or not and perceived economic
strain, emotional support from one's spouse, and internal and external
family coping strategies on change in degree of displaced workers' marital happiness (Table 3.2. Part 1, equations 1a-1d).

The data indicate that there was no gender effect on marital happiness: Women workers' marriages were affected in comparable fashion to
those of displaced men. Similarly, number of life events experienced in
the year prior to the plant closing did not significantly influence marriages after job displacement. Of particular interest here is the finding that
neither the amount of economic strain experienced nor the fact of having

taken a new job caused change in workers' assessments of their marital happiness (compare equations 1a and 1b).

On the other hand, use of an internal coping strategy whereby the family members reframed the situation in more positive terms and had confidence in their ability to solve problems contributed to increased happiness in marriage (equation 1c). Marital happiness was also increased by families' use of an external coping strategy that involved use and mobilization of union, company, and community resources. Similarly, perception that one had a caring spouse led to increased marital happiness (equation 1d).

Family Relationships
Following the Closing

In order to determine whether and how the plant closing experience affected families, we examined (1) displaced workers' perceptions of stability and change in their relationships with their extended families and (2) their assessments of family cohesiveness and adaptability.

In response to our second questionnaire five months after the plant closing, a large majority (82.7%) of the displaced workers indicated that unemployment had not affected their relationships with extended families. About 5% said that their extended family ties worsened; whereas, 12% perceived that theirs had changed for the better.

There was also considerable stability in workers' family cohesiveness and adaptability. For cohesiveness, 20.0% indicated no change from Wave 1 to Wave 3 of our study, and another 40% changed only one or two points on the 24-point scale. For adaptability, 18.4% indicated no change and another 43% changed only one or two points on the 20-point scale.

To explain the change over time that occurred in family cohesiveness, we regressed cohesiveness at Wave 3 on cohesiveness at Wave 1, gender, life events, reemployment status, perceived economic strain, perceived emotional support from one's spouse, and internal and external family coping strategies (see Table 3.2, Part 2, equations 2a-2d). As was the case for equations predicting change in marital happiness (Part 1) results here indicate no significant effects of gender and life events in addition to the plant closing. There was also no impact of reemployment status. On the other hand, the greater the perceived economic strain, the greater decline in cohesiveness of workers' families.

TABLE 3.2

Regressions of Marriage and Family Changes on Gender, Adverse Events, and Coping for Displaced Blue-Collar Workers (N = 52)[a]

Equation	Gender	Life Events	Reemployment Status	Economic Strain	Spouse Care	Internal Coping: Family	External Coping: Social	External Coping: Community	Marital Happiness at Time 1	Cohesion at Time 1	Adaptability at Time 1	R^2
(1a) Marital Happiness at Time 2 regressed on:	-.17	.06	.21	–	–	.23	.05	–	.37**	–	–	.26
(1b) Marital Happiness at Time 2 regressed on:	-.18	.06	–	-.07	–	.20	-.08	–	.34*	–	–	.23
(1c) Marital Happiness at Time 2 regressed on:	-.13	-.02	–	-.06	–	.23+	–	.28*	.32*	–	–	.30
(1d) Marital Happiness at Time 2 regressed on:	-.18	.10	–	-.10	.23+	–	-.07	–	.29*	–	–	.24
(2a) Family Cohesion at Time 2 regressed on:	.06	.01	.06	–	–	.14	-.06	–	–	.56***	–	.31
(2b) Family Cohesion at Time 2 regressed on:	.12	.08	–	-.39**	–	.12	-.23+	–	–	.52***	–	.44

(2c) Family Cohesion at Time 2 regressed on:	.12	-.02	—	-.32**	.12	.18	—	—	.50***	—	.42
(2d) Family Cohesion at Time 2 regressed on:	.11	.16	—	-.42**	.19	—	-.22+	—	.45***	—	.45
(3a) Family Adaptability at Time 2 regressed on:	-.06	.01	.04	—	.16	—	.04	—	—	.62***	.45
(3b) Family Adaptability at Time 2 regressed on:	-.03	.04	—	-.20	.14	—	-.05	—	—	.62***	.48
(3c) Family Adaptability at Time 2 regressed on:	-.01	.01	—	-.18+	.16	.12	—	—	—	.60***	.49
(3d) Family Adaptability at Time 2 regressed on:	-.03	.09	—	-.22+	.30**	—	-.03	—	—	.51***	.53

a. Standardized regression coefficients are presented.
+p ≤ .10; *p < .05; **p < .01; ***p < .001.

Interestingly, enlisting social support from friends and neighbors as a coping strategy was marginally related to decreased family cohesion. Neither use of a psychological coping strategy within the family nor more active coping in terms of engagement in union, company, or community activities significantly affected change in family cohesiveness. Similarly, perception that one's spouse was emotionally supportive had no impact on cohesiveness of the family.

Regarding family adaptability, we regressed adaptability at Wave 3 on adaptability at Wave 1, gender, life events, reemployment status, economic strain, emotional support from spouse, and internal and external family coping strategies (see Table 3.2, Part 3, equations 3a-3d). Once again, neither gender of worker nor number of negative life events nor reemployment status affected change in the dependent variable. As was true for equations predicting change in family cohesion (Part 2), results here indicate that the greater the perceived economic strain, the greater the decline in adaptability of workers' families. Moreover, similar to equation 1d, predicting change in marital happiness, results here indicate that the greater the perception that one's spouse was emotionally supportive, the greater the increase in adaptability of workers' families. Unlike equations predicting either marital happiness or family cohesion, results for change in family adaptability show no impact of any coping strategy—internal or external.

SUMMARY AND CONCLUSIONS

For a sample of 75 blue-collar women and men workers displaced by a midwestern plant closing, we found considerable stability in the structure and quality of their marriages and family relationships over an eight-month period subsequent to the shutdown. In evaluating the relatively small impact of the plant closure, we note the way in which we assessed change, and reflect on the social context in which the shutdown occurred. First, unlike most life events research, our study controlled for initial marriage and family functioning (i.e., Wave 1 scores on happiness, cohesiveness, and adaptability) in an empirical examination of the stress process. Doing so resulted in attributing smaller, but more warranted, effects to stressors (see Cronkite and Moos, 1984; McFarlane et al., 1983).

Second, in terms of the context of the closure, the workers were given six months advance notification of the closure. An assumption of life event researchers and policymakers alike is that "to be forewarned is to be forearmed." Clearly, workers' Wave 1 scores were generally high on marital happiness, and family cohesiveness and adaptability. Moreover, emotional support from the spouse was perceived to be abundant and steadfast. Workers' families were particularly prone to turn inwards upon themselves with respect to coping strategies, in comparison to contributing to and using union, company, or community resources, -although both approaches augmented marital happiness. Overall, then, it appears that our sample benefited from being able to face job displacement from a position of considerable family strengths. They could have benefited further by using and developing community resources as well.

In addition to advance notification, our sample of workers received a relatively generous package of benefits from the closing company, including severance pay, continuation of health care benefits during the severance pay period, retirement benefits, and job search and retirement workshops. These benefits delayed the adverse effects of economic strain for many for several months following the shutdown. Also, the workers may have been positively affected by the announcement six weeks after the closing that the plant had been sold to another candy manufacturer.

Not unlike some other groups of displaced blue-collar workers, however, many in our sample remained unemployed nine months after the closure, and those who were reemployed were getting lower hourly wages than in their preshutdown jobs, on the average (Perrucci et al., 1985; Office of Technology Assessment, 1986). Whether this represents the beginning of unstable, dead-end work that will eventually negatively influence workers' family life we do not know (Furstenberg, 1974). Our data do indicate that economic strain led to decreased family cohesion and adaptability and that reemployment per se did not augment the quality of marriage and family relationships. To bolster family life, unemployment assistance, and, eventually, new jobs for blue-collar workers must provide an acceptable standard of living.

We underscore the finding that job loss from a plant closing was experienced similarly for the families of displaced women in comparison with those of displaced men. The incidence of household unemployment doubled from the time of the 1958-1959 recession to 1980, with the most substantial increase in the unemployment experience occurring for married women, rather than for married men or single household heads (Curtin, Gordon, and Ponza, 1981). Plant closings were an increasingly important cause of this unemployment (Bluestone and Harrison, 1982). Economic planning and policy should, therefore, take account of the effects of plant closings on both women and men.

In light of the above, it is unfortunate that only a minority of all U.S. workers have advance notification of shutdowns or severance pay provisions with their employing companies. Only 20% of U.S. workers are unionized and have contracts (Harrison, 1984). Less than half of these workers are covered by early warning or severance pay clauses (Margolis and Farran, 1984). Moreover, only a minority of the unemployed have unemployment compensation or retraining available to them (Office of Technology Assessment, 1986). And quite likely there is a reduction in public assistance resources at the time that the displaced have an increased need for human services (see, e.g., Ferman, 1984).

Therefore, these underutilized strategies and additional ways of reducing unemployment and assisting unemployed workers, their families and communities are being proposed and deserve serious consideration. These include (1) job maintenance initiatives such as employee ownership of firms, job-sharing, and plant closing legislation; (2) improvement of economic assistance to displaced workers including larger unemployment benefits for longer periods of time, extension of deadlines for bill payments, and job retraining and relocation programs; and (3) expansion of social welfare programs, such as national health insurance, to assist all low-income individuals and families whether unemployed or underemployed (Perrucci and Perrucci, 1986). Primary emphasis has been placed on the economic consequences of plant closings. Programs to meet the noneconomic consequences, such as disruption of social networks (Margolis and Farran, 1984), difficulty in identifying and dealing with social service agencies, and general individual and family problems are also needed (Perrucci et al., 1985).

NOTES

1. At Wave 1, displaced workers indicated whether their jobs at the plant had held any of a list of twelve meanings, ranging from a way to "make a decent living," to "have recreational activities." For only one item was there a significant difference between men and women.

2. As was suggested in the studies on the effects of the Depression on families (Angell, 1936; Bakke, 1940; Cavan and Ranck, 1938), we posit that a high level of cohesion and adaptability are positive factors in enabling families to respond well to the aftermath of a plant shutdown. This may seem to contrast with the work of the authors of FACES and their colleagues (i.e., Olson et al., 1982; Olson, Sprenkle, and Russell, 1979) who point to moderate levels of adaptability and cohesion as the most functional for marriage and family development. However, we have used only five subgroups of FACES items—three of the eight categories of cohesion items and two of the six categories of adaptability items. In addition, Olson's meaning of "moderate" needs to be taken into account. For example,

there is evidence (Sprenkle and Olson, 1978) that under stressful circumstances, better adjusted couples have a more egalitarian leadership pattern—one neither husband-dominated (one extreme) nor wife-dominated (another extreme). Families exhibiting egalitarian sharing of roles in our study were scored as high (rather than moderate) on those measures.

3. No information is available for nonrespondents.

4. The table of Pearson zero-order correlations, means and standard deviations for all variables in the regression equations is available on request from the authors.

PART II

Coping with Economic Distress

Parts II and III examine processes and mechanisms through which economic dislocation and distress affect the nature of quality of family life. Part II deals with the role of coping resources and behaviors in dealing with economic distress while Part III focuses on interpretive processes used by family members in responding to economic distress.

The chapters in Part II further elaborate the relationship between economic dislocation and economic distress and examine the diverse impacts of economic distress on family life. Phillip J. Bowman discusses economic dislocation among black male workers whose unskilled factory jobs are being eliminated by deindustrialization. He discusses the intensifying effects of blacks males' lack of preparation for newly emerging positions, the effects of successive recessions on black male labor force participation, and the concentration of blacks in central cities as new job opportunities are created increasingly in suburban areas.

In the second chapter, Voydanoff and Donnelly examine the effects of economic distress on quality of family life among the general population of an urban industrial area. They study four types of economic distress: employment instability and uncertainty and economic deprivation and strain. Among men, economic strain and employment instability are most strongly associated with quality of family life while spouse's employment instability and uncertainty are most significant among women.

Bowman analyzes the repercussions of economic distress on families by mapping out the ripple effects of deindustrialization and job loss on black families. Economic dislocation creates provider role strain among black men who are unable to find stable employment and thus can not serve as primary providers for their families. This situation is reflected in multiple-role strain among employed black mothers who become responsible for both economic support and child rearing. Since many black women work at low-paying service jobs, most single-parent families live in poverty. The high incidence of poverty in black families creates a job search strain among adolescents who attempt to contribute to family income. With levels of black teenage unemployment approaching 50%, these adolescents experience considerable difficulty and discouragement.

Voydanoff and Donnelly discuss the role of coping resources and behaviors in alleviating the effects of economic distress on family life. Those experiencing economic distress tend to have fewer family coping resources, for example, family pride and accord; however, having these resources is associated with higher levels of marital/family satisfaction. Economic distress is positively related to the use of family coping behaviors, namely, family financial improvement efforts. The use of these coping behaviors, however, is not related to higher marital/family satisfaction.

These chapters also present implications for policies and programs that address economic distress. Bowman suggests interventions on three levels: training programs to prepare prime working age and young blacks for changed employment opportunities; a redistribution of paid employment, income, and child-rearing activities among family members; and the encouragement of informal coping strategies that alleviate the effects of economic distress on families. Voydanoff and Donnelly suggest that programs to build family coping resources should improve the quality of family life among the economically distressed. They further point out that those who conduct programs oriented to financial improvement efforts must recognize that, although these efforts may be necessary to reduce economic distress, they should not necessarily be expected to result in greater marital/family satisfaction.

4

Postindustrial Displacement and Family Role Strains: Challenges to the Black Family

Phillip J. Bowman

The Industrial Revolution not only provided the basis for the United States to become a twentieth-century economic power, but it also had a stabilizing impact on black family life that was unprecedented. E. Franklin Frazier (1939), in his classic study of "The Negro Family in the United States," described the stabilizing effects of early industrialization on black family structure and relationships:

> Though many urban Negro workers must still seek a living in domestic and personal service, the number of skilled as well as unskilled workers and laborers is growing. It appears that, as the Negro worker becomes an industrial worker, he assumes responsibility for support of his family and acquires new authority in family relations [p. 355].

AUTHOR'S NOTE: The preparation of this chapter was supported by a postdoctoral fellowship from the Rockefeller Foundation. I would also like to acknowledge the technical support provided by several members of the Program for Research on Black Americans at the University of Michigan's Institute for Social Research.

The willingness of black Americans, particularly men, to meet a critical demand for unskilled blue-collar workers has been an important ingredient in the emergence of industrial America as the world's preeminent economic power. Frazier aptly pointed out that the pressing demand for unskilled industrial workers also created unprecedented opportunities for black males to become responsible economic providers within stable, working-class black families.

As we approach the twenty-first century, technological innovation in the form of massive deindustrialization is again impinging upon the black family. However, the rapid introduction of new manufacturing technology now threatens virtually to eliminate precisely the industrial job categories where black males have been concentrated for decades (Ayres and Miller, 1982; Hunt and Hunt, 1983; Luria, 1981). Robotics, automation, and related labor market changes appear to be displacing black males into the ranks of the unemployed in larger proportions than other workers. It may well become an irony of twentieth-century history that industrial innovation once touted as a major stabilizing force in black family life, ends up being a central destabilizing factor.

The differential vulnerability of black males to postindustrial displacement does not merely effect their own personal lives, but also produces a succession of provider role strains within the family unit. Growing joblessness among displaced black husband-fathers intensifies pressure on both mothers and children to participate in the family work effort as a matter of economic survival. Hence the diffusion of provider role responsibilities from black men to women to children represents crucial ripple effects of postindustrial displacement. These ripple effects within black families may further accentuate high labor force participation, severe unemployment, and related psychosocial distress among both black mothers and teenage children.

To help guide responsive public policy and intervention, theory-driven studies must build on existing research to link postindustrial displacement systematically to psychosocial problems within families (Bowman, 1985; Catalano and Dooley, 1980; Pearlin, 1983). We need to better understand how provider role problems experienced by displaced black males produce a specific sequelae of interrelated role strains among other family members. Specifically, studies should be carefully designed to clarify the intrafamilial effects of massive deindustrialization that ripple from primary provider role strain among displaced husband-fathers, to multiple-role strain among working mothers, to job search strain among unemployed teenage children. The ability to cope effectively with this succession of family role strains, which appears to escalate as labor-saving technology eliminates unskilled industrial jobs, represents a growing challenge to black families as we approach the twenty-first century. To provide a better basis for understanding the nature of this challenge, the sections below include (1) a more detailed discussion of the differential impact of accelerating technological changes on black males, (2) a conceptual model to guide future inquiry on how a sequelae of intra-familial role strains may mediate the psychosocial consequences of post-industrial displacement, and (3) some specific directions for future research and related public policy implications.

IMPACT OF MASSIVE DEINDUSTRIALIZATION

Increasingly, labor-saving technology is changing production processes, particularly in basic American industries such as steel and automobile manufacturing (Buckingham, 1961; Luria, 1981; Mansfield, 1971; Martin, 1982a; Sahal, 1981). The sense of urgency with which advanced technology is currently being introduced rests on its potential to promote greater profits and efficiency, and to meet the challenge of foreign competition. Many industrial planners now envision rapid automation in declining industries with robotics and other computer-controlled machines virtually eliminating the need for unskilled labor (Ayres and Miller, 1981-1982; Hunt and Hunt, 1983). Emerging industrial technology not only eliminates jobs for unskilled laborers but also reduces demand for operatives and other semiskilled workers. For example, researchers estimate that the next generation of industrial robots may alone replace 3 million operatives (Ayres and Miller, 1982). Moreover, recent data from the U.S. Department of Labor on permanent job losses during the 1980s reveal that 5.1 million workers, mostly in steel and automobile manufacturing, were displaced between 1981 and 1985 due to plant closings or layoffs. [1]

Current deindustrialization in America must be understood as a phase in a long history of innovation in production processes, but the rate of technological change has accelerated dramatically over the past two decades (Haber, Ferman, and Hudson, 1963; Mansfield, 1971; Martin, 1982a, 1982b; Sahal, 1981). Shifting social values and increasingly sophisticated technology both promise to accelerate further the displacement of unskilled industrial jobs in the future. The dramatic increase in the pace at which new manufacturing technology has been adopted over the past decade reflects decreasing societal resistance. Initially, postindustrial automation was gradually implemented with phased reduction of workers through early retirement and normal attrition, due largely to strong resistance from organized labor. This union resistance was buttressed by a general societal fear that widespread unemployment would result from rapid automation. However, national concern over foreign competition and related events over the past two decades have offset initial fears of catastrophic human consequences and made way for more dramatic structural changes (Buckingham, 1961; Luria, 1981; Hunt and Hunt, 1983). In terms of technology, the application of automated manufacturing systems in industry will be further accelerated by ongoing research and development on artificial intelligence that is crucial to future generations of "smart robots" (Alexander, 1982; Gevarter, 1982).

Black Male Vulnerability: Unskilled Laborers and Operatives

Deindustrialization and related postindustrial changes have both positive and negative consequences. The adoption of labor-saving technology in the new industrial sector results in greater corporate profits, more efficient production, and the creation of new jobs. However, the adverse impact is not evenly distributed and black males appear especially vulnerable (Ayres and Miller, 1981-1982, 1982; Drucker, 1981; Hunt and Hunt, 1983). Racial minorities in general and black males in particular are grossly overrepresented in the blue-collar occupational categories being displaced.

After the mechanization of southern agriculture displaced farm labor, black males were recruited in massive numbers to the urban north to fill precisely those job categories that are currently being eliminated by rapid deindustrialization (Briggs, 1970; Ernst and Hugg, 1976; Guzda, 1982; Harrison, 1974). For example, 92% of blacks working in the automotive industry during 1966 were in blue-collar categories of laborer, operative or maintenance service (Briggs, 1970). More recently, the 1980 census revealed that 52.9% of all black males who still have a job are employed in the unskilled labor or semiskilled categories that are most vulnerable to industrial automation. This compares with 19.1% of black females who, although seriously underemployed, tend to work in unskilled service and clerical jobs that are hit less hard by deindustrialization. The increasing numbers of white women in the labor force, because of gender segmentation, are confronted with patterns of underemployment similar to black women. Therefore, while white men remain overrepresented in highly skilled occupations, the concentration of white and black women in service and clerical jobs makes them less vulnerable than black males to growing postindustrial obsolescence.

To be sure, the number of jobless black males will continue to increase disproportionately as accelerating deindustrialization results in more permanent layoffs, plant closings, and factory relocations. It is important to note that technological change also reduces the number of new unskilled laborers and operatives hired. In intergenerational terms, two generations of black males must adapt to the rapid displacement of unskilled manufacturing jobs. While prime working age black men increasingly face permanent layoffs from industrial jobs similar to those held by their fathers, their own sons no longer have such jobs as employment options (Drucker, 1981; Hunt and Hunt, 1983; Mangum and Seninger, 1978).

Additional Risk Factors:
Precursors of Economic Obsolescence

In addition to their overrepresentation as unskilled laborers and operatives, other factors may amplify the adverse impact of postindustrial changes on black males and their families well into the twenty-first century. While all blue-collar workers are hard hit, the impacts on black males are even more severe because of several factors including (1) a postindustrial "skill twist" with new jobs created requiring far greater skills than those displaced, (2) a tendency for economic recession to have differential impact on the labor force attrition of displaced black males, and (3) isolation of displaced black males in depressed central cities away from growing suburban job options. Hence accelerating displacement of unskilled industrial jobs tends to interact with these other risk factors to exacerbate further the vulnerability of black males to economic obsolescence and their families to long-term poverty.

SKILL TWIST AND
ACADEMIC UNDERACHIEVEMENT

Postindustrial technology will eliminate more jobs than it creates, and black males are least likely to be successful in actually attaining the newly created jobs for several reasons. First of all, because of the poor quality of education they receive, black males are grossly underprepared to compete for the new jobs that will require a much better educated labor force. While eliminating unskilled jobs, deindustrialization produces highly skilled jobs in such areas as electrical engineering, computer technology, robot technology, laser technology, and energy technology (Cetron, 1982; Leon, 1982; Leontief, 1982; Martin, 1982a, 1982b). Displaced workers who successfully retrain for these new jobs with expanding opportunities must have sufficiently strong academic backgrounds to develop specialized skills readily. Both younger and prime working aged black men, being among the most unskilled products of American public education, face a distinct disadvantage. Indeed, they must overcome substantial barriers to compete successfully for these new skilled jobs. For example, the black male high school dropout rate in the city of New York is 72%. Nationally, many black males who do graduate from high school are functionally illiterate, and they are not as likely as black females to enter college, and those who do attend college are also less likely to graduate (Jones et al., 1986). Career preparation, retraining, and employment transition become even greater challenges for displaced black males—given their level of academic unpreparedness in a labor market with increasing skill demands.

ECONOMIC RECESSION AND
LABOR FORCE ATTRITION

Greater vulnerability of black males to postindustrial displacement may also help explain why recent economic recessions have had particularly devastating effects on their labor force attrition. The eminent economist Andrew Brimmer (1973) noted that every economic downturn since the Great Depression has made black workers, who have always been concentrated in marginal secondary jobs, lag even further behind whites. Brimmer observes that the resulting "lag can be seen on several measures—including a slower growth in the black labor force, the smaller share of new jobs obtained by blacks, and the continued climb in black unemployment." Hence, largely because of their dependency on vulnerable industrial jobs, black males are at higher risk for job loss during recessions and are less likely to regain employment when economic recovery occurs. Recent data from the U.S. Department of Labor show that black workers who lost their jobs between 1981 and 1985 are about twice as likely as whites to remain unemployed.

While official unemployment statistics represent one indicator of black male vulnerability to the joint impact of economic recession and postindustrial changes, recent labor force dropout trends may express this impact even more dramatically. Although black males have been historically underemployed in menial jobs, their severe joblessness appears to be a more recent phenomenon. In fact, governmental data show that black males were more likely to be employed than white males or any other group during the 55-year period from 1890 to 1945 (see Note 1). However, every economic recession since the Great Depression has been accompanied by disproportionate numbers of jobless black males dropping out of the labor force (Brimmer, 1973, 1974, 1976; Cross, 1985). High labor demands during World War II somewhat mitigated labor force attrition for all groups, but more recent trends reveal a dramatic drop in the proportion of black males employed between 1950 and 1980. These trends suggest that as deindustrialization accelerates, recurring economic recession will result in disproportionate numbers of black males being displaced from unskilled jobs, becoming discouraged in their search for new jobs, and dropping out of the labor force. Black teenage boys, older black men, and those with little formal education appear especially vulnerable (Wool, 1978). Cross (1985) projected that this disturbing problem is likely to become even worse by the end of the century, and concludes "of all observed statistical trends affecting the black race—other than the sharp increase in black women receiving public relief—none is more alarming than the steep decline in the labor force participation of black men" (p. 245).

RACIAL ISOLATION AND THE URBAN UNDERCLASS

Despite problems created by interpersonal racial discrimination, structural changes linked with deindustrialization may have indirect discriminatory effects on black workers that are even more deleterious. The ability of black males to cope effectively with postindustrial displacement is restricted by the systematic relocation of basic manufacturing away from central cities in the northeast-northcentral quadrant of the nation where black Americans are highly concentrated (Ernst and Hugg, 1976; Gordus, Jarley, and Ferman, 1981; Rees, 1979). As the proportion of blacks increases in northern cities, there is a clear tendency for nearby manufacturing facilities to close and new plants to be built in other locations to attract different labor markets. Such practices may well represent a rational business choice by productivity-minded corporate management seeking to build modernized plants in areas with more "desirable" labor markets. However, the impact of such decisions on displaced black workers and their families may be devastating.

While growing numbers of urban black males are displaced from relatively high-paying industrial jobs, those unskilled jobs with expanding opportunities tend to be low paying and increasingly located in middle-class suburban areas. However, prosperous suburban areas are not readily accessible to displaced black males from the inner city because of both transportation barriers and racial friction. Massive white flight from black cities to white suburban areas has created what some researchers have called the growing "chocolate city-vanilla suburb" phenomenon (Ernst and Hugg, 1976; Farley et al., 1978). This phenomenon, which researchers have found to be spurred by negative racial attitudes that blacks lower property values and increase crime rates, has resulted in the North replacing the South as the most segregated region in the nation.

Thus the movement of industrial jobs away from the urban North has been even more devastating to displaced black males because of their isolation in depressed central cities away from prosperous suburbs (Mangum and Seninger, 1978). This isolation contributes to what some have called a permanent and growing black underclass of jobless men and welfare dependent women in northern cities such as Detroit, Chicago, and New York (Anderson, 1978; Auletta, 1982; Wilson, 1978). Relocation efforts of displaced industrial workers have usually resulted in an exodus from the "Snowbelt" seeking opportunities in the more prosperous "Sunbelt." However, most have found little demand for unskilled blue-collar workers in cities such as Atlanta, Houston, or Los Angeles. Instead, they too often find themselves among the Sunbelt's own emerging urban black underclass (Glasgow, 1980).

Growing obsolescence among urban black males displaced by labor-saving technological changes may produce a sense of hopelessness when their job search efforts repeatedly fail. Moreover, diminishing employment opportunities in depressed central cities may threaten the self-esteem of displaced black males and leave very few options for legitimate modes of coping (Anderson, 1978; Gary, 1981; Green, 1981). For example, severe joblessness and job search discouragement may intensify provider role strain experienced by black husband-fathers and, in turn, increase their vulnerability to familial estrangement, drugs, crime, and other psychosocial problems. Some analysts who have documented the prevalence of negative psychosocial symptoms among black males have also emphasized their relationship to family pathologies (Auletta, 1982; Liebow, 1967; Moynihan, 1965). However, few have adequately addressed the spurious nature of this relationship and how psychosocial problems that plague black males and related family instability may both be adverse by-products of ongoing industrial transformations.

It is shortsighted to reduce current black family instability, poverty, and related psychosocial problems to the distal evils of slavery or self-perpetuating subcultural deficits (Ryan, 1971). The distinct psychosocial problems experienced by black males and their families, although historically rooted in southern slavery, have been maintained by persistent dual labor market barriers and are currently being exacerbated by growing postindustrial obsolescence (Cross, 1985; Green, 1980; Guzda, 1982; Harrison, 1974; Wilson, 1978).

RIPPLE EFFECTS WITHIN HIGH-RISK FAMILIES

The particular vulnerability of black males to deindustrialization is based largely on their concentration in vulnerable blue-collar jobs, a growing tendency for technology to replace such unskilled jobs with highly skilled positions, and their lack of preparation to compete in skilled labor markets. Moreover, recurring economic recessions and growing isolation in depressed inner cities further exacerbate the tendency for postindustrial displacement to give rise to growing labor force attrition among black males and the feminization of black family poverty.

The differential vulnerability of black males to deindustrialization is critical to understanding the growing feminization of black family poverty and related provider role problems of black mothers and teenage children (Beale, 1986; Bowman, 1984, 1985; McAdoo, 1984). When increasing numbers of black males become discouraged in job search, drop out of the labor force, and lose personal income—they find it difficult to meet expectations as primary providers for their families. As husbands and fathers, such provider role strain is personally distressful for displaced black males, but may also produce an enduring economic crisis and related psychosocial problems within the black family unit. Therefore, the rapid displacement of unskilled industrial jobs places black males and their families, already at higher risk for economic and related psychosocial distress, at even greater risk.

If the black family and other high-risk families are to cope effectively with provider role problems produced by accelerating postindustrial changes, more responsive public policy must be developed (Catalano and Dooley, 1980; Leontief, 1982; Luria, 1981). Effective strategies must be devised to avoid, interrupt, and reverse the progression of provider role strains and related psychosocial problems within high-risk families. To guide the development of more responsive strategies, theory-driven empirical studies must better clarify the manner in which economic difficulties faced by displaced black men have ripple effects within their families.

Such systematic studies can also provide an empirical base to develop more coherent social psychological theory on role strain-adaptation processes (Barnett and Baruch, 1985; Bowman, 1985; Goode, 1960; Pearlin, 1983; Sarbin and Allen, 1968). A viable theoretical model must identify specific factors and processes that mediate harmful psychosocial consequences of job displacement among displaced males, their wives and children. In addition, a useful model would clarify the operation of informal and formal resources that might mitigate harmful effects or promote effective coping.

Role Strain-Adaptation:
Toward a Theoretical Model

Figure 4.1 presents a three-stage conceptual model as a guide to future research, theory development, and intervention. A basic premise incorporated in this heuristic model is that negative psychosocial effects of postindustrial displacement within high-risk families are mediated by a succession of family-based role strains. More specifically, harmful ripple effects occur as provider role strain experienced by displaced males diffuses further within the family to intensify multiple-role strain among working mothers, and, in turn, job search strain among unemployed teenage children. Another central premise is that the harmful effects of these intrafamilial role strains may be buffered by informal sociocultural coping resources, but more proactive public policy is necessary to prevent such ripple effects from occurring. Building on stress-adaptation theory and research, two basic propositions can be extrapolated to guide future inquiry: (1) a sequelae of intrafamilial role strains increase the vulnerability of individual family members to postindustrial displacement, while (2) informal and formal coping resources may both operate to reduce the vulnerability of family members to such role strains (Beale, 1986; Bowman, 1984, 1985; Fried, 1979; Harrison, Bowman and Beale, 1985; Kaplan, 1983; Moos, 1976).

Family role strains may be defined as objective difficulties, or subjective reactions to such difficulties, that occur when family members face obstacles in meeting family role expectations (Barnett and Baruch, 1985; Croog, 1970; Goode, 1960; Pearlin, 1983). A basic assumption is that fathers, mothers, and children want to do what they are expected to do within families but it is not always easy or even possible. For example, unemployed or underemployed black men, who are increasingly displaced from unskilled industrial jobs, find it difficult to be primary economic providers for their families (Bowman, 1985). Black working

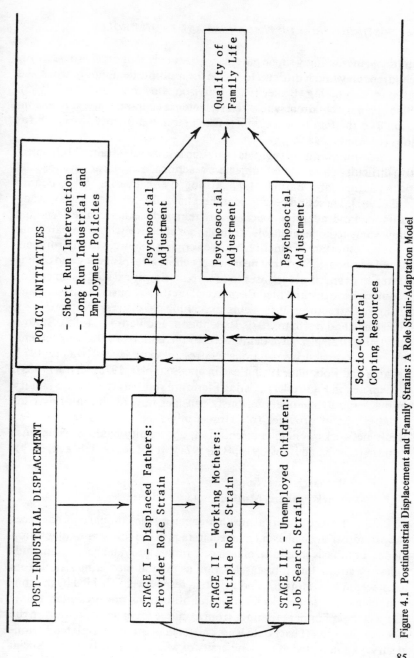

Figure 4.1 Postindustrial Displacement and Family Strains: A Role Strain-Adaptation Model

85

mothers, increasingly single parents who are sole economic providers for children, may find it difficult to juggle the multiple demands of work and primary caretaking (Beale, 1986; Harrison, Bowman, and Beal, 1985). Black teenage children, who often feel intense economic pressure to contribute to the family work effort, face extreme difficulty searching for jobs (Bowman, 1984).

A growing literature suggests that such family role strains, both objective difficulties and related subjective reactions, carry clear psychosocial risks (Barnett and Baruch, 1985; Croog, 1970; Pearlin, 1983; Pearlin et al., 1981). These and other researchers have also found that it is crucial to understand adaptive mechanisms that reduce harmful effects and allow some to cope with role strains more effectively. Past research has made an important distinction between coping resources as environmental and personal factors that promote psychological resiliency and coping strategies as specific responses to life stress. Empirical studies on coping resources have documented the particular efficacy of social support and strong self-structures in reducing psychological distress (Kaplan, 1983; Lieberman and Borman, 1979; Rosenbaum and Ben-Ari, 1985). Studies on coping strategies have demonstrated the adaptive value of problem-focused over defensive reactions to stressful experiences (Haans, 1977; Lazarus and Folkman, 1980; Pearlin and Schooler, 1978; Taylor, 1983). As depicted in Figure 4.1, existing literature suggests that future inquiry on black family members seriously consider how the harmful psychosocial effects of provider role strains might be reversed by extended family networks, religious orientation, and reality-based attributional patterns (Gurin and Epps, 1974; Hill, 1971; McAdoo, 1981; Stack, 1974).

Research Directions:
Black Fathers, Mothers, and Children

Future research must better clarify the familial consequences of postindustrial displacement at each stage in the role strain-adaptation model. Emphasis should be placed on primary provider role strain, multiple-role strain, and job search strain as pivotal mediating risk factors for black fathers, mothers, and children, respectively. Guided by the conceptual model, some specific research directions are presented below along with preliminary findings from a unique set of national data on the black population. These data were collected in three interrelated national surveys conducted at the University of Michigan's Institute for Social Research between 1979 and 1983: (1) the Study of Black American Life—a national cross-section survey of 2,107 black adults—that was sponsored by the National Institute of Mental Health; (2) the Three-Generational Black Family Study—a survey of over 1,000 three-generational black families that used family members of the national cross-section respondents as the sampling frame—sponsored by the National Institute on Aging; and (3) the Panel Study of Black Youth—a survey of 200 black youth from the third generation of the three-generational family study who were interviewed in 1980 and 1983—sponsored by the U.S. Department of Health and Human Services (Bowman, 1983a; Bowman, Gurin, and Howard, 1984; Jackson, Tucker, and Bowman, 1982; Jackson and Hatchett, 1986).

STAGE I: BLACK FATHERS AND PROVIDER ROLE STRAIN

The foregoing discussion indicates that black males are hardest hit by growing postindustrial displacement that increases their unemployment levels, labor force attrition, and economic obsolescence. As fathers and husbands, this increasing economic marginality strains their ability to operate as primary providers for their families. Figure 4.1 suggests that future research at Stage I builds on past studies of black males and examines how family provider role strain mediates the adverse impact of displacement on their personal lives as well as the quality of black family-life (Cazenave, 1981; Gary, 1981; Heckler, 1985; Wilkinson and Taylor, 1977). In line with a role strain-adaptation perspective, studies should also seek to identify coping resources and strategies that might act to ameliorate the harmful effects of the strain they experience as primary family providers.

To begin to examine these issues, analyses have begun on data from a sample of 372 black husband-fathers who were interviewed in the period 1979-1980 as part of a national cross-section survey of 2,107 adults (Bowman, 1983b, 1985). First, the data indicate that black husband-fathers who remained with their families were more likely to have jobs (72%) than black fathers who were separated from their families (58%). Although only correlational, these findings reveal a rather clear link between unemployment and familial estrangement among black fathers. Multivariate analyses further suggest that the harmful impact of unemployment status, an objective aspect of provider role strain, is exacerbated by various subjective dimensions among black husband-fathers. An expectancy of failure in efforts to be good husbands to their wives was particularly distressful, accounting for more negative variance in a measure of life happiness than actual joblessness. Moreover, other subjective dimensions of provider role strain also had adverse effects on their psychosocial adjustment, including expectancy of failure as a father, expectancy of failure as primary family provider, and anxiety about family economic subsistence. With respect to coping resources, cohesive family bonds and strong religious beliefs both reduced but failed to off-set entirely the adverse effects of provider role strain. Other sociocultural coping mechanisms such as multiple family earners, para-kin friendships and system-blame attributions failed to have significant effects that were psychosocially enhancing for black husband-fathers.

To expand upon the findings summarized above, future research must examine in greater detail how the effects of postindustrial displacement on black fathers are mediated by specific role strain-adaptation processes. How is the impact of actual joblessness mediated by cognitive and affective dimensions of provider role strain and various coping resources? Do subjective dimensions of provider role strain affect various indicators of psychological distress and family life quality in the same manner? Is the stability of existing black husband-wife families threatened by the intense psychological distress produced when husbands come to expect failure in efforts to provide for their wives? Are the psychosocial effects of provider role strain the same when black fathers live in traditional husband-wife households as when they live apart from their families? How might public policy or intervention operate to reinforce sociocultural resources such as cohesive families to encourage more adaptive modes of coping?

STAGE II: WORKING MOTHERS AND MULTIPLE-ROLE STRAIN

As depicted in Figure 4.1, provider role strain experienced by displaced fathers ripples further within the black family to exacerbate multiple-role strain faced by working mothers. Black women have long worked to contribute to the economic well-being of both low-income and middle-income black families, while white women have only recently entered the labor force in large numbers. Because of the relatively low-income levels of black men, economically stable black families have always been far more dependent on two or more earners. The wife in a black household typically contributes about 60% more to the family income than the wife in a white household (Dingle, 1985).

With postindustrial displacement increasing the economic marginality of black fathers, large numbers of black mothers find themselves in the role of primary or sole economic provider for their children

(McAdoo, 1984). For example, data from the 1980 census indicate that nearly half (47%) of all black families with children under 18 years old do not have a man present to act as primary provider, compared to only 14% of white families. Despite persistently high levels of unemployment among black women, it is important to focus on the experience of black working mothers because of their desire to avoid welfare dependency and several related trends. As black men continue to lose their relatively high-paying jobs in industrial manufacturing, black women will find it increasingly imperative to take low-level service and clerical jobs as alternatives to welfare dependency. Moreover, the relevance of black working mothers is further increased by social welfare policy directions toward workfare provisions, and the tendency for black women to compete successfully for low-level jobs in the expanding service sector. By 1995, it is estimated that a full 58% of all employment will be service-oriented, while manufacturing jobs will shrink to a mere 19% (Martin, 1982a, 1982b; Hunt and Hunt, 1983).

Some recent research has emphasized "enhancing" effects of multiple-role involvement (Baruch and Barnett, 1986), but studies of black women suggest that consideration also be given to the harmful impact of multiple-role strain as well as the mitigating influence of various coping mechanisms (McAdoo, 1981, 1984; Rodgers-Rose, 1980). While objective indicators of role overload, such as the number of hours worked and number of dependent children under 18, are important, studies of multiple-role strain among black working mothers should also explore the operation of more subjective dimensions. To investigate these issues, analyses have begun on data from black working mothers in the national cross-section survey of the black adult population (Beale, 1986; Harrison, Bowman, and Beale, 1985). Preliminary findings suggest that an expectancy of failure in the mother role is a particularly distressful dimension of multiple-role strain for black working mothers. Multivariate analysis shows that a working mother's belief that efforts to be a good mother to her children will fail is even more deleterious than perceptions of role overload. The findings further suggest that strong religious belief is a powerful coping resource for black working mothers, and appears to reduce the negative psychosocial effects of multiple-role strain even more than extended family bonds and para-kin friendships.

Are the harmful effects of multiple-role strain on black working mothers reduced in traditional husband-wife families where the father has gainful employment? Does expectancy of failure in the mother role have the same severe effects if black working mothers are married as when they are single parents? Do the enhancing effects of strong religious belief operate directly or indirectly by reinforcing cohesive family bonds or para-kin friendships among church members? Should public policy to deal with the feminization of black family poverty and related strains on single mothers include provisions directed at provider role problems of displaced black fathers? Such questions represent fertile ground for future inquiry.

STAGE III: UNEMPLOYED
CHILDREN AND JOB SEARCH STRAIN

As shown in Figure 4.1, the third stage of the conceptual model considers how provider role strain among displaced fathers and working mothers ripple even deeper into the black family by intensifying job search strain faced by unemployed teenage children. Thanks to sometimes dramatic media accounts, few would disagree that black teenage unemployment has reached crisis proportions with no immediate solution in sight. Unemployment among black teenagers is consistently higher than among any other national subpopulation and remains over 50% in some areas (Freeman and Wise, 1982; Green, 1980; Mangum and Seninger, 1978). Even President Reagan called black teenage joblessness "a national tragedy," although he has failed to provide adequate support for Job Corps or other programs responsive to their unique plight.

What is particularly surprising is a tendency for both researchers and policymakers to neglect the critical link between severe black teenage unemployment and family-based pressure to enter the labor force prematurely to compensate for provider role difficulties of their displaced fathers. Most analyses of high black youth unemployment focus on problems with a high minimum wage, improper work attitudes, inadequate skills, and entrapment within depressed inner-city neighborhoods away from booming suburbs (Freeman and Wise, 1982; Mangum and Seninger, 1978). To be sure, these factors contribute significantly to the high unemployment rate among black as compared to white teenagers. However, while white youth tend to seek jobs more casually, black teenagers are compelled in larger proportions to find jobs in order to contribute to the family work effort and economic subsistence.

Despite their strong economic motivation for jobs, black teenage children face discouraging odds as they enter the labor force. As suggested earlier, the accelerated pace of postindustrial labor market changes makes job search among the current generation of young black males particularly problematic. Some even predict that many black teenagers, especially urban males, will never find a regular job but must find alternative means to survive as members of a permanent underclass (Glasgow, 1980; Green, 1980; Wilson, 1978). Psychological distress produced by intense pressure on black youth to contribute to family economic survival and related job search frustration may be linked to the serious psychosocial adjustment problems they experience, including school failure, teenage parenting, and homicidal violence (Bowman, 1980; Green, 1982; Greenberger and Steinberg, 1987; Jones et al., 1986). Future studies must build on existing research to investigate early labor market entry, severe job search strain, and related psychosocial problems among black teenagers. To guide the development of more coherent theory and responsive intervention, studies should be carefully designed to unravel the specific psychosocial effects of actual joblessness, various subjective reactions to job search difficulties, and related coping processes.

A series of studies using national data on black adults and youth have begun to provide some direction for future inquiry on how the harmful effects of unemployment may be exacerbated by subjective reactions such as low job search expectancies. While the majority of unemployed black youth in a recent study expressed some level of hopelessness in their job search, almost all continued to actively look for work (Bowman, 1984; Bowman, Gurin, and Howard, 1984). Compared to jobless black adults, unemployed black youth were far less likely to stop active job search when discouraged (Bowman et al., 1982). In line with learned helplessness theory, becoming so discouraged that they gave up hope was associated with higher levels of psychological distress even when black youth continued to look for a job (Garber and Seligman, 1980). Findings also suggest that, in addition to job search expectancy, causal attributions may be another important ingredient in adaptive coping among jobless black youth. Blaming oneself, especially stable personal traits such as ability, for job search failure was associated with increased discouragement and maladaptive psychological reactions. In contrast to self-blame, attributions that job search failure was due to external factors such as job market limitations or racial barriers appeared to be less psychologically debilitating. Moreover, attributing job search difficulties to changeable factors such as effort, age, or education rather than blaming unchangeable causes tended to reduce their level of discouragement in job search. There is also some evidence that parental socialization that transmits proactive postures toward racial barriers may help black teenagers become less intrapunative, less helpless, and more efficacious in their coping (Bowman and Howard, 1985).

Are the harmful effects of discouragement, which appear to be a pivotal aspect of job search strain for black teenagers, reduced if they live in husband-wife families with adequate economic resources? Would cognitive adaptation strategies, which reduce intrapunative self-blame, make black youth feel less helpless and more resourceful in the face of job search discouragement? How might extended family networks, peer support, or religious orientation enable some jobless black teenagers to cope more effectively? If career preparation interventions helped high-risk black males navigate the difficult school to work transition, would job search strain promote more adaptive rather than maladaptive responses? Such questions should be addressed in future research and intervention activities.

SUMMARY AND IMPLICATIONS

This chapter has discussed the sources, nature, and pace of recent labor saving changes in American industrial technology. Rapid displacement of specific industrial job categories is identified as a growing psychosocial risk factor with differential impact. Although all blue-collar workers are "at risk," racial minorities in general and black men in particular are hardest hit because of their concentration in the most vulnerable jobs. Other risk factors including an increasingly skilled labor market, pervasive academic underachievement, recurring economic recession, and urban racial segregation interact with deindustrialization to increase the economic marginality of displaced black males. The differential impact of postindustrial labor market changes on black males not only affects their personal lives but also has crucial ripple effects with black families. A role strain-adaptation model is presented that conceptualizes intrafamilial ripple effects in terms of a succession of provider role strains and related psychosocial processes. This model links rapid postindustrial displacement and related family-based role strains to growing psychosocial problems experienced by high-risk fathers, mothers, and children.

Research directions deduced from the role strain-adaptation model have important theoretical and practical implications. Related research can provide a coherent basis for advancing basic social psychological knowledge on the nature and consequences of role strains in complex social settings (Barnett and Baruch, 1985; Baruch and Barnett, 1986; Fried, 1979; Pearlin, 1983; Sarbin and Allen, 1968). Guided by the proposed model, empirical studies can systematically link crucial aspects of individual role behavior with forces at the group and societal level. The general focus is on how the psychosocial effects of structured inequalities or stressful life events are mediated by individual role strain and coping processes within social groups. Psychological studies on unemployment, and other socially structured stressors in natural settings, would do well to focus on the nature and consequences of related role strains (Catalano and Dooley, 1980; Cohn, 1978; Feather and Davenport, 1981; Ferman and Gordus, 1979; Jahoda, 1982; Kelvin and Jarrett, 1985).

As a basis to develop further the role strain-adaptation model, future research on postindustrial displacement should investigate how its psychosocial consequences are mediated by a sequelae of intrafamilial role strains: How are the harmful effects of displacement mediated by actual provider role difficulties faced by family members and their subjective reactions to such difficulties? How might formal intervention combine with informal sociocultural coping mechanisms to eliminate harmful intrafamilial effects of displacement? Research on these questions offer potential to incorporate ideas from learned helplessness and learned resourcefulness theories within the role strain-adaptation framework to specify better social psychological factors that mediate both maladaptive and adaptive consequences (Barnett and Baruch, 1985; Baruch and Barnett, 1986; Fried, 1979; Garber and Seligman, 1980; Pearlin, 1983; Rosenbaum and Ben-Ari, 1985). Preliminary studies suggest that an expectancy of failure in the family provider role, a cognitive dimension of provider role strain, operates to exacerbate harmful psychosocial effects of objective provider role difficulties in distinct ways for fathers, mothers, and children (Beale, 1986; Bowman, 1983b, 1984, 1985; Bowman et al., 1982; Harrison, Bowman, and Beal, 1985). These studies further suggest that cohesive families, religious orientation, and causal attributions may reduce but fail to eliminate such deleterious psychosocial effects.

The theoretical model, together with future empirical research, have practical relevance for guiding responsive public policy to support black family members in their efforts to cope effectively with postindustrial changes. Careful planning is necessary to prevent the potentially devastating effects of labor-saving industrial technology on high-risk black males and, in turn, on their families. A viable national strategy would not only ensure that massive deindustrialization improve economic productivity, but also that inevitable job displacement does not have catastrophic human consequences on any sector of society (Ayres and

Miller, 1981-1982, 1982; Choates, 1982; Luria, 1981). For example, Japanese industrial policy has encouraged the acceptance of automation largely because employers have been responsible for employee retraining and in some cases workers have even received a share of the profits (Hunt and Hunt, 1983). In contrast, neither the U.S. government nor private industry has adequately addressed issues related to the differential impact or psychosocial costs of modern labor-saving technology for black fathers, mothers, and teenage children.

Urban black males, who were often recruited to northern industrial cities earlier in the century to meet pressing labor market demands, now face growing obsolescence largely because they are not being prepared for rapid displacement or employment transition. Moreover, social welfare policy has yet to address adequately intrafamilial ripple effects of postindustrial displacement that make growing labor force attrition of black males, feminization of black family poverty, and black teenage unemployment inseparable issues. The role strain-adaptation model and related research suggest that responsive public policy must include provisions for intervention at three levels: (1) *employment-training* interventions that prevent the permanent displacement of growing numbers of high-risk black males into a jobless underclass, (2) *family work-sharing* interventions that interrupt the intrafamilial ripple effects of postindustrial displacement and promote self-reliant black families rather than welfare dependency, and (3) *personal empowerment* interventions that reverse the harmful psychosocial effects of displacement-related role strains on individual family members and reinforce their efforts to cope effectively.

In the long run, socially responsible industrial and employment policy initiatives must expand upon provisions for other high-risk groups and target strategies toward the specific risk factors that result in growing numbers of black males being permanently displaced into economic obsolescence (Ayres and Miller, 1982; Luria, 1981; Wool, 1978). For example, rather than broad notions of full employment, intervention must incorporate intensive training and employment transition strategies specifically targeted to the unique plight of displaced black males in postindustrial America (Etzioni, 1983; Leontief, 1982). Strategies must include innovative pedagogy to reverse and prevent the pervasive pattern of failure among black males in traditional educational and retraining settings. Moreover, employment transition intervention must go beyond supported work provisions and include strategies to (1) remove or circumvent various barriers that have restricted the access of black males to higher-status industrial jobs, and (2) facilitate the movement of more black males into service jobs or other economic sectors with expanding job opportunities. Employment-training intervention should also consider the crucial intergenerational dimension of postindustrial displacement and target distinct strategies toward (a) prime working age black men who have lost blue-collar industrial jobs, and (b) their sons and grandsons who may increasingly find themselves entrapped in urban areas where such unskilled jobs are no longer an option. To be effective, such long-run strategies would require a unique combination of government leadership, private sector commitment, and local community support.

In order to interrupt the devastating ripple effects postindustrial displacement is already having on black families, the employment-training strategies discussed above need to be further incorporated into a more comprehensive family work-sharing policy. Although there are likely multiple causes for growing poverty and instability within black families, two factors appear especially crucial: (1) the lack of economic support from growing numbers of displaced black fathers, and (2) a family welfare system that discourages the sharing of resources and stable relationships between displaced fathers and mothers (Auletta, 1982; Bane and Ellwood, 1984; Duncan, 1984; Ellwood and Bane, 1983; McAdoo, 1984). It follows that black family poverty and instability could be substantially reduced by a responsible work-sharing policy that (a) increased employment among displaced fathers and the mothers of their children, (b) required black fathers and mothers to share earned resources to provide child support, and (c) developed incentives to increase the involvement of black fathers in child rearing. Such work-sharing provisions would reduce provider role strain among displaced black fathers, while also reducing multiple-role strain among working mothers. Moreover, parental work-sharing could also reduce the pressure on black teenage children to seek jobs prematurely for family economic survival, while providing a more stable and supportive family environment for improving their academic and career preparation. It is also important to note that emphases in family work-sharing on jobs, earned entitlements and self-reliance over welfare, government handouts, and dependency represent a potential convergence of conservative "workfare," liberal "supported work," and black "self-reliance" policy agendas (Hamilton, 1986). The concept of work sharing also provides an integrative family policy framework within which to address economic problems of disparate underclass groups including displaced men, single welfare mothers, and jobless teenagers (Kelly, 1985).

While employment and family work-sharing policies offer promise for long-run prevention, the growing psychosocial consequences of provider role strains experienced by displaced males and their families require more immediate intervention. In the short run, personal empowerment interventions can be designed to mobilize naturally occurring resources that mitigate harmful psychosocial effects of role strains and promote adaptive coping among high-risk black fathers, mothers, and children. Guided by ongoing role strain-adaptation research, formal services and self-help efforts should seek to enhance coping capacity by reinforcing both sociocultural resources such as cohesive families and cognitive adaptation strategies such as reality-based attributions. Policymakers, human service workers, and mental health professionals might also find helpful guidance from exemplary intervention activities being developed and evaluated at the Michigan Prevention Research Center. [2] To avert the growing destabilization of black families and communities by accelerating postindustrial changes, both short- and long-run policy agendas seem imperative as we move into the twenty-first century (Ayres and Miller, 1982; Etzioni, 1983; Leontief, 1982; Luria, 1981). While the employment and work-sharing policies represent more "proactive" preventive measures in the long run, short-run efforts can reduce the severity of existing psychosocial consequences (Catalano and Dooley, 1980).

NOTES

1. The sources of official governmental statistics reported in this chapter are the decennial censuses and Current Population Surveys both conducted by the Bureau of the Census. Several periodic reports provided recent data while historical data were obtained from a special report published by the U.S. Bureau of the Census (1979). Also, monthly statistical tabulations and larger summaries from the Bureau of Labor Statistics, a division of the U.S. Department of Labor, were utilized including a quarterly report on *Employment in Perspective: Minority Workers.*

2. For additional information on strategies for such preventive intervention and related research activities, contact Dr. Richard H. Price at the Michigan Prevention Intervention Research Center, Institute for Social Research, Ann Arbor, Michigan.

5

Economic Distress, Family Coping, and Quality of Family Life

Patricia Voydanoff
Brenda W. Donnelly

The nation's economy has entered a period of long-term structural change. Technological developments, shifts in the geographic location of jobs, and the closing of obsolete plants have resulted in declining employment levels in several manufacturing industries and created new opportunities in the information and service sectors of the economy. Effects on the labor force are pervasive and deep, affecting both white-collar and blue-collar workers. Many of those displaced by declining manufacturing industries are either underqualified or overqualified for jobs in the growing sectors of the economy.

These changes are creating high levels of economic distress for families. This distress is reflected in family tensions and instability. Thus there is a need to know how families deal with economic distress and which approaches are most effective in preventing or reducing problems associated with economic distress. This chapter examines the impact of economic distress on quality of family life and assesses the role of family coping resources and behaviors in alleviating the negative effects of economic distress on family life.

A TYPOLOGY OF ECONOMIC DISTRESS

Economic distress is a multidimensional concept including objective and subjective aspects of employment and income (Voydanoff, 1984). The following figure shows a typology of economic distress based on these distinctions:

	Objective	*Subjective*
Employment	Employment Instability	Employment Uncertainty
Income	Economic Deprivation	Economic Strain

Employment instability consists of several dimensions including the number and length of periods of employment and unemployment, underemployment, downward job mobility, inability to obtain entry-level positions, and forced early retirement. Employment uncertainty is a subjective assessment of the probability of unemployment, its likely length, and prospects for reemployment. The employed may be concerned about possible layoffs or cuts in work hours while the unemployed may be discouraged about prospects for reemployment.

The objective aspect of income, economic deprivation, includes low income, insufficient financial resources, and a decrease in income over time. Economic deprivation may result from the inability to work, unemployment, or inadequate pay while employed. Economic strain is a subjective evaluation of one's current financial situation. It includes the perceived adequacy of financial resources, financial concerns and worries, and expectations regarding one's future economic situation.

EFFECTS OF ECONOMIC DISTRESS ON FAMILY LIFE

Research since the depression of the 1930s indicates that economic distress has pervasive effects on families. Unemployment is associated with lower levels of family stability, marital adjustment, family cohesion, marital communication, and harmony in family relations (Atkinson, Liem, and Liem, 1986; Larson, 1984; Scholzman, 1979). Families in which workers experience relatively few periods of unemployment have greater intrafamily integration (Siddique, 1981). Children of the unemployed are at higher risk of illness, child abuse, and infant mortality (Kelly, Sheldon, and Fox, 1985; Margolis, 1982a; Rayman, 1988; Steinberg, Catalano, and Dooley, 1981). Children in families experiencing employment uncertainty also are at risk for illness (Margolis and Farran, 1984). In addition, income loss and insufficient financial resources are associated with family financial disputes and marital tensions (Liker and Elder, 1983; Nowak and Snyder, 1984).

Most earlier work focuses on a single period of unemployment, for example, a plant closing. A number of other aspects of economic distress have been neglected. Therefore, this study tests the following hypothesis:

Hypothesis 1: Economic distress is negatively related to the quality of family life.

FAMILY COPING RESOURCES

Not all families respond in the same way to economic distress. Family stress theory spells out conditions under which stressors, such as unemployment, serious illness, and other life events, are associated with family crisis or disrupted family functioning (Burr, 1973; Hill, 1958; McCubbin and Patterson, 1983; McCubbin et al., 1980; Menaghan, 1983b). It suggests that family coping resources and behaviors influence the effects of stressors on family life.

Family coping resources are characteristics of the family system that facilitate effective problem-solving approaches in response to difficulties, for example, family adaptability and cohesion. Limited research suggests that these resources may be decreased when unemployment occurs (Perrucci and Targ, 1988). More extensive research indicates that family coping resources are associated with higher levels of family functioning during unemployment. Studies of families during the Depression found that family adaptation, family cohesion, and strong marital bonds prior to unemployment were associated with the maintenance of family organization and marital relationships during unemployment (Angell, 1936; Cavan and Ranck, 1938; Liker and Elder, 1983). Larson (1984) reports that, among couples with unemployed husbands, equalitarian role expectations are associated with higher scores on marital adjustment, consensus, quality of marital communication, and harmony in family relations.

This literature suggests the following hypotheses regarding family coping resources:

Hypothesis 2a: Economic distress is negatively associated with family coping resources.

Hypothesis 2b: Family coping resources are positively related to quality of family life.

Hypothesis 2c: Family coping resources mediate the relationship between economic distress and quality of family life.

Hypothesis 3: Family coping resources buffer the effects of economic distress on quality of family life.

FAMILY COPING BEHAVIORS

Families also engage in several types of coping behaviors to deal with stressors. The major types referred to in the family stress literature include (1) managing family resources to decrease vulnerability to stressors, (2) maintaining and strengthening family resources, (3) reducing or eliminating stressors and their hardships, and (4) actively influencing ingthe environment by changing social circumstances (McCubbin et al., 1980). Coping behaviors are actions directed toward specific stressors whereas coping resources are generalizable across stressors.

Research has documented the use of several family coping behaviors designed to improve the financial situation of families experiencing economic distress. These behaviors include cutting expenditures, increasing home production, spouses taking jobs, and spending savings and/or going into debt (Curtin, Gordon, and Ponza, 1981; Larson, 1984; Perrucci et al., 1985; Rayman, 1983; Root, 1983). Despite the documentation of these behaviors, we know little about their effects on the quality of family life. Nowak and Snyder (1984) find that cutbacks in household expenditures are negatively related to marital satisfaction and positively related to family tensions among both men and women. Family problems result from role shifts when the wives of unemployed professionals become employed (Kaufman, 1982; Leventman, 1981).

This chapter tests the following hypotheses regarding family coping behaviors:

Hypothesis 4a: Economic distress is positively associated with family coping behaviors.

Hypothesis 4b: Family coping behaviors are positively related to quality of family life.

Hypothesis 4c: Family coping behaviors counteract the effects of economic distress on quality of family life.

Hypothesis 5: Family coping behaviors buffer the effects of economic distress on quality of family life.

Because of the preliminary nature of previous research in this area, these hypotheses are stated in general and exploratory terms.

THE PRESENT STUDY

The major objectives of this chapter are (1) to examine the effects of economic distress on quality of family life and family coping resources and behaviors, (2) to determine the direct and indirect effects of family coping resources and behaviors on quality of family life, and (3) to assess the moderating effects of family coping resources and behaviors on relationships between economic distress and quality of family life. The quality of family life is a subjective evaluation in which individuals indicate their degree of satisfaction with their marriage and family life.

This study moves beyond previous research by articulating and investigating the effects of several components of economic distress on quality of family life among both men and women by developing hypotheses regarding the effects of coping resources and behaviors on relationships between economic distress and quality of family life and by testing the hypotheses on a large representative sample of an urban area undergoing significant economic change.

METHODS

Sample Characteristics

The analysis is based on a probability sample of 630 adults between the ages of 18 and 65 in the Dayton, Ohio, metropolitan area. Telephone numbers were drawn randomly from the residential population of the area; nonresidential numbers were eliminated from the sampling lists. Interviewers chose respondents in multi-adult households according to the Bryant modification of the Troldahl and Carter grid (Bryant, 1975) that is designed to provide a sample closely representing the age and sex characteristics of the population. The telephone interviews, conducted during the summer of 1984, averaged 45 minutes in length. The response rate is 64%.

Basic demographic characteristics of the sample include the following: 52% female; 82% white; 64% married; 58% with more than a high school education; and 35% with family incomes of less than $20,000. The median age is 34.7 years. These figures are generally comparable with

1980 census figures for the area although women, 18-19-year-olds, the never married, those with a high school education or less, and families with incomes under $20,000 are slightly underrepresented (see Voydanoff and Donnelly, 1986, for more detailed information regarding the survey and sampling procedures).

This study draws on data for the 203 married men and 207 married women.

Measures

QUALITY OF FAMILY LIFE

The indicator of quality of family life, marital/family satisfaction (MFSAT), consists of answers to the following two questions: "All in all, how satisfied would you say you are with your marriage?" and "All in all, how satisfied would you say you are with your family life?" The response categories include extremely satisfied, very satisfied, somewhat satisfied, and not too satisfied. The alpha coefficient of reliability is .81.

ECONOMIC DISTRESS

The study includes measures of the four components of economic distress—economic deprivation, employment instability, economic strain, and employment uncertainty. The indicator of *economic deprivation* is the total income available to the respondent's household during the past year (FAM.INC). Five response categories were presented to respondents: (1) under $10,000, (2) between $10,000 and $20,000, (3) over $20,000 but less than $35,000, (4) between $35,000 and $50,000, and (5) over $50,000.

The measure of *employment instability* consists of a dummy variable in which respondents who are currently unemployed or have been unemployed at some time during the past three years are coded 1 (SOME.UNEMP). A comparable dummy variable was computed for spouses (SOME.UNEMP.SP).

Insecurity (INSEC), the indicator of *economic strain*, is a summated scale consisting of responses to two questions: "In general, how hard is it *now* for you and your family to live on its present income—very hard, fairly hard, not too hard, not hard at all?" and "When you think of your family's financial situation, how secure do you feel—very secure, somewhat secure, not too secure, not at all secure?" The alpha coefficient of reliability is .75.

Employment uncertainty is a dummy variable indicating responses of certain, very likely, and somewhat likely to the following question: "How likely is it that during the next three years you will lose your present job and have to look for a job with another employer—certain, very likely, somewhat likely, or not at all likely?" (LOSE). A comparable question was used to compute LOSE.SP for spouses.

FAMILY COPING RESOURCES AND BEHAVIORS

Questions used to assess *family coping resources* are adapted from the Family Strengths Scale developed by Olson et al. (1982). The Family Strengths Scale includes two subscales, pride (F.PRIDE) and accord (F.ACCORD). The items for each summated scale are presented in Appendix A. The alpha coefficient of reliability is .88 for pride and .74 for accord.

An additional set of questions examines whether respondents perceive that the allocation of outside employment responsibilities and family decision making are equalitarian in their families. The items are listed in Appendix A. The alpha coefficient of reliability for the summated scale of equalitarian roles (EQ.ROLES) is .62.

A major type of problem-focused *family coping behavior* relevant to economic distress involves efforts to improve the family's financial situation. Responses to 16 financial improvement efforts were entered into a factor analysis. The resulting five factors were used to form the following summated scales: financial management (FIN.MANAGE), alpha coefficient of reliability = .56; informal economy (INF.ECON), alpha = .54; do-it-yourself (DO.IT.SELF), alpha = .44; family work effort (FAM.WORK), alpha = .34; and financial overextension (OVEREXT), alpha = .79. The items for these scales are presented in Appendix A.

DEMOGRAPHIC CONTROLS

Four demographic controls are included in the analyses: age, education, race, and the presence of children. Age (AGE) is coded in number of years. Education (EDUCATION) is categorized as follows: (1) grades 1-7, (2) grade 8, (3) grades 9-11, (4) grade 12, (5) some college without degree, (5.1) junior college degree, (6) college degree, and (7) graduate or professional education. Race (RACE) is a dummy variable indicating white (1) or nonwhite (0). The final demographic control (KIDS) is a dummy variable indicating respondents having one or more children under 18 living in their households.

RESULTS

Appendix B presents the bivariate correlations, means, and standard deviations for the variables included in the analysis. With some exceptions, the correlations among predictors are low. Correlations higher than .35 are found for both men and women between insecurity and income; pride and accord; and insecurity and accord. Relatively high correlations for men include family income and respondent's unemployment; informal economy and insecurity; informal economy and family work effort; and informal economy and do-it-yourself. Spouse's unemployment and family income show a relatively high correlation for women.

Economic Distress and
Quality of Family Life

Table 5.1 presents findings testing Hypothesis 1: Economic distress is negatively related to quality of family life. These findings indicate that, for men, insecurity, respondent's unemployment, and spouse's unemployment show significant negative correlations and regression coefficients for marital/family satisfaction. Among women, negative regression coefficients are significant for spouse's unemployment and spouse's employment uncertainty. Significant correlations for family income, insecurity, and respondent's employment uncertainty are not important in the regression equations.

These results support Hypothesis 1; several indicators of economic distress are associated with lower levels of marital/family satisfaction among men and women. However, not all components of economic distress are equally significant. Economic strain and respondent's and spouse's employment instability are most important for men; spouse's employment uncertainty and instability are most important for women.

Relationships Between Economic Distress
and Family Coping Resources and Behaviors

A portion of Table 5.2 examines Hypothesis 2a: Economic distress is negatively associated with family coping resources. The data

TABLE 5.1
Regressions of Marital/Family Satisfaction on
Economic Distress for Married Men and Women

	Men		*Women*	
	r	beta	r	beta
Demographic Controls				
AGE	−.08	−.17	−.18**	−.22**
EDUCATION	.14*	.00	.19**	.08
RACE	.13*	.03	.24**	.22**
KIDS	.00	.06	.06	.02
Economic Deprivation				
FAM.INC	.13*	.01	.16*	.01
Economic Strain				
INSEC	−.25**	−.22*	−.21**	−.08
Employment Uncertainty				
LOSE	−.02	.06	−.13*	−.05
LOSE.SP	−.06	−.07	−.26**	−.20**
Employment Instability				
SOME.UNEMP	−.23**	−.21*	.06	.04
SOME.UNEMP.SP	−.26**	−.20**	−.21**	−.17*
N	170-180		187-199	
R^2	.19		.22	

*p ≤ .05, 2-tailed test; **p ≤ .01, 2-tailed test.

indicate that several aspects of economic distress are negatively related to family coping resources among men and women. Among men, the correlations are strongest for family income, insecurity, and respondent's employment uncertainty in relation to pride and accord. Among women, the correlations are strongest for several indicators of economic distress and family accord. These data provide support for Hypothesis 2a. Several aspects of economic distress are associated with lower levels of coping resources, especially low income, insecurity, and respondent's employment uncertainty among men and low income, insecurity, and spouse's employment instability and uncertainty among women.

Table 5.2 also presents data relevant to Hypothesis 4a: Economic distress is positively associated with family coping behaviors. The significant correlations indicate positive relationships between several aspects of economic distress and financial improvement efforts. These corre-

TABLE 5.2

Correlations Between Family Coping Resources and Behaviors and Economic Distress for Married Men and Women

	FAM.INC	INSEC	LOSE	LOSE.SP	SOME.UNEMP	SOME.UNEMP.SP
Men						
Family Coping Resources						
F. PRIDE	.19**	-.24**	-.12*	-.11	-.04	-.14*
F. ACCORD	.16*	-.40**	-.12*	.02	-.09	-.05
EQ. ROLES	.25**	-.11	.01	.15*	.04	.01
Family Coping Behaviors						
FIN.MANAGE	.12*	-.04	.08	-.03	-.04	-.01
INF.ECON	-.37**	.43**	.25**	.01	.22**	.00
DO.IT.SELF	-.13*	.21**	.15	.03	.03	-.10
OVEREXT	.07	.23**	-.08	.15*	.01	.03
FAM.WORK	-.08	.18**	.17*	.20**	.17*	.15*
N	162-170	171-178	172-180	172-180	172-180	176-180
Women						
Family Coping Resources						
F. PRIDE	.10	-.15*	-.11	-.11	.01	-.12
F. ACCORD	.27**	-.41**	-.16*	-.27**	.02	-.19**
EQ. ROLES	.16*	-.09	.01	-.01	.03	.05
Family Coping Behaviors						
FIN.MANAGE	.04	-.01	-.12	.04	.03	.06
INF.ECON	-.27**	.22**	.26**	.18**	.06	.34*
DO.IT.SELF	.01	.07	.05	.05	-.02	.03
OVEREXT	.17*	-.10	.13*	.18**	-.03	-.11
FAM.WORK	-.05	.05	.19**	.20**	.14*	.08
N	174-186	183-197	184-198	184-198	184-198	184-198

*p ≤ .05, 2-tailed test; **p ≤ .01, 2-tailed test.

lations are strongest for informal economy and family work effort among men and informal economy, overextension, and family work effort among women. Among men, informal economy and family work effort are most likely to be used by those reporting insecurity, employment uncertainty, and unemployment. Among women, use of the informal economy, overextension, and family work effort are most closely associated with respondent's and spouse's employment uncertainty. Hypothesis 4a is supported most strongly for insecurity among men and respondent and spouse employment uncertainty among women.

Both hypotheses are supported for some components of economic distress and indicators of family coping resources and behaviors. In general, economic distress is associated with lower levels of family coping resources and higher levels of family coping behaviors.

Relationships Between Family
Coping Resources and Behaviors
and Quality of Family Life

Table 5.3 presents data that test Hypotheses 2b and 4b: Family coping resources and behaviors are positively related to quality of family life. The data show that two family coping resources, pride and accord, are positively related to marital/family satisfaction in both the correlation and regression analyses for men and women. However, equalitarian roles shows modest negative associations with marital/family satisfaction in the regression equations. Among men, one family coping behavior, financial management, is positively related to marital/family satisfaction in the correlation and regression analyses. However, two other coping behaviors, informal economy and family work effort, are associated with lower levels of marital/family satisfaction. Family coping behaviors are not related to marital/family satisfaction among women.

The findings for pride and accord support Hypothesis 3; both of these family coping resources are associated with higher levels of marital/family satisfaction. With one exception, the findings for coping behaviors do not support Hypothesis 4b. Thus family coping resources generally are positively related to marital/family satisfaction whereas coping behaviors are not.

TABLE 5.3

Regressions of Marital/Family Satisfaction on Family Coping
Resources and Behaviors for Married Men and Women

	Men		Women	
	r	beta	r	beta
Demographic Controls				
AGE	−.08	−.06	−.18**	−.15
EDUCATION	−.14*	−.03	.19**	.07
RACE	.13*	.10	.24**	.19**
KIDS	.00	.03	.06	.01
Family Coping Resources				
F. PRIDE	.32**	.22**	.53**	.37**
F. ACCORD	.28**	.14	.44**	.27**
EQ. ROLES	−.01	−.08	.04	−.09
Family Coping Behaviors				
FIN. MANAGE	.23**	.18*	.07	−.00
INF. ECON	−.18**	−.13	−.07	.00
DO. IT. SELF	−.02	.08	.07	.05
OVEREXT	−.02	−.00	−.02	−.07
FAM. WORK	−.19**	−.12	−.03	.01
N	172-180		184-199	
R^2	.21		.40	

*p ≤ .05, 2-tailed test; **p ≤ .01, 2-tailed test.

Do Family Coping Resources Mediate the Relationship Between Economic Distress and Quality of Family Life?

Path analysis is used to test Hypothesis 2c: Family coping resources mediate the relationship between economic distress and quality of family life. Path analysis is a statistical technique based on multiple-regression analysis that tests additive causal models and allows one to determine the extent to which relationships between variables are direct or indirect, that is, operate through other variables. Hypothesis 2c indicates an expectation that most of the relationship between economic distress and quality of family life will be accounted for by the negative relationship between economic distress and family coping resources and the positive relationship between coping resources and quality of family life.

Separate path analyses were computed for all combinations of the indicators of economic distress and pride and accord (data are available from the authors). These analyses provide limited support for the hypothesis. Among women, accord mediated the relationships between insecurity and income and marital/family satisfaction. Among men, pride and accord were independent contributors to high marital/family satisfaction among those experiencing unemployment and those whose spouses had been unemployed. The bulk of the analyses reveal that family coping resources are partial mediators of the relationship between economic distress and quality of family life, that is, they show both direct and indirect effects of economic distress on quality of family life.

Do Family Coping Behaviors Counteract the Effects of Economic Distress on Quality of Family Life?

Additional path analyses test Hypothesis 4c: Family coping behaviors counteract the effects of economic distress on quality of family life, that is, the effects of economic distress on quality of family life are reduced by using family coping behaviors. Separate analyses were computed for each combination of the indicators of economic distress and informal economy and family work effort. These analyses do not support Hypothesis 4c. Among men, family coping behaviors tend to intensify the effects of economic distress on quality of family life, that is, economic distress is associated with higher levels of informal economy and family work effort that in turn are associated with lower marital/family satisfaction. However, most of the relationship between economic distress and marital/family satisfaction is direct and does not operate indirectly through family coping behaviors. Since family coping behaviors are not related to marital/family satisfaction among women, the relationship between economic distress and quality of family life is direct and not influenced by family coping behaviors.

Buffering the Effects of Economic Distress on Quality of Family Life

Hypotheses 3 and 5 propose that family coping resources and behaviors buffer the effects of economic distress on marital/family satisfaction. When buffering effects occur, economic distress does not have negative effects on marital/family satisfaction among those with high levels of coping resources and behaviors. Negative relationships between economic distress and marital/family satisfaction occur only among those with low levels of coping resources and behaviors and disappear among those with high levels. The moderating effects of coping resources and behaviors are examined by entering control variables, an economic distress measure, a coping measure, and the cross-product of the two measures in a separate regression equation. These regression equations are calculated for economic distress measures with direct effects on marital/family satisfaction, that is insecurity, SOME.UNEMP, and SOME. UNEMP.SP for men and LOSE.SP and SOME.UNEMP.SP for women (data are available from the authors).

The analyses reveal one significant interaction for family coping resources among men. Family pride buffers the negative effects of respondent's unemployment on marital/family satisfaction. Several nonsignificant interactions indicate a mixture of buffering and exacerbating effects. When exacerbating effects occur, negative relationships between economic uncertainty and marital/family satisfaction are stronger rather than weaker among those with family coping resources. The data for women reveal no significant interactions; however, most nonsignificant interactions suggest buffering effects.

These results provide little support for Hypothesis 3. Family coping resources have nonsignificant buffering effects among women; for men coping resources have buffering effects in some cases and exacerbating effects in others.

No significant interactions for family coping behaviors are found for either men or women. Among men, coping behaviors either have no effect on relationships between economic distress and marital/family satisfaction or nonsignificant exacerbating effects. Coping behaviors generally show nonsignificant buffering effects on relationships between spouse uncertainty and unemployment and marital/family satisfaction among women. These results do not support Hypothesis 5.

DISCUSSION

The results provide varying levels of support for the hypotheses. Economic distress is negatively related to marital/family satisfaction. This relationship is strongest for economic strain and respondent's and spouse's employment instability among men; spouse's employment uncertainty and instability are most important for women.

Several aspects of economic distress are associated with lower levels of coping resources, especially economic deprivation, economic strain, and respondent's employment uncertainty among men and economic deprivation, economic strain, and spouse's employment instability and uncertainty among women. In addition, family coping resources are positively related to marital/family satisfaction. Family coping resources partially mediate relationships between economic distress and quality of family life.

Economic distress also is positively associated with the use of several coping behaviors, especially informal economy and family work effort. These relationships are stronger for economic strain among men and respondent and spouse employment uncertainty among women. Among men, some coping behaviors are negatively related to quality of family life suggesting that the use of coping behaviors intensifies the effects of economic distress on quality of family life. Family coping behaviors are not related to quality of family life among women.

Neither family coping resources nor family coping behaviors are significant buffers for the effects of economic distress on marital/family satisfaction. Coping resources and behaviors have nonsignificant buffering effects on relationships among spouse uncertainty and unemployment and marital/family satisfaction among women.

These results have several important implications for understanding economic distress and family life. First, they point out the need to specify components of economic distress. The various components differ in the significance of their relationships with quality of family life, the availablity of coping resources, and the use of coping behaviors. The strength of relationships vary among men and women. Among men, economic strain and respondent's employment uncertainty and instability are relatively important. For women, spouse employment uncertainty and instability are relatively more important. Thus the impact of economic distress among men is closely tied to their employment situation and to their family's general economic well-being while the impact for women is most closely related to their husbands' employment situation.

Second, these results indicate the importance of studying relationships among economic distress, coping resources and behaviors, and quality of family life among both men and women. Although the general pattern of support for the hypotheses applies to both men and women, the details differ considerably throughout the analysis. The relative importance of various components of economic distress differ in relation to quality of family life, family coping resources, and family coping behaviors. In addition, coping resources and behaviors are more likely to show buffering effects among women than men.

Lastly, patterns of relationships differ for family coping resources and family coping behaviors. Economic distress is associated with lower levels of family coping resources; however, those with greater resources have higher marital/family satisfaction. Thus lower family coping resources partially explain the relationship between economic distress and marital/family satisfaction. Coping resources have weak, nonsignificant buffering effects on relationships between economic distress and marital/family satisfaction among women and weak buffering and exacerbating effects among men. On the other hand, economic distress is positively related to the use of family coping behaviors; however, the use of these behaviors is not consistently related to marital/family satisfaction. Family coping behaviors slightly intensify relationships between economic distress and marital/family satisfaction among men and have no effect on marital/family satisfaction among women. Coping behaviors show weak buffering effects among women.

Therefore, family coping resources and behaviors generally expected to alleviate the effects of economic distress on marital/family satisfaction do not always have the desired effects. Although family coping resources are associated with higher levels of marital/family satisfaction, the level of coping resources is generally lower among those experiencing economic distress. Family coping behaviors may address the financial problems associated with economic distress; however, they do not have positive effects on marital/family satisfaction. Coping resources and behaviors are generally not successful in buffering the effects of economic distress on marital/family satisfaction.

Policies and programs designed to address the effects of economic distress on family life need to take such findings into account. Since family coping resources generally have positive effects on marital/family satisfaction, programs to build family coping resources will have relatively direct beneficial effects. Policies and programs oriented toward coping behaviors must be more carefully articulated. Although family coping behaviors may reduce economic distress, their effects on marital/family satisfaction are less positive. Those designing programs to develop the use of these family coping behaviors must take into account that such behaviors are not necessarily associated with positive family outcomes even though they reduce economic distress.

In addition, the findings of this study have bearing on the extent to which programs should be targeted to those experiencing economic distress. Results indicating additive effects of coping resources and behaviors on marital/family satisfaction suggest that general policies and programs designed to increase these resources and behaviors will benefit everyone regardless of the level of economic distress. On the other hand, data indicating buffering effects suggest that policies targeted to those experiencing economic distress would be particularly effective for these families and of lesser value to those not experiencing economic distress. This chapter provides more support for a broad-based approach since the findings for direct additive relationships are stronger than those for buffering effects.

This study provides a relatively comprehensive analysis of relationships between economic distress and quality of family life. It examines the impact of family coping resources and behaviors on relationships between several aspects of economic distress and marital/family satisfaction. The approach used in this study represents a beginning effort to isolate processes and mechanisms through which economic distress affects family life; more work is needed to continue to map out the processes through which these relationships occur.

APPENDIX A
Items in Multiple-Item Scales

Family Strengths

Respondents were asked, "Here are some statements about families. Please say whether or not you agree with the statements for your family." Response categories include (4) strongly agree, (3) agree, (2) disagree, and (1) strongly disagree. Family pride includes the following items:

We can express our feelings.
We really do trust and confide in each other.
Family members feel loyal to the family.
We share similar values and beliefs as a family.
Things work out well for us as a family.
Members respect one another.
We are proud of our family.

Family accord consists of:

We tend to worry about many things.
We have the same problems over and over.
Accomplishing what we want to do seems difficult for us.
We are critical of each other.
There are many conflicts in our family.

The items in this scale were coded in the reverse direction.

Equalitarian Roles

The introduction and response categories are the same as those for family strengths. The following items make up the scale of equalitarian roles:

In our family, the wife should not work outside the home unless it is an absolute financial necessity.

The husband should have the final word in most of the important decisions in our family.

For us, the husband's occupation is always regarded as more important than the wife's.

The items were coded in the reverse direction.

Financial Improvement Efforts

Respondents were asked, "People have different ways of improving their financial situation. Have you and your family tried to improve your financial situation in any of these ways?" Possible responses were (4) yes or (1) no.

The financial management scale includes the following items:

Keep records of spending so you can budget money.

Decide what is most important to spend your money on.

Make advance plans about how to use your time and money.

Informal economy:

Shop at food co-op.

Buy used goods, for example, clothing/garage sales.

Exchange help with others (repairs, babysitting, clothing).

Sell personal items (clothing, furniture, household items).

Do odd jobs to earn money (painting, child care).

Do-it-yourself:

Do own household repairs and work.

Grow fruit and vegetables in order to save money.

Make clothing.

Family work effort:

> Someone in your family took a second or third job.
> Family member worked overtime.
> Family member who was not working went to work.

Overextension:

> Buy on credit/borrow money.
> Spend savings.

APPENDIX B
Bivariate Correlations, Means, and Standard Deviations for Married Men (Upper Triangle) and Married Women (Lower Triangle)

	1	2	3	4	5	6	7	8	9	10	11	12	13	14	15	16	17	18	19	Mean	Standard Deviation
FAM. INC		-.40	-.05	-.49	-.20	.09	.19	.16	.24	.14	-.33	-.07	-.10	-.10	.21	.51	.19	-.11	.13	3.27	1.00
SOME. UNEMP	-.07		.15	.31	.21	-.04	-.05	-.09	.04	-.12	.26	.01	.01	.17	-.26	-.22	-.11	.23	.23	.18	.38
SOME. UNEMP. SP	-.37	-.00		.19	.01	.13	-.15	-.06	-.01	-.01	.02	-.05	.00	.18	-.13	-.03	-.16	.16	-.26	.14	.35
INSEC	-.50	.06	.31		.21	-.06	-.23	-.39	-.13	-.03	.42	.19	.18	.18	-.22	-.31	-.25	.32	-.25	4.10	1.46
LOSE	.00	.18	.07	.20		.25	-.14	-.11	-.02	.05	.25	.11	-.10	.15	-.17	-.20	-.15	.12	-.02	.27	.44
LOSE. SP	-.12	.07	.29	.22	.24		-.08	.39	.15	.00	.00	.06	.12	.22	-.02	-.07	-.01	.09	-.06	.19	.39
F. PRIDE	.10	.03	-.12	-.15	-.12	-.12		-.08	.16	.13	.13	-.10	.04	-.17	-.16	.28	.01	.09	.32	23.21	2.73
F. ACCORD	.25	.04	-.20	-.41	-.16	-.28	.45		.06	.09	-.25	-.03	-.14	-.15	.15	.20	.11	-.05	.28	13.28	2.10
EQ. ROLES	.15	.05	.05	-.08	-.01	-.01	.11	.13		.11	-.07	.01	.08	-.08	-.15	.25	-.10	.02	-.01	8.01	1.49
FIN. MANAGE	.07	.02	.04	-.04	-.08	.03	.10	.08	.12		.07	.09	.01	-.04	-.21	.17	.00	.25	.23	10.68	2.20
INF. ECON	-.25	.08	.32	.20	.20	.16	-.15	-.27	-.10	.06		.41	.11	.36	-.13	-.27	-.14	.00	-.18	9.38	3.81
DO. IT. SELF	.04	-.01	.03	.04	.04	.04	.10	-.07	-.03	.05	.23		.17	.28	.04	-.09	-.06	.21	-.02	7.09	2.84
OVEREXT	.21	-.03	-.14	-.10	.11	.17	.01	.04	.10	-.00	-.01	.13		.18	-.19	.07	.01	.19	-.19	5.37	2.21
FAM. WORK	-.01	.16	.05	.02	.17	.19	.00	-.18	.05	-.05	.23	.26	.18		-.01	-.09	.02	.19	-.08	5.53	2.66
AGE	.06	-.20	-.21	.07	-.05	-.20	-.15	.02	-.28	-.14	-.23	.14	-.13	-.16		-.10	.07	.05	.14	40.44	12.19
EDUCATION	.47	-.02	-.13	-.31	.04	-.08	.16	.25	.37	-.01	-.14	.05	.22	.02	-.13		.26	.01	.13	4.96	1.23
RACE	.14	.00	.03	-.05	-.10	.01	.05	.02	-.03	.02	.04	.16	.02	-.02	-.04	.11		-.04	.00	.89	.32
KIDS	-.06	.11	.15	.09	.01	.06	-.02	.04	.04	.12	.20	.00	.04	.12	-.45	-.04	-.04		.06	.57	.50
MFSAT	.16	.06	-.21	-.21	-.13	-.24	.53	.44	.44	.07	-.07	.07	-.02	-.03	-.18	.19	.24	.06		3.44	.69
Mean	3.06	.16	.22	4.31	.24	.28	23.25	13.07	7.92	10.58	10.35	7.32	5.39	5.97	39.18	4.75	.87	.57	3.40		
Standard Deviation	1.00	.37	.42	1.57	.43	.45	3.35	2.49	1.88	2.15	4.01	3.00	2.34	2.64	11.61	1.22	.32	.50	.72		

NOTE: Pairwise missing data results in Ns ranging from 176 to 180 for married men and 184 to 199 for married women.

PART III

Understanding Unemployment

Compared with previous sections, the chapters in Part III provide a more qualitative view of unemployment and its effects on individuals and families. The authors present case studies to highlight individuals' subjective responses to unemployment and their interpretation of the consequences of unemployment for their lives. In this way these chapters enrich our understanding of the meaning of unemployment to the unemployed and members of their families. This understanding is needed for the development of policies and programs that effectively address the concerns of those experiencing economic distress.

Rayman's analysis of the meaning of unemployment for children describes a chain reaction in which unemployment first affects the unemployed parent followed in turn by effects on family relationships and children's mental and physical health. This process is similar to the ripple-effect discussed by Bowman in the previous section. It illustrates the complex processes involved in relationships between economic distress and family life. Rayman further documents this complexity by presenting case studies of unemployment in three types of families: unemployed male families, feminization of poverty families, and general hardship families.

The Liem chapter views the subjectivity and meaning of unemployment from a different perspective, namely, by examining the extent to which the unemployed are victims or critics of their situation. He looks beyond the frequently documented emotional and family strain associated with unemployment and focuses on individual and spouse perceptions of the causes and solutions of unemployment. Liem describes the ways in which the unemployed assert their interests rather than perceiving themselves as helpless victims. He discusses how actions such as resisting reemployment at lower skill levels and postponing application for Unemployment Insurance and other benefits can be perceived as the avoidance of demeaning solutions to problems rather than as self-defeating refusal to accept one's unfortunate circumstances.

Rayman's case studies demonstrate various effects of deprivation on families and children and point to the need for preventive and ameliorative interventions. Rayman suggests that these interventions should focus on eliminating the source of problems through changes in the social and economic order, providing job-skill training to low-income women, addressing the special needs of families experiencing long-term unemployment, and providing adequate health care and social services.

Liem discusses the importance of viewing policy from a perspective that takes into account both the objective and subjective interests of the unemployed and creating programs that address the needs of the unemployed without fostering dependence. He also stresses the need for the unemployed to participate in the formulation and enactment of policies and programs to address unemployment. This chapter anticipates the chapters in Part IV which discuss responses to economic distress in political, cultural, and institutional terms.

6

Unemployment and Family Life: The Meaning for Children

Paula Rayman

You will get new shoes when you get to heaven [Carl Sandberg, 1936].

Due to recent economic events in the industrialized world, social scientists have given renewed attention to the issue of unemployment. In the early 1980s unemployment rates reached levels not experienced since the Depression Era, going into double digits and stabilized in the United States at between 6% and 7% of the labor force. The official unemployment rates, however, ignore not only those who are termed "discouraged workers" and those involuntarily working part time but also family members affected by a wage-earner's job loss. [1] In particular we know very little about the significance of parental unemployment for children in "unemployed families"—the short- and long-range consequences for child health, safety, and development.

With 100 million people in the U.S. labor force, each 1% rise in the unemployment rate translates to another one million people out of work. Lewis Margolis (1982a) estimated that during the 1981-1982 recession, with nearly one out of five workers experiencing some unemployment,

119

the number of children affected was substantially over 10 million. The classic Depression studies of unemployment (Bakke, 1933, 1940; Komarovsky, 1940; Jahoda, Lazarsfeld, and Zeisel, 1971; Angell, 1936) provide strong evidence of the ways in which job loss produces stressful change in families. These stresses include decline in both financial and social status, changes in family role patterns, and absence of security and hope for the future. The task of research on the relationship of unemployment and child welfare is to broaden our understanding of how such job loss family stress is experienced by children, what mediating factors exist within the family, and what are the implications for those concerned with family programs and public policy. This chapter will address each of these research questions.

The heart of this chapter is a series of case studies of children from unemployed and economically distressed families who came to use the medical facilities of Boston's Children's Hospital during the period 1982-1984. Research was conducted at the Family Development Study Unit at the Hospital, which has been interested in the concept of pediatric social illness, which includes child abuse and neglect, failure to thrive, and accidents. This concept directs attention to a broad range of childhood pathologies in which family functioning and social context play a significant etiologic role. [2] Unemployment can be seen as a potentially traumatic experience for a family, which in turn can lead to pain and distress for a child, from short-term impairment of function to a longer-term threat to developmental potential. A study of unemployment and children's lives thus goes beyond individual clinical conditions of the child and encompasses issues of public health.

Before turning to the case studies, a review of previous research on children and unemployment will be presented that establishes a theoretical "chain-reaction" analysis. In addition, recent statistics on relevant factors such as women in the labor force, infant mortality, and single-parent households will provide a contrast with the Depression Era and emphasize the importance of having a historical perspective for social science investigation.

LEARNING FROM THE PAST

The studies of individuals and families during the Depression provide important clues regarding how economic distress is experienced by children. While not establishing causal, definitive patterns of job loss and childhood development, they present clear, often detailed evidence of how parental unemployment changes children's lives. Among the issues raised by the Depression Era research are the consequences of change in parental authority, the movement from wishfulness and hope to feelings of resignation and impotency, and that children of different classes and ages may have different abilities to react and adapt to family difficulties.

> The father was sitting on a low stool with a pile of worn-out children's shoes in front of him that he was trying to mend with roofing felt. . . . The father explained with embarrassment, "You see, this is my Sunday job. On Sundays I have to patch the shoes up a bit so that the children can go off to school again on Monday" [Jahoda, Lazarsfeld, and Zeisel, 1971].

This chapter began with a quote from Carl Sandberg, which reflects what a parent tells a child when the parent cannot provide the basic clothes that the family members need. The above lines are from a study of 1930s unemployment in an Austrian community, *Marienthal*. Unusual for unemployment research, the authors of *Marienthal* actually collected data directly from children as well as adults. Their primary findings were that prolonged unemployment leads to apathy and a "breakdown of social personality structure." For fathers this translated into an inability to be the breadwinner and properly take care of the family. Authority patterns altered in the family, especially as fathers could not literally "earn" their respect from achieving their prescribed role. Because the entire community was so devastated by the factory closedown, fathers and mothers had few places to go for outside support. As unemployment dragged on in Marienthal, families moved closer and closer to the last stages of weariness and catastrophe. Children's responses to this skidding transition were captured by an essay, "What I want for Christmas," that the authors asked children to write. Compared to children of working parents, the Marienthal children asked for gifts costing only one-third as much. Moreover, they hesitated to ask for anything at all. And even when they asked for relatively little, what they actually received was even less. The discrepancy between wish and fulfillment was enormous, fostering sentiments among the children of resignation to a world offering scarcity. Children were learning not to expect toys or new shoes as parents grew increasingly embarrassed and depressed about becoming nonproviders.

On the other side of the ocean at the same time period children were also seeking shoes:

> Dear Mrs. Rossvelt my mother can not read nor write and she have to take
> care of five in family. I have no shoe and we are suffin sometime we is with
> no fire and I am bare foot [McElvaine, 1983].

This letter, one of many compiled by Robert McElvaine, was written by
a child in St. Louis, Missouri, in 1936. McElvaine (1983) comments in
his section on the "Forgotten Children" that while children did not blame
themselves for the unemployment of their parents, they did try to make
things better by writing letters to people they thought could help or
by going out to get whatever work they could find if they were old
enough. The letters from children show a belief that someone in power
will come to their rescue. They also suggest that children of different
ages attempt different activities depending on what they understand of
their situation. Older children, for example, can assume more of an adult
role, which may have positive maturing effects as well as more negative
consequences.

Glen H. Elder (1974) in *Children of the Great Depression* goes farther
than most other works concerned with that era to establish what in fact
happened to children, reinterpreting data concerning adolescents from
working and middle classes during the Depression in a California community. Elder utilizes an analytic model that posits that crises do not
reside within a particular individual or situation but from the interaction
between the individual and social events. Thus individuals can adapt to
crises in various ways as they try to achieve control over their life situation and solve problems stemming from economic deprivation. His work
demonstrates that the Depression influenced families in different ways,
with children from middle-class homes generally faring better in the long
run than children, especially boys, from working-class backgrounds.

To link economic loss and the child, Elder studied changes in three
categories: family division of labor, family relationships, and social
strains. In terms of family relations, he found that severe economic loss
caused children to diminish their view of their father and increase the
mother's centrality as decision maker and primary family resource. As
family losses increased, children were more apt to think erroneously that
their peers thought less of them. From data collected on these same children as adults, Elder discovered that class played an important differentiating role in eventual outcomes of the Depression experiences, with
working-class youth suffering more lasting impairment of health, self-
confidence, and resiliency. For all children of the Depression, Elder
found that, as adults, values of family life and raising children were
paramount.

Finally, regarding the Depression Era research, the work by Mirra Komarovsky (1940) sheds additional light on the pain in family relations caused by the erosion of father authority and the ascension of new roles assumed by the spouse of the unemployed.

Komarovsky pays close attention to the ways in which the wife and mother becomes the heart and soul of family life and that much depends on her resiliency. Children throughout early socialization are taught the importance of work and how identity and self-esteem are centrally caught up in the work process. When, therefore, a father becomes unemployed, the linkage is called into question and to the child the father may seem shattered. How a child reacts may in part depend on what other family members can contribute to a sense of rebuilding, coping, and possible hope.

RECENT STUDIES

The 1970s and 1980s have marked another major historical period producing unemployment research. This is not surprising as it was not until this moment in the post-World War II era that so many workers experienced being out of work. At the same time more general research on stress and child development had occurred since the 1940s, which has informed the theoretical and empirical framework of the more recent explorations. The most useful analysis seems to develop the idea of a "chain-reaction" approach to understanding the link between job loss and child welfare: an unemployment event—parental stress—family disruption—child stress. At each juncture there are possibilities for negative and positive adaptations.

An exciting ongoing study of the children of Martha's Vineyard, Massachusetts, is providing new knowledge about the effects of stress on families and disorders in children (Collins, 1983). The study concentrates on 400 children, assessing what kinds of stress are most damaging to children and how families and health care professionals can best cope with it. Preliminary results state that among families reporting chronic stress-producing difficulties, the most prevalent worry was financial security; also chronic continual stress, such as that caused by long-term unemployment, is suspected to be a significant factor in causing psychiatric and behavioral disorders in children.

Robert Kelly and others at Wayne State University (Kelly, Sheldon, and Fox, 1985) have looked at economic dislocation and child health during the early 1980s recession in the hard-hit automobile industry region of the Midwest. They find, through interviews of parents about their children, that job loss has an indirect and subtle relationship to child health. Specifically, they found that unemployment, while not the sole source of economic insecurity, is strongly associated with subjective economic stress, which in turn is strongly predictive of health problems for parents, which is the strongest predictor of health problems for children.

Margolis and Farran (1981) also examined the health effects on children of parental job loss and found that the children of laid-off hourly workers, when compared to the children of retrained workers, appeared to be at greater risk for illness in general, infectious illness and illnesses of longer duration.

Additional recent research focusing on children and unemployment has employed macrodata analysis to associate child health and job loss often complicated by poverty. Research that shows an association between child abuse and unemployment (Gil, 1971, 1973; Catalano, 1982; Brenner, 1976) does not usually distinguish between temporary and chronic unemployment and how poverty itself may be a source of family stress. Others researching relationships between more general economic change and family and child well-being (Justice and Duncan, 1977; Brenner, 1973; Cherlin, 1979) conclude that indeed economic instability of a family is associated with increases in infant mortality, child abuse, and marital difficulties.

There are very few studies in which the voices of children themselves are heard. Paulter and Lewko (1983) administered a 75-item worry inventory to 538 boys and 483 girls from grades 6, 9, and 12 in an economically distressed community of Canada. They found that worries were heightened for those children living in unemployed households. The unemployment effect was most pronounced in children grade 6. For these children, economic uncertainty was posited as a source of multiple worries.

Artie Morris-Vann (1984), an elementary guidance counselor for the Detroit Public Schools, presented Congressional testimony reviewing her work with children of the unemployed. She stated that children are often confused by the unemployment event, not comprehending why a parent may suddenly be emotionally upset or why tension mounts in the household. Some children felt their bad behavior had somehow sparked their parent's dismissal from a job. Many children expressed fear regarding the outcome of unemployment, including eviction, having to wear ragged clothes, starving, selling their toys, and having other children laugh at them. Embarrassment and loneliness were common concerns, with children feeling badly about making up excuses for not being able to go places with better-off friends.

HISTORICAL CONTEXT

In comparing what we have learned regarding unemployment and children's lives from the Depression Era to research done more recently, there are a number of salient similarities and a few major differences. The importance of working in our culture has remained constant, upholding Freud's notion that love and work are the two primary pillars that constitute a person's foundation and interface with society. Both periods have been focused on the loss of work for male breadwinners and rarely include people of color or from rural locations. Those studies that have taken a more family-oriented approach view women in terms of their spouse role, assessing how well women assume new roles to aid family adaptations. Concerning how children fare, there seems agreement that the longer the duration of job loss, the more children are negatively affected, with factors of class and age of child also influencing outcomes.

However, the terrain in which unemployment exists in the United States has greatly shifted between the 1930s and the 1980s. Maternal employment is common in most households now with a majority of women with preschool children in the labor force. Families in which there are two parents present are reliant on both incomes for family support.

Moreover, there are increasing numbers of children living in single-parent households. It is projected that by the time children born during the period 1975-1980 reach age 17, over 40% of white children and nearly-twice that for black children will be in households without two natural parents present. What constitutes a family has also been affected by a decreasing birth rate, the break up of extended family household arrangements, and the decreasing tendency by families to take in boarders.

Despite the emergence of social welfare programs since the Depression, more children are living in poverty today than ever. One in five children under 3 years of age lives in poverty today—half of all black children and more than half of all children living in female-headed households (Miller, 1983). Thus, in numbers, 22 million children live in poverty. For those who became unemployed in the mid-1970s, only 47% received unemployment compensation and only 5% received welfare/AFDC benefits (Moen, Kain, and Elder, 1983). The longer the unemployment period, the less likely a family was to receive benefits. By the 1980s, 3.5 million children were cut off school food programs and Head Start programs. Finally, infant mortality rates increased in the 1980s in economically distressed regions, as families had fewer resources for food and medical coverage and government programs to aid pregnant women and young children (WIC) were reduced. Thus though there was an expectation of a social safety net in place in recent years that was not there in the Depression, in fact no net seemed to be there for many of the unemployed.

CHILDREN'S HOSPITAL STUDY

In 1983, a team of researchers at the Family Development Study Unit at Children's Hospital, Boston, began a seminar series to discuss the consequences of unemployment for families and children and how these families could be helped to cope with related problems. The Family Development Study Unit, working often with colleagues in the Family Trauma team, the Sexual Abuse team, and Emergency Room services, does short-term family therapy for families referred to the clinic from the greater Boston metropolitan area. Child psychiatrists, pediatricians, nurses, and social workers all confer together on intakes and the type of treatment to be offered to a family. Referrals are made to outside agencies when appropriate. Consultations often take place with representatives from governmental social services agencies, legal services, church associations, and community welfare institutions.

From December 1982 to March 1984, there were 52 family intakes in the unit. As a social scientist on a postdoctoral fellowship at the unit, my research was focused on exploring the relationship of economic dislocation, particularly unemployment, with family stress and child health. In total, 37 of the cases had enough collected data available to warrant examination and became the basis of the case-study research. The perspective shaping the overall analysis of the study was gleaned from the work of Robert Coles (1967) in his excellent series of *Children in Crisis*: Socioeconomic issues are not just parenthetically important, but rather they play a significant role in how family members and children see themselves in the world. Whether a child has proper shoes shapes his or her life experience.

Of the 37 documented cases, 12 families demonstrated severe economic hardship. These can be further categorized for analysis of linking specific economic distress patterns and family outcomes. Three categories emerged: the unemployed male families, the feminization of poverty families, and the general hardship or couples-in-struggle families. For all the families, children were responding with health problems, sometimes physical, sometimes emotional, usually both. The fact that the families came to the clinic was hopeful, at least a recognition of something going wrong. However, coming to the clinic did not necessarily ease the problems much, depending on a family's ability to reconstruct itself in a new way to cope better with ongoing hard realities.

Following are case-history summaries of two families in each category to provide a close-up look at family and child events.

Unemployed Male Household

PEAL FAMILY

Mr. and Mrs. Peal live with their five children. After being unemployed for over one year, Mr. Peal entered a retraining program at a local computer firm. During his job loss he began drinking heavily, started gambling and separated from his wife briefly. They live in a crowded five-room apartment and Mr. Peal states, "I have been a bad provider for my family." While at home one day doing the laundry, the mother, who is depressed, left the baby, 1-year-old, in the bathtub unattended. The child drowned. The other children are scared and feel guilty but do not know what to do. One of the older boys reports being hit by the father. After the clinic visit, the children are removed under a care and protection act to a foster home.

CLAUDE FAMILY

The mother is in her late 30s, the father has been out of work for two years. The 1-year-old child became too much for the mother to deal with. The mother tried to get help for herself; there are no extended family members nearby. The father has begun to drink and is intolerant of the toddler's playing. The mother fears for the child and asks for him to be temporarily placed in foster care until the father finds work.

Feminization of Poverty Families

DAWSON FAMILY

Ms. Dawson lives with her 4-year-old son. They were referred to the clinic by a social worker from the school who noticed Billy's behavior problems and his mother's inability to control him. Ms. Dawson is 22, unemployed with a 10th grade education and has never had a steady job. She was married for a short time to Billy's father who was in the Army. She now lives with her parents, her single-parent sister and her 3-year-old niece. Ms. Dawson wants to have her own place and get a job so she can properly support Billy. She worries about her ability to be a mother but feels if she had some security she would manage fine.

HALL FAMILY

The mother is a single parent with four children. She has no training for a job. She and her children have lived in temporary shelters for one year. The children have been going to school with inappropriate clothing. Mother reports that she has no money for bringing kids to the doctor. Social workers report she may have abused her youngest, a 3-year-old. They question whether to remove the children from the mother. Mother wants to keep children but knows right now she cannot give proper care.

General Hardship Families

POLLO FAMILY

Mother was only 17 when child was born and baby lived with paternal grandparents. Mother recently married a man who has a steady job. He told clinic workers of his pride in his work and his hope that he can make a good home for his stepdaughter. Mother feels she can now make a new start in life after being an unwed mother. She feels her child is very loved but has been through a rough beginning of life. She says that she now has economic security and that makes all the difference.

KATES FAMILY

Mr. and Mrs. Kates live with three children, two of their own, ages 3 and 10, and one older son, 18, from Mrs. Kates's former marriage. Janelle was reported to be doing poorly in school and seems unhappy and depressed. Mrs. Kates thinks the reason why Janelle is having a hard time is because she and her husband are rarely at home in order to make ends meet. Mrs. Kates, after being out of work, finally found a job from four to midnight; Mr. Kates, who also was recently laid off, now is driving a truck and is away a lot. Older son is in charge of caring for Janelle and she says he brings over girlfriends and pays no attention to her. Younger child is watched by Mrs. Kates's sister. Mrs. Kates knows their situation is not good but sees no way out. Their unemployment devoured their savings; any job they get she thinks they need to take. She does not like to go on welfare.

CASE-STUDY DISCUSSION

It can be seen from these cases that unemployment takes on different faces within families. Just as there are various forms of unemployment (i.e., chronic, short and long term, and teenage inability to even enter the labor force) there are also many varieties of family structure (i.e., single-headed households, male-headed families, extended families). When we turn our attention to how children fare within an environment of unemployment, therefore, our understanding will be thwarted unless these variations are noted.

The social science unemployment literature, as discussed earlier, has given us the most information regarding unemployed male families, in which the father was the traditional head of household. Depression Era studies supported the view that a father's loss of work resulted in an erosion of his usual authority within the family, a decrease in his self-esteem, and often sparked a deterioration in mental health.

A very interesting account of unemployed males' "loss-of-self" is presented in the *Marienthal* study. Men and women who had been laid off from a textile mill in Austria were asked to keep a diary of what they did with their time during the day now that they were jobless. As mothers and wives, most of the women had no trouble filling out detailed accounts of busy daily activity—in effect they had plenty of work to do. But the fathers and husbands presented another picture. They could not account for hours at a time, often stating they stood idling on street corners or in parks waiting to go home for dinner. They could not seem to reshape their energies around new constructive tasks.

While the classic unemployment research of the 1930s did offer images of the unemployed father, there was little elaboration of how the father acted out or coped with depression, embarrassment, and anger. The case studies at Children's Hospital begin to demonstrate the link between the father's personal and mental health and outcomes for children and the family.

In the Peal family, the father's job loss was interwoven with alcoholism and gambling. Epidemiologist Harvey Brenner, utilizing national survey data, has demonstrated that alcohol-related illnesses are positively correlated to periods of economic decline. On the more micro family level, the Peal family case suggests a convergence of distress, including a depressed mother, child death due to accident (neglect), physical abuse of children, and an overall tone of fear, guilt, and worry in the home.

Although the outcome of an unemployed father is not as severe for the Claude family, there is also evidence of father alcoholism and possible physical abuse of a small child. In both family situations, the mother appears unable to cope with the distress and the new economic and psychological realities of living in an unemployed household. She can protect neither herself nor her children. For both these families outside aid is necessary, with families at least temporarily broken up for basic physical and mental health reasons.

The Dawson and Hall family cases each represent the economic and social and psychological stresses confronting women who singly head households. In both families, the mother's difficult situation is compounded by her lack of job skills. An excellent recent book, *Women and Children Last* (Sidel, 1986), delineates the daily struggles for women not adequately prepared to raise families alone. Economically, these women are especially vulnerable as are their children. While families headed by women in 1983 accounted for 16% of all families, they account for 48% of all *poor* families.

In 1984, the poverty line for a family of four was set at $10,609. For urban households headed by women, it is almost impossible to meet the housing, shelter, food, and health costs for that amount. For example, if a woman works at a minimum-pay job ($3.35/hour), her yearly income would only be $6,968. Because of their lack of job skills and the structure of occupations in our economy, many women can find work only with low pay. They usually have no career mobility with jobs primarily in the service sector. They face a future of raising families in poverty whether they work or not.

One important difference among women who head households is the degree to which they have available support systems. Ms. Dawson, for instance, was able to seek shelter and a home for her child with her parents. While extended family networks were very available and active during the Depression Era, they have been steadily eroded in recent decades. A partial exception to this loss of family and community support systems occurs in the black and Hispanic cultures. Here, as Carol Stack (1974) documented in *All Our Kin*, networking with blood relatives and friends enables women heads of households to cope better with daily life's economic and social difficulties. Without such a web of support, mothers such as Ms. Hall are likely to be at the mercy of the existing (and often nonexistent) public welfare system. Ms. Dawson's son has a steady home place while Ms. Hall's four children have a history of temporary shelters and a future of foster homes.

The two "general hardship" family cases present contrasting evidence of families in transition. For the Pollo family, life is beginning to brighten. Coming from the hardships of being an unwed teenage mother, Ms. Pollo has recently married and is able now to offer her child the possibilities of a secure economic and family environment. She comes to the family clinic seeking help in undoing some of the damage inflicted on her child during the early years of general hardship. Her new husband stresses that his pride in his work will help create a good and secure home.

Both parents in the Kates family had unemployment experiences and their precarious economic situation is having clear negative impacts on their children. The jobless periods ate up their savings, and to make ends meet now both parents work odd hours. This results in parents rarely being at home, and the younger children are left in the care of an inattentive older sibling or outside the home by a relative. Mrs. Kates realizes the family is hardly existing as a viable unit; there is no time for building relationships, nurturing, and having any fun together. The middle child is demonstrating her unhappiness in school by doing poorly and her affect is one of depression. Artie Morris-Vann, as noted earlier, comments on how children in economically distressed households often display their problems in school. In the case of the Kates family, it was a school counselor that brought the family to the Children's Hospital unit in order to address the failing child's difficulties.

Some of the specifics of each of these case studies suggest the variety of issues faced by different categories of unemployed families. However, it is important to note that a salient common theme surfaced among the children during family therapy sessions at the hospital: deprivation. As children participated in "play therapy" with the family development staff, their underlying worries and concerns emerged. [3] One child drew pictures of houses being upside down and trees missing limbs. Another small child drew a self-portrait with himself very tiny, with no arms or legs, and a father standing nearby looming large and angry. Other children engaged in puppet play or played with dolls and blocks to act out events. One 8-year-old boy devised a castle where he constantly looked for the king who had gone away without explanation. The queen was very worried about money and where they would have to live. This boy came from an impoverished single-parent home. Another child built a series of rooms out of blocks—a living room, kitchen, and bedroom. When the father arrived home, the child hid near a chair. Later the child made believe he went out to the store to get food so he "could take care of everybody so no one will be hungry." This boy's father had been laid off for two years, was full of anger and embarrassment, and seemed unable to communicate caring anymore to his family.

Deprivation—the lack of a secure, safe haven at home—took on shapes of absent parents, physical and mental abuse, fears of homelessness, loneliness, powerlessness, and depression. The depth of deprivation was mediated in each case by the extent of economic distress, the duration of job loss, the availability of support systems, and the presence or absence of a nurturing, caring person in the child's life. Yet all of the children had a taste of the bitter pill of unemployment, the causes of which may have been outside their comprehension, but left degrees of scars nonetheless.

SOCIAL POLICY CONSIDERATIONS

There are short- and long-term perspectives when considering appropriate social policy responses to the needs of unemployed families and children. The most adequate solutions would necessarily embrace fundamental change in our social and economic order. An example of this long-range view has been clearly set forth in the U.S. Bishops' Pastoral "Economic Justice for All." Its call for full employment policies is a primary "prevention" treatment prescription for the problems of children's welfare due to parental job loss.

The long-term prescription also mandates a national health care system that would guarantee all children access to decent medical attention regardless of class standing. As Ruth Sidel (1986) states, only through universal entitlement will high-quality services be provided for all. As long as such services are provided only to those labeled "truly needy," they will be of lower quality and subject to cutbacks. Though there is general agreement in our society that regular health care is essential for children, it is estimated that nearly nine million children in the United States have no regular source of health care, less than one-half of all poor children are immunized against preventable disease, and many children living in poverty remain ineligible for Medicaid.

The circumstances at Children's Hospital, where our cases of children from unemployed families were seen, add another ironic dimension to the inadequacies of the present economic order. In the midst of the 1980s recession and the rising demand for clinic services and emergency treatment, the hospital was reducing staff to meet cost reductions. Simultaneously, funding from governmental agencies for support of the Family Development Unit was curtailed. Far too many families similar to the case-study examples were referred to the unit only to be turned away. Other backup social service agencies were also experiencing strain, making it very difficult to provide needed follow-up services for the families and children. While long-range, sweeping social policy changes would offer the best "treatment" (including learning from programs already in existence in many other industrialized nations such as Sweden and Canada), shorter-range, remedial policies would allow more immediate relief and aid. Our case-studies strongly suggest two categories for social policy programming that would directly or indirectly help the lives of children in unemployed families. The first, job-skill training, is targeted at the increasing population of single women heads of households. If Ms. Dawson and Ms. Hall could enter a job-skills program, helping them to secure future steady income, much would be gained. The economic standing of their families would improve, the mother's self-esteem would be given a boost, the family's environment and degree of well-being and self-sufficiency would be enhanced, and the sense of deprivation and worry experienced by the children decreased. The Employment and Training Program or "E.T." was set up in 1983 by the Massachusetts Department of Public Welfare as a way to help women out of poverty and into jobs. Since its inception, over 13,000 have been placed in jobs. Moreover, while enrolled in E.T., women receive day care vouchers from the state and keep Medicaid benefits for 15 months after going into the program. The child care and health insurance coverages are especially important features for single-parent women and it is hoped that it will be adopted in national legislation on job training sponsored by Representative Nancy Johnson from Connecticut.

Second, the male head of household cases and the general hardship cases highlight the issue of the duration of job loss and the need for a transitional or stage approach for unemployed families. Much of the depression literature implicitly acknowledges the positive correlation between length of job loss and the severity of family problems: the longer unemployed, the more devastation for the family. In both the male head of household cases, the father had been out of work over a year with severe problems evident in each family. These long-time unemployed families need to be identified so that intervention would be instituted earlier (i.e., counseling support, medical attention for children, availability of financial aid to help families not lose homes), thereby preventing later more severe losses. Programs set up in the Mon Valley, Pennsylvania, to aid families of unemployed steel workers have in fact mobilized resources along these lines. Families such as the Kates need to make the transition from the frying pan of unemployment without jumping into the fire of family breakdown. Unfortunately, it is often not until a child of such a family is in deep distress that intervention occurs. More creative remedial action by all those concerned with family and child well-being, including school personnel, pediatricians, clergy, and state agency representatives is necessary to reduce the scarring of children of the unemployed.

NOTES

1. According to the Department of Labor, unemployed persons make up all persons who did not work during the survey week, who made specific efforts to find a job within the past four weeks, and who were available for work during the survey week. This definition does not include discouraged workers no longer actively seeking work and those "engaged in own home housework," "in school," "unable to work" because of long-term physical or mental illness, and "other." The "other" group includes for the most part retired and seasonal workers for whom the survey week fell in an "off" season and who were not reported as unemployed. Persons doing incidental unpaid family work (less than 15 hours) are also classified as not in the labor force.

2. For more on the concept of pediatric social illness, see Bowles and Newberger (1982).

3. Sessions were conducted behind a one-way view mirror so other staff and researchers could observe. Families were asked permission before observation was allowed.

7

Unemployed Workers and Their Families: Social Victims or Social Critics?

Ramsay Liem

The central question in this chapter—unemployed workers and their families: social victims or social critics?—is a departure from the kinds of issues I and my colleagues have been focusing on in our research on problems of dislocation. As psychologists with longstanding interests in the relation between broad social structures and processes and psychological well-being, our main concerns have emphasized the social distribution of emotional impairment as influenced by one's fate in the marketplace. Like others we have been stimulated by Brenner's (1973, 1976, 1979) macro studies of economic change and well-being to investigate the impacts of unemployment as they are experienced directly by workers. We have also emphasized the response of the family unit as mediating these effects.

AUTHOR'S NOTE: Some of the research reported in this chapter was supported by the National Institute of Mental Health, research grant number MH31316. I would like to thank Richard Balzer, Ali Banuazizi, Lois Biener, Joan Liem, Brinton Lykes, S. M. Miller, Elliot Mishler, and Paula Rayman for their helpful review of earlier drafts of this chapter and related pieces.

The answers to questions regarding the significance of job loss as a risk factor for physical and emotional health are admittedly imprecise. Even more problematic are the complex processes through which workers and their families cope with unemployment drawing on personal, socially distributed, and human service resources. Nonetheless, a substantial number of investigations in the United States and abroad make a strong case that under many conditions of significant economic contraction job loss is relevant for health as well as economic and social functioning (Horowitz, 1984; Warr, 1984). The work we are doing with others on the Work and Unemployment Project similarly points to a rather clear pattern of material loss, threat to the family's customary routine, disruption of family relationships, and emotional strain in adult family members following unemployment (Atkinson, Liem, and Liem, 1986; Liem and Rayman, 1982; Liem, 1983b).

It is important to pursue this line of research and to clarify issues such as the particular economic and social conditions under which the impacts of joblessness are most severe. This chapter will share several observations regarding these questions. There is, however, another level of concern that deserves an equal hearing but is rarely addressed. As the title of this chapter implies, the issue centers on the subjectivity of workers who experience job loss, that is, their intentionality and social efficacy.

It is not surprising that this question should emerge in the context of research on the emotional impacts of unemployment. As we have discussed elsewhere (Liem, 1983a), unemployed workers are labeled, intentionally or not, as helpless victims of uncontrollable economic circumstances when the scope of their reactions to unemployment is limited to effects such as anxiety and despair. The quality of hopelessness is especially problematic and yet is the most common attribute associated with the long-term response to job loss. Virtually all attempts to identify stages of response to joblessness culminate in defeat, apathy and despair, resignation, or reorganization and acceptance (Eisenberg and Lazarsfeld, 1938; Jahoda, Lazarsfeld, and Zeisel, 1971; Powell and Driscoll, 1973). Our own research further underscores this conception of victimization by noting a tendency to blame oneself or to internalize responsibility for job loss among the unemployed.

The concept of social victim is important in that it signifies the social basis of the hardships and distress faced by workers and their families. However, this characterization of workers is narrow and one sided in a very critical sense. It implies the loss of a fundamental prerequisite of social enfranchisement and human dignity, the capacity to assert one's interests and to act on them. Even the most sympathetic description of job losers as victims can imply dependency and helplessness.

A similar point has been made by Bramel and Friend (1981) in a discussion of the famous Hawthorne studies at the Chicago Western Electric Plant. The title of the paper, "Hawthorne, the Myth of the Docile Worker, and Class Bias in Psychology," succinctly conveys the essence of the argument. The authors challenge the common belief that these studies demonstrated that the productivity and satisfaction of workers increased simply as a result of the close and sympathetic attention paid to workers by researchers and supervisors. The following quote from a popular textbook on social psychology is typical of mainstream descriptions of the significance of the Hawthorne studies:

> Regardless of the conditions, whether there were more or fewer rest periods, longer or shorter workdays, each experimental period produced a higher rate of work than the one before. Although this effect was probably due to several reasons, the most important was that the women felt they were something special, that they were being treated particularly well, that they were in an interesting experiment, and that they were expected to perform exceptionally. They were happy, a lot of attention was paid to them, and they complied with what they thought the experimenter wanted [Freedman, Sears, and Carlsmith, 1981, p. 338].

Through a careful review of primary data, Bramel and Friend extract a different picture of these workers. Rather than docile, simple-minded individuals, these workers resisted arbitrary demands for increased productivity, opposed changes in working conditions, such as the elimination of rest periods, and revealed a clear understanding of the implications of experimental manipulations for their interests. Examples of this tension between researchers and subjects range from talking and socializing during work periods, to work slowdowns, to direct, hostile confrontations. In fact, the researchers were forced on several occasions to adopt coercive methods of control (e.g., the firing of two women workers) to maintain production goals.

The Hawthorne experiments apparently involved significant struggle and accommodation on the part of researchers and workers. Productivity, therefore, resulted from *mutual* efforts to control the situation. Yet the intentional, determinative aspect of these workers is so thoroughly obscured in reports of this study that workers appear to be thoroughly passive, compliant objects of the situation as defined by the researchers.

As we have noted before, similar distortions can occur in descriptions of unemployed workers especially where stress and health are the primary concerns. Fryer and Payne (1984), British psychologists, have made a related observation suggesting that more attention be paid to proactive behavior among the unemployed. They stress the identification of a special group of unemployed, those who are "using their unemployment in an *exceptionally* positive and creative way" (Fryer and Payne, 1984, p. 282). They locate proactivity in a special group of highly "self actualizing individuals." This dichotomy implies that although "apathy, decline, and deterioration" may be a fair description of the morale of many of the jobless, at least some individuals escape this extreme alienation.

Michael Frisch and Dorothy Watts address the same point from a more universalistic perspective, that is in regard to the unemployed as a whole. In a remarkable article describing the preparation of a feature report for the *New York Times Magazine,* they reconstruct the editorial process that shaped the content of the article, a compendium of excerpts from an oral history project of the Buffalo area unemployed (Frisch and Watts, 1980).

What is striking about this analysis is the almost imperceptible grooming of these stories of job loss by the *Times* editorial board such that their end product

> resulted in the core [of the article] being emotion and exclamation rather than . . . reflection and intelligent discussion . . . it emphasized the revelation of experience rather than its instrumental, even didactic communication and it tended to sever that experience from the social and class context with which it had been invested by our subjects . . ." [Frisch and Watts, 1980, p. 98].

Rather than hearing *from* the unemployed, the editors preferred to hear *about them* as objects of the recessionary economy.

The following excerpt of an interview with a domestic worker provides an example of the contrasting images of workers as implied by the editors' as opposed to the researchers' choice of interview material (portions selected by the *Times'* editors are in standard type; the fuller text proposed by the Buffalo researchers includes this material as well as the statements in bold print):

> About the people. They got the wrong type people for the wrong type jobs to make Buffalo come up. Buffalo could be number one, it could be done.

If they put the right type people in, they'd see how Buffalo would bloom. **You have to spend to make, that's all there is to it. In Buffalo, it seems like they don't want to put out money, they just want to hold money, and they're just killing it. If we could put our money in something good, why we could get something out of it. But we got to put it in first. They're going to have to do something, people can only go hungry for so long. I don't know what the cause is, but it's something to think about. I'm telling you.** It looks like people, we pull against each other so much now. We're not like we used to be; more together. We're divided, and it looks like all we care for is, if I live. I don't care what becomes of you. **But we can't be like that. Until we get together we're gonna be this way, and farther apart, in worser shape.**

Frisch and Watts argue that the briefer passage chosen by the *Times* is emotive, exclamatory, ungrounded, and seemingly arbitrary whereas the fuller text provides the grounding and reveals conscious reflection. In particular, this woman informs us of the absence of serious financial investment in Buffalo, a necessity in her view for turning things around. One could add that her more complete statement also expresses a commitment to collective solutions as essential to meeting personal needs and not the individualism that is often attributed to workers.

Contrast the following two versions of a union representative's story:

But then Litton came in, in 1965. They loaded the plant with salaried workers; these out of towners would be walking around here and we couldn't even find out what their jobs were. . . . Most people know that Litton is a holding company. They get in, they make a buck, they get out. **I don't think it's fair. I don't think it's right to the community. You're not only talking 750 jobs. Add their families, their warehouses, and other interests all over the country. There's truckers involved, there's railroads involved, people getting cut back all over. Now, when you're talking 750 jobs, you might be talking 10,000 people before you're done.**

Although the shortened version captures much of the essential content of this worker's remarks, it does so at the cost of downplaying this man's thoughtful and informed analysis of the ripple effects of a major layoff. His comments are also indicative of a sensitivity to the interdependence of workers by virtue of the interdependence of their jobs. These are not the thoughts of a man for whom the experience of being out of work is only one of emotional strain.

Frisch and Watts note, however, that the editors' choices of passages repeatedly emphasize emotional responses to unemployment abstracted from workers' analyses of local and national conditions affecting the job market and the quality of their lives. This critical review reveals conflicting sentiments about those who are not working, views that differ fundamentally in their assumptions about the efficacy of the unemployed.

This difference is most clearly expressed in the contrasting preferences for the title of the article on the Buffalo unemployed. The authors proposed "America Not Working"—a reference both to workers and to the broader economic system. The *Times* insisted on "Down and Out in America."

These opposing perceptions of unemployed workers can also be found in the work of Piven and Cloward (1977), on the one hand, and Garrity (1978), on the other, regarding unemployment during the Great Depression. Whereas Garrity tends to focus on the wearing down of workers, Piven and Cloward document in great detail the role of rank and file workers in agitating for economic assistance and relief services. Much of the early success in winning local and later national relief can be directly attributed to the spontaneous as well as organized efforts of the unemployed.

The emphasis on the subjective features of workers' experiences of unemployment also shares common theoretical ground with approaches to social analysis in other areas. One example is the work of Apple (1982) on the social functions of public schooling. His point of departure is the radical critique of public education that emphasizes the role of schools in socializing students to meet class-based normative expectations of the workplace, e.g., punctuality, deference to authority, acquisition of skills versus critical thinking for working-class children (Bowles and Gintis, 1976). In this analysis, schools aid in the social reproduction of unequal, stratified social and economic relations.

Although a past contributor to this critique, Apple suggests that this perspective overstates the determination of students by schools, thereby reducing them to mere pawns in the face of institutional imperatives. While preserving in large part the structural analysis of the role of schools in social reproduction, Apple (1983, p. 104) observes significant tension in the schools attributable in part to challenges to the formal and informal demands of the system.

> Most of the time these students are in school is spent not on "work" (what teachers think school is for) but on regenerating a specific lived culture— talking about sports, discussing and planning outside activities done with friends, talking about the "nonacademic" things they do in school . . . a large amount of time was spent finding ways to "goof off," to make class

more interesting, to gain some measure of *control* over the pattern of day to day interaction that was so standard in the school.

Apple calls this dialectic between school system and student sub-culture "contestation" and argues that social reproduction must contend with these significant sources of opposition. Transforming students into workers is, therefore, a tension-filled dialectic process. Schools are contested terrains and not simply institutions for the transmission of skills and norms to a passive, receptive student body. "Lived subcultures" provide students with some measure of autonomy within which to gain perspective on their experience in school, to deal with contradictions inherent in the school experience (e.g., egalitarian ideals versus class-based tracking), and to evolve a response to them. This is not to say that the relation between students and school system is egalitarian. But it does acknowledge an important dynamic through which the process of social reproduction must operate. The broader theoretical discussion to which this work belongs is resistance theory (Giddens, 1979) and it is this framework that is also most relevant to the reexamination of the experience of unemployed workers that follows.

THE BOSTON UNEMPLOYED

Our own efforts to apply this line of analysis involves interviews that we conducted as part of our study of unemployed families. Briefly, the Work and Unemployment project was designed as a panel study of involuntarily unemployed men and their families during the national recession of the late 1970s and early 1980s. As noted earlier, it was intended initially to help resolve the question of the health risk associated with economic downturns suggested by the research of Brenner (1973, 1976, 1979).

The study includes 80 families with recently unemployed men and 80 matched controls, all with at least one child in the home. Both blue- and white-collar workers are represented in the sample. All families were seen (husbands and wives together) four times during a one-year period. About a third of these families were reemployed within three months, another third within 6 months, and all but 15% of the sample by the end of the year. Average length of unemployment was 18 weeks. Equal numbers of wives worked full or part time outside the home, or full time in the home. Although some of the unemployment occurred in the context of large company layoffs (e.g., Polaroid), most workers were let go from smaller service and manufacturing sites where layoffs generally numbered fewer than 100 workers.

The stress of unemployment. It is not our intention to report extensively on the emotional impacts of dislocation experienced by this group of families. However, it is important to note that our findings indicate that many of these families experienced significant emotional strain during the period of unemployment. Husbands and wives experienced greater anxiety and depression than their controls and these responses were frequently exacerbated by the severity of financial loss, length of joblessness, conflicts between spouses regarding the husband's job hunt, and a tendency to internalize responsibility for the loss of work. Paranoia and hostility were also acknowledged by unemployed men and many wives experienced phobiclike fears and self-consciousness in the presence of others.

This is not to imply that the response to job loss was uniform for all families. There are notable exceptions to the usual pattern of emotional distress. In these cases, flexibility regarding the sharing of domestic responsibilities and breadwinning coupled with ease and openness of communication within the family are associated with a much more benign experience of the unemployment. For these families the success in weathering this hardship seemed to reaffirm and further strengthen existing bonds among family members.

Nevertheless, on the whole it would be fair to say that joblessness was more often a major hardship for this group of people. For seven of the families with unemployed men the marriages ended in separation or divorce during the study year as compared with a similar result in two control families.

Subjectivity among the unemployed. The central concern in this discussion, however, is whether there is also a subjective aspect to the response of these families to the job loss; that is, a positive assertion of interests and needs as well as a stress reaction. Does the elevation of anxiety and depression mean that these workers and their spouses experienced only the imposition of strain or are there other important aspects of the response to unemployment that fall outside the scope of our initial research questions?

Currently, we are reexamining a small number of randomly selected interviews with these families guided by the illustrations of efficacy among workers provided by Frisch and Watts and our own sense of a positive, self-affirming quality in workers' response to job loss. What we have found can be described by referring to the following areas of inquiry: workers' reflections on their work conditions, their understanding of their layoffs, their observations regarding the job hunt, and their assessment of public supports for the unemployed. The information is based on responses to open-ended questions in each of these areas, followed, when needed, by more focused probes.

The examples we have found are intended to illustrate rather than validate the kinds of responses to unemployment from which we can reasonably infer agency and subjectivity among workers. It remains to be discovered how frequently these different expressions of efficacy occur among the unemployed and what factors influence the form they take.

Social critics and social victims. The reflections of a number of families touch on several of these areas. One example is provided by an older, middle-aged couple who experienced a very difficult adjustment throughout the husband's unemployment. The couple ultimately separated during the year of the interviews and the husband experienced a brief psychiatric hospitalization. The wife also developed agoraphobia for a short period following the separation. The following quotes give a flavor of this more negative aspect of the unemployment.

> [Husband] I've been getting depressed and that isn't really dealing with it. Just worrying about the future while I try to improve it at the same time which isn't quite that easy to do especially when you're in job interviews. You're just not at your psychological best when you know that you don't have any income and you need a job and you want a job. You come across, I come across, as somewhat desperate, which is what I am and it just about kills your chances for getting a job.

> [Wife] I'm giving 400% of myself to him and my daughter to maintain normalcy and I'm tired, very tired. I find myself jealous of my friends because they are now where we would have been financially and it hurts.

> [Husband in response to a question about financial problems] Fuel; foreclosure on my house, foreclosure on my car, foreclosure on my life [mumbles]; I have created a mess.

> [Husband regarding the meaning of unemployment] It means being without power to control the things you normally like to have control over in your life like happiness, for me anyway. I lost a lot of confidence. . . . I'm actually scared to go on a job interview.

These remarks convey much of the sense of the burden of unemployment and of the battering of two people by this experience. They suggest helplessness and victimization.

There is more to this couple's encounter with joblessness, however, suggesting that the strain of unemployment is only one aspect of their experience. Consider the following comments:

[Husband regarding things better and worse since his unemployment] . . . doesn't mean anything for better. For worse: poverty and the possibility of lower paying jobs for doing the hardest work. Those who move paper get big money and those who sweat are exploited.

People in positions to help me have not come forward; blue-collar workers have offered more help and given me more leads. The white-collar professionals never offered me anything—except sympathy which I didn't want.

[Wife, also regarding positive and negative aspects of unemployment] It's better in a sense because I've become much more politically aware; doing a lot of reading about the system of government. I've become interested in socialism . . . opening up my eyes to corporate and government corruption.

[Husband regarding support for the job hunt] Help wasn't available because in my opinion the corporate system from government on down is not really concerned with the plight of the unemployed person be they white collar or blue collar.

[Husband commenting on what he is looking for in a job] I have been trying to resolve whether or not I should take a job at which I would be unhappy; make a week's pay or continue to go for the American dream of an executive position which is what I understand I am qualified to do but no one else understands it.

What is striking about these two sets of responses is that even in the midst of the virtual collapse of this family, the husband and wife have not completely internalized their difficulties. There is a clear sense of the inequities in the system and an emerging identification with blue-collar workers in a man whose job history includes both white-collar, public relations work and unskilled manual labor. Similarly, the fearfulness of agoraphobia does not negate a developing political awareness in the wife. Social criticism and victimization exist together in this couple's experience of unemployment.

The job hunt. Another element of assertiveness in the face of unemployment can be found in this worker's unwillingness to give up his desire to find meaningful, remunerative work. This tendency to maintain one's own agenda for acceptable work in line with one's status and salary expectations is very common in this group of workers. In spite of very active job searches, these men often resisted taking a job for the sake of being employed even if their prospects for reemployment were extremely limited. One of the most common manifestations of this response was to maintain the belief that one would be recalled to his previous job, the preferred resolution to unemployment for many of these workers. Job counselors frequently complain that this type of reaction is self-defeating and compounds the stress of being out of work. It is also behavior that leads those who have never been unemployed to attribute much of the blame for joblessness to dislocated workers, themselves.

There is a very different way to understand this approach to the job hunt, however. The material well-being and social standing of most people and their families is principally derived from their position in the marketplace. Consequently, to resist the downward skidding typically associated with the reemployment of industrial workers today is to affirm one's sense of material and social worth. In view of the substantial hardships imposed by the job loss in our sample, it is actually remarkable that the overwhelming majority of workers chose to "hold out" when faced with reemployment in marginal positions. Several direct quotes convey the spirit of these "hold outs":

In my profession, marine electrician, there's nothing available. I've gone to companies to train as an apprentice electrician, commercial, and they're only paying $3-4/hr. I was making $8.50. You can't take that!

[Wife of assembly line worker] I was nervous before but this adds to it. We should be ahead, not behind, but we're behind . . . we want to buy a house someday, send both children to college.

[Her husband] I haven't been offered a job that is acceptable to what I want, we need. Something that would pay better and have medical benefits, retirement.

[An electrical worker] I could get any amount of jobs as an electrician's helper or minor maintenance man changing light bulbs when in fact I'm more qualified to design the systems that they're changing the parts in. If I wanted to cut my income by 2/3rds, I could go to work tomorrow.

These comments, we think, reflect a clear positive self-regard and not the unrealistic, self-defeating outlook that is often assumed to motivate this kind of response.

This is not to say that holding out for the right job can not also be problematic. In fact, conflicts between spouses over how readily a worker should take a job frequently contributed to the tension in marriages that ended in separation and divorce. The point is that with reference to worker's esteem and sense of authorship over their working lives, holding out has positive significance. In the context of marital or family dynamics, however, the same actions take on other meanings. This paradox is what we believe makes the issue of the family's response to unemployment an extremely complex question. A negative outcome, for example, may not simply be the direct result of accumulating stresses among family members. It may instead be the product of new incompatibilities created by the way family members are able to express their self-respect and personal needs.

Engaging in a selective job hunt is only one way that workers maintain their own agendas regarding work. They also create other opportunities to meet their social and material needs *in spite of* the formal options provided by the job market. They patch together part time jobs, participate in the underground economy, and invest more time and energy in domestic and child-care responsibilities as new sources of gratification. Although far from ideal, these activities can meet a worker's needs in the short run and often at less cost to one's esteem and sense of efficacy than one would pay by taking the kinds of jobs that are readily available. Failing to recognize that people are constantly creating alternatives to unsatisfactory and even degrading options afforded by our formal institutions makes it difficult to appreciate holding out by the unemployed as a rational and self-serving act.

Emotions versus critical reflection. Another aspect of the discrediting of unemployed workers is implied by the attention paid to workers' visceral, emotional reactions to their layoffs rather than their knowledge about or comprehension of the circumstances surrounding their unemployment. In the words of Frisch and Watts (1980, p. 100):

> The *Times* sought to offer its readers stimulating fare, not uninvited guests. While they were quite willing to serve up the pain and suffering of the working class, they were less inclined to open their pages to the ideas, values, reflections, advice, and social consciousness of these people. Nor were they interested . . . in sharing the right to *interpret their experience*. Tell us what happened and what you feel . . . and our readers will worry about what it means and how to think about it [emphasis added].

This negation of workers as reflective and knowledgeable is part of the more basic conception of them as passive, helpless victims. Victims emote and vent whereas those who resist and assert also analyze, plan, and act. Understanding, strategizing, and problem solving are the things policymakers, service providers, and political activists do *for* the unemployed.

Our interviews suggest that these workers were not simply reactive and emotive. They were knowledgeable about conditions in their industries and particular places of work and especially aware of conflicts of interest between themselves and those in control of management decisions. For example,

[Assembly line worker] Polaroid goofed a lot of things. They overproduced and overspeculated. Some guy making $100,000 a year made a film cartridge for $27 [a piece]. They had to sell it by government standards for $10 and also the chemicals leaked into the camera. Suddenly, making of that camera ceased and the people making that camera were higher than us [in seniority]; so they had to get rid of the excess and we were the excess baggage. Those people got our jobs.

[Hospital maintenance worker] Hospital said they could save money by bringing in an outside firm. Two months after I started, the shop signed cards to have a union come in for elections; everybody in the shop was in court except for two guys. Hospital went to court, spent $30,000 to keep the union out. The union won and the hospital fired the whole crew and brought in an outside firm which offered you a job, cut in pay and less benefits, and I would have to cross a picket line.

[Retail worker] There's a change in the nature of the business such that they don't hire trained people in my job; because of the economy, they're firing instead of hiring and using less qualified people.

[Wife of hospital worker shortly before her own lay off from a department store clerical position] We could have been receiving a full pay check; would make it a lot easier to deal with unemployment. Everything takes money. In my employment, I don't know if they could do it, but cut hours rather than lay off. If we could work three days a week all year (it would be a lot better), but they let you go for an undetermined amount of time.

Had we inquired further, it is likely that we would have discovered these workers to have had even more detailed knowledge and understanding of the circumstances of their layoffs. These were not docile, uninformed workers out of touch with the deskilling, union busting, and planning failures in their industries. On the contrary, they were outspoken critics of these conditions as well as promoters of solutions more sympathetic to workers.

Perceptions of service providers. A fourth observation from our interviews concerns the reactions of these workers to the service sector. These tend to be noncommittal at best and highly critical at their worst. The following is a sample of descriptions of different types of service providers:

> [Regarding unemployment compensation] The worst thing, . . . they'll send your employer a statement asking why you're not working and you'll have to wait until your employer decides to send it back . . . if he doesn't, they just fine him $20 and they give me the benefits; but anytime later he could say he fired me and they would ask for the money back; . . . a bureaucratic mess. What you have to go through to get that stipend, it's so demeaning, degrading.

> I was only a pawn. I found the personnel people down there [division of employment security] unrealistic, unsympathetic.

> Maybe someone next door wants something done, someone offers $20 for fixing a car. But if you go and tell unemployment they cut it off from what you're making. Then they wonder why people are thieving and I sure as hell ain't thieving. They'll take it off from $116/week for a family of four.

> The fuel assistance program. That's the one that gave me the run around. I made $2,000 too much *last year*. They go by last year's income! Either you starve and they save you while you're dying or you make a little too much—crazy.

> We got food stamps but $54 for one month for a family of four is not sufficient. They don't base it on enough of the money you have to spend out. If you tell them you have to pay your own insurance, they don't count this or health payments. They only go for gas, lights, telephone, rent. You don't just live on utilities.

It is no wonder that these workers refrain from seeking help as much as possible. Uniformly, the people we interviewed described the process of collecting unemployment compensation as a ritual in public self-degradation. Their only defense was to avoid public services as much as possible, which they appeared to do with considerable determination. For example, 90% of the workers who expressed a need for some kind of counseling help (about half of the sample) refused to seek it out. A smaller but significant number of families also delayed their application for unemployment compensation. While this type of response again appears to reflect contradictory, self-defeating behavior, it can also be understood as a refusal to expose one's self to demeaning attributions and situations. The paradox is that the only means for contesting these perceptions deprives workers of help they both deserve and can use.

Personal resistance. A final example from our interviews provides a brief illustration of several additional dimensions of worker resistance and subjectivity. It involves a man who serviced large, industrial electrical equipment. His wife was a full-time homemaker. He remarked about his layoff:

> The longer you work at a job the more cataclysmic the occurrence is when you are finally terminated. And the more successful you feel in your job the worse off you are. I mean the first two days, I mean like, are really out of sight . . . if you're lucky you snap out of it . . . but if not you begin the long road down the hill.

This worker, however, did not go downhill. On the contrary, he was one of the most resourceful and confident people we interviewed. A sense of this quality is captured in the following comment:

> And if I had to walk out tomorrow morning and find another line of work remotely connected and it interested me, I'd start at the bottom and go all the way to the top. See, I started working at this place five years ago for $3.20/hr. as the bottom man on the totem pole and when I was laid off I was at the top.

This confidence was also expressed in this man's no nonsense approach to getting the help from public agencies he felt was his due from the schools by way of special educational services for his daughter, from Medicaid to help cover medical bills, and from the division of employment security for unemployment compensation. In this example, one need not infer subjectivity from behavior; it is expressed directly and forthrightly.

These, then, are some of the examples of the "other side" of the experience of job loss. In different ways they portray unemployed workers not simply as objects of their circumstances but as contesting their diminished work options and loss of access to resources. This is by no means to suggest that the family strain resulting from unemployment or the worker's emotional distress are trivial or that dislocated workers are not victims of powerful market forces. But these kinds of impacts do not constitute the entire experience of being out of work nor do they necessarily mean that workers and their families have been rendered helpless and passive by their unemployment. On the contrary, we believe the evidence strongly suggests that there are many ways in which "victims" of unemployment also maintain their agendas and contest their loss of options.

POLICY IMPLICATIONS

The interviews we have conducted suggest a variety of considerations for economic and human service policy. They imply that the more retraining and relocation programs define their tasks in purely technical terms (e.g., replacing obsolete skills with new, marketable skills), and disregard the broader agendas that workers attach to their jobs, the more they will encounter significant resistance. They also draw attention to what may be an inherent problem in human service delivery, the attribution of dependence and helplessness through the act of helping.

Common to these implications is the basic question of control and authorship. Our current reading of our interviews raises doubts about the extent to which the very act of policy formulation and enactment can and should be done completely outside the experience of unemployment. As a problem-solving practice, to separate policymaking as well as help giving from the activity of those who experience the problem would simply reproduce on the largest scale the undermining of worker subjectivity.

Rappaport (1985) has raised a similar point although from a somewhat different perspective. The objective as he construes it is to empower people implying the need to restore efficacy. We would argue that the issue of efficacy is *made* problematic by research and policy constructions that ignore workers' acts of problem definition and resistance. Nevertheless, Rappaport's distinction between the provision of services *for* versus the development of help giving *with* clients is relevant to the problem of unemployment as it is reflected in our interviews. Collaboration between service providers and the unemployed rather than prescription by the former is clearly most appropriate given the central dynamic of workers' efforts to maintain their own agendas during the job loss.

Organizations such as the Mon Valley Unemployed Workers Association (Deitch, 1984) provide opportunities to put this principle into practice. This group has developed special credit programs, health care packages, and political action strategies to advance the needs of the unemployed. Services provided directly by the association or in collaboration with professional caregivers resolve the problem of ownership by incorporating help giving within an organizational base identified with workers. An alternative is a union affiliation that has been developed extensively by Schore (1984). Her program of counseling services also relies heavily on peer counselors often drawn from the ranks of the unemployed, themselves.

The difficult question is how to develop this kind of practice on a larger scale given a human service sector, public or private, that is unaccustomed to formal accountability to client groups. If past experience is to provide the answer (Piven and Cloward, 1977), it is likely that organized pressure from the jobless, themselves, will be a necessary ingredient for accomplishing this objective. However, the more there are pockets of caregivers committed to the logic and principle of such practice, the more likely it is that this pressure will be effective.

PART IV

Political Responses to Economic Distress

This section is concerned with the need for an adequate level of employment in our society as an essential prerequisite for human dignity and family living. Each chapter addresses the importance to individuals and families of meaningful work at a decent standard of living.

While a wide range of policy approaches exist for coping with economic dislocations, two central and contrasting themes are highlighted in this section. One array of recommendations is oriented toward the goal of reprivatization: Activities that were once a source of government action are shifted to private initiative. The other set of recommendations is oriented toward economic democracy: Citizen participation is necessary to stimulate government and other collective efforts to create economic justice for all.

The arguments given by neoconservatives and laissez-faire proponents for economic reprivatization are criticized in these and later chapters. Individualistic and neoconservative perspectives are rejected in the chapters by Linda Majka and Margaret Hohman. Fred Block criticizes the assumption of "false necessity," by which harmful economic consequences are justified by the claim that no alternatives exist. The viewpoints supporting reprivatization set up an illusory economic goal of absolute independence, while most individuals are left vulnerable to the harsh effects of economic change. They fail to balance the satisfaction of personal wants at the expense of others with a respect for the human dignity of all individuals and families.

The authors of the following chapters question the ability of unplanned economic behavior to provide adequately for human needs. They emphasize especially the need for sufficient numbers of jobs at adequate wages, as well as adequate levels of social services. In addition, other collective actions independent of government are required to cope with the negative consequences of economic restructuring. Recognizing full employment as a desirable social goal, the chapters are concerned in diverse ways with how an attainable social program can be formulated and what would be effective mobilizing strategies.

Arguments supporting the principle of economic justice are explored in each essay. The authors examine concepts of what is fair, right, and efficient in economic life. They question how the division might be mended between family life and employment, and private life and public actions. They see responsibility for others as a necessary consequence of our interdependence in the economy and society.

Social movements for economic and political change are needed to make economic justice a reality. Linda Majka emphasizes the importance of alternative perspectives to utilitarian individualism. She believes we must engage in collective efforts to create long-run solutions to economic distress and reduce economic inequalities among families. She proposes that this will require improvements in the nature, content, and compensation of both full-time and part-time work, family support services, and sex equity in employment. Margaret Hohman emphasizes the importance of moral and religious traditions in judging society and stimulating social action. She asserts that the well-being of all the people is an appropriate standard for evaluating public policy, and revives the search for common moral commitments, especially sharing, cooperation, and generosity toward others as essential to an ethical life. Fred Block proposes that an efficient society is one that avoids the social and economic damage resulting from an irrational economy. He believes that alternatives exist to the current pattern of unmet needs while resources stand idle or are used wastefully. He feels that the goal of additional employment can be supported and the importance of unpaid labor in families, local communities, and voluntary groups can be recognized by reducing the hours of the work week. All of the chapters in this section perceive a larger role for an informed and concerned citizenry in effecting the necessary changes.

8

Neoconservative Perspectives on Economic Inequalities Among Families

Linda C. Majka

The well-being of the family in the last quarter of the twentieth century has become a critical social issue in recent years. From many points in the political spectrum come expressions of concern over family distress. The apparent sources of concern are similar: The traditional family system is in decline. In Europe and the United States, we are gradually no longer living in the family lifestyles traditional to our societies in the past. This creates a lag between what we assume we ought to be and what we actually are in terms of real relationships.

Several underlying economic conditions have recently heightened the perception and reality of family distress: Two incomes have often become necessary to maintain the standard of living for families that was established 25 years ago; economic dislocations have created mass unemployment in many regions; high unemployment rates extending over a decade are unconducive to procreation and marital stability; and continuing racial and gender inequalities have promoted the feminization of poverty.

One response to the underlying economic dislocations has been the current conservative direction of public policies under the Reagan administration. Considering the extent to which the family is now regarded as an endangered institution, it is not surprising that the conservative

155

political agenda is accompanied by an insistence on a return to traditional familial values.

This chapter examines what have been defined as "neoconservative" accounts of our present circumstances, their conclusions on solutions to perceived social problems, and recommendations for change. It focuses on the intellectuals who have recently published on social issues, the family, and public policies with the support of the American Enterprise Institute (AEI). The views of AEI scholars are significant because of the influence of the AEI across a wide array of government initiatives. During the Reagan administration the AEI has emerged as a major source of information for media, Congress, and agency staffs in Washington. Its publications are at present as well promoted, circulated, and accessible as those of any intellectual resource or think tank of its type in Washington. This chapter offers a critical analysis of the neoconservative accounts of American social institutions, especially the family, and concludes with reflections on alternatives.

THE ECONOMIC CONTEXT
OF FAMILY LIFE

Why study the viewpoints of the neoconservatives on the current state of American social institutions? It has been suggested that they might be the most prominent group of American intellectuals during the Reagan administration (Green, 1981, p. 8). Many have become regarded as experts in fields relevant to the formation of public policy. By entering actively into the marketplace of ideas in their own disciplines, they help shape the agenda of current public debate; they participate in setting the limits of "responsible" opinion on social issues; and they build the credibility of sets of policies. The neoconservatives are primarily associated with elite universities, and their ideas are well circulated in journals and popular periodicals. They have more access to political decision makers than most intellectuals (Edsall, 1984, p. 218; Rosenthal, 1985, pp. 7-8). Finally, their views hold additional currency by being congenial to political and economic elites (see Steinfels, 1979, pp. 6-13; Coser and Howe, 1974).

This chapter surveys four leading neoconservative intellectuals. Irving Kristol has been editor of *The Public Interest*, columnist for the *Wall Street Journal*, Henry Luce Professor of Urban Values at New York University, and director of a conservative foundation, The Institute for Educational Affairs. Michael Novak was the Watson-Ledden Professor

of Religious Studies at Syracuse University and now is a Resident
Scholar of the American Enterprise Institute. Brigitte Berger is a Professor of Sociology at Wellesley College. Peter Berger is University Professor at Boston University. Significant continuities appear among their
concerns in no small part because the American Enterprise Institute has
assisted them through its functioning as a neoconservative support base
since the 1970s. Peter Berger was codirector of the Mediating Structures
Project of the AEI from 1976 to 1979. In their preface to *The War Over
the Family*, Berger and Berger thank Michael Novak. In his acknowl-
edgment in *The Spirit of Democratic Capitalism*, Michael Novak thanks
Irving Kristol. In his preface to *Two Cheers for Capitalism*, Irving Kristol, also a former Resident Scholar of the AEI, does not thank anyone
at all.

While there are differences in the interests of those groups who com-
pose conservatism in the 1980s, the neoconservatives share many of the
assumptions held by the current movement of family traditionalists.
Several free-market economists who offer distinctive viewpoints on the
family also typically share the same assumptions (see Majka, 1988).
Berger and Berger characterize these assumptions as endorsement of the
traditional family and traditional roles between the sexes, spouses, and
generations. They emphasize conventional norms of moral responsibility, not only in sexuality but wide areas of social behavior. They
espouse conventional viewpoints on military defense, welfare, crime,
and/or capitalist system (Berger and Berger, 1983, p. 31). Finally, they
agree that government has only a very limited power to solve social problems (p. 203).

At times the neoconservatives attempt to distinguish their views from
the free-market economists, but significant continuities exist between
them, nevertheless. Both tend to caricature their political opponents on
the left as "antifamily" (B. Berger, 1980, p. 151; Berger and Berger, 1983,
p. 140; Kristol, 1978, pp. 66-67; Novak, 1982, pp. 156, 159). All profess
admiration for the old ideals of the "bourgeois family" as the source of
Protestant virtues and last refuge of decency (Berger and Berger, 1983,
pp. 172, 183-184; Novak, 1982, pp. 159 ff.; Kristol, 1978, pp. 86, 138-139;
Kristol, 1983, p. 77). All see the family as a primary source of economic
motivation: The desire to enrich one's family is the underlying motive behind attachment to private property and the work ethic (Novak, 1982,
pp. 148, 162-164; Berger and Berger, 1983, p. 175; Kristol, 1978, p. 224).

It has been argued that the primary distinction between the neoconservatives and free-market economists is the willingness of neoconservatives

to accept the utility of such New Deal reforms as the creation of a welfare state, a practical attitude toward government participation in the economy, and only muted support for big business (Steinfels, 1979, p. 10; Kristol, 1978, p. 136; Kristol, 1983, pp. 76-77). In neoconservative publications in the 1980s, however, the authors claim to support New Deal reforms while at the same time condemn welfare activities as "state interventionism." They directly endorse the free-market economists' assertions that the expansion of the welfare state created a crisis and weakened the economy. Also, they view economic growth and "the creative powers of the market" as important means of solving social problems (e.g., Novak, 1985, 1982, pp. 122-126, 218; Kristol, 1983, pp. 76, 193; Berger and Berger, 1983, p. 207).

In a rare reference to the possibility of a major malfunctioning within the capitalist economic system, Irving Kristol regrets the lack of a spirit of stoicism in bourgeois society. Premodern societies, in contrast, prepared for suffering with a stoic mood in the public sphere. We are told they believed, "Life is hard, fortune is fickle, bad luck is more likely than good luck and a better life is more probable after death than before" (Kristol, 1978, p. 163). Today we are supposedly hampered with the attitude that nothing should be permitted to go very wrong for very long. When calamity does strike, it finds the society morally and intellectually unprepared (p. 163).

The neoconservatives are uncomfortably silent about the social impact of the three recessions that have taken place in the last fifteen years. Indeed, terms such as *unemployment, layoff, plant closure,* and *recession* are completely absent from the indexes for their books. They seem to imply that the undesirable personal and family consequences of economic policies are insignificant or ought to be dismissed as irrelevant to policy considerations.

The nearest the neoconservatives come to dealing with the economic well-being of families is in their treatment of income inequalities. Berger and Berger (1983, p. 183) view class differences among families as declining, especially in terms of lifestyle comparisons. Novak (1982, p. 124) regards inequality as necessary, and argues that the pursuit of equality only makes the public sullen and resentful. Besides, security and equality run counter to the human condition. Novak (1985) reassures us that poverty is normal: "Poverty is the immemorial condition of the human race." Kristol (1985) denies that greater income inequalities have any clear relationship to individual and social pathology. He declares that income inequality cannot even be tied to economic well-being since poverty and affluence have their "ambiguities" (p. 195). After all, capitalism incites ever more unreasonable material expectations, and all income groups feel deprived (Kristol, 1983, p. 167). He invites us to consider the human costs for those who are condemned to affluence, he asserts that affluence can be as demoralizing as poverty. Thus we ought to be cautious about overestimating the economic well-being of those who are, statistically speaking, rich (p. 167).

The neoconservatives perceive virtue underlying the social status of the rich. They claim that many who are now wealthy were born poor (Novak, 1982, p. 214). Also, inequalities of wealth directly reflect inequalities in human talents and abilities (Kristol, 1978, p. 184). Novak (1982) celebrates the social contributions of the rich. For example, their tastes enhance urban architecture; their ambition for public immortality creates museums, galleries, symphony halls, and libraries; they build mansions and gardens that the public may admire from a distance, and churches, monuments, and universities that allow one close enough to make donations. Also, the wealthy, unlike the poor, do more than their share of economic investment and patronage of new technology (p. 213).

The neoconservatives agree that when it comes to family income distribution, no one is able to know what is the "common good." In fact, attempts to do so often make matters worse. (This is also the central thesis of Charles Murray [1984] in his well-publicized book, *Losing Ground*, the product of another conservative establishment, the Manhattan Institute for Social Research.) Berger and Berger (1983, pp. 35-36) regard attempts to find solutions to the problems of income distribution and unemployment as "revolutionary scenarios," having little to do with the "concrete problems of families." Brigitte Berger (1980, p. 151) asserts that most claims to equality, including racial and sexual as well as economic, "serve only to intensify these inequalities." Kristol (1983, p. 200) regards egalitarian criteria as inappropriate means of evaluating capitalist society. Echoing Adam Smith, Kristol (1978) instead argues that a "fair" distribution of income is one that is allocated according to a person's input into the economy. This input is best measured by the marketplace and the transactions that take place there (pp. 191-192). He seems to imply that activities that take place outside the market are, by definition, leisure. The contradictions in this view are readily visible for women's work. Doing housework, taking care of children, and carrying out assorted tasks for husbands are major forms of unpaid domestic labor and take place outside the market. Perhaps he believes women's work in the home has no more economic value than it receives, and possibility deserves even less.

Economic growth pure and simple offers the best prospect for families at low-income levels, according to the neoconservatives. This argument is common to both liberals and conservatives. What distinguishes the neoconservatives in part is their lack of concern with the uneven pattern of growth and its impact on specific human populations. For example, the growth of U.S. Steel by way of divesting of its steel plants and expanding into other investment avenues via corporate takeovers may have improved profitability, but it has been devastating for residents of the Monongahela Valley. However, for the neoconservatives, these kinds of realities are nonproblematic. Novak (1982, p. 126), for example, simply states that growth guarantees larger future income resources so that people at every level of society can reasonably hope for material gains. Similarly, Kristol (1983) sees in economic growth the opportunity to improve everyone's condition, although the improvements are admittedly unequal in extent and the timing of the gains. It is asserted that one of the "bedrock of truths about the human condition" is that economic growth assures a huge expansion of the property-owning middle classes (p. 193). Presumably, by its capacity to bring the deserving poor and working class into the middle class, economic growth "solves" the problem of poverty (p. 322).

The neoconservatives find little to challenge their views in the problem of poverty. If families are poor, it is either a temporary matter or their own fault. Berger and Berger (1983, p. 5) reduce the problem of the economic deprivation experienced by children to the lack of "a properly bourgeois childhood." Novak (1982, p. 125) argues that ours is a society where people need feel trapped only by their own misjudgments or behavior. The poor have no reason to interpret their condition as permanent, according to Kristol (1983), because of the critical role of talent and sheer luck. In any case, poverty does not always dehumanize (pp. 196-197). The neoconservatives agree that in actuality the number of "needy families" is few: Kristol (1983, p. 197) estimates the proportion of the American people who qualify as "problematically poor" as well under 10% (see also Berger and Berger, 1983, p. 208).

The disproportionate location of black families among the poor also presents no difficulty for the neoconservatives. Novak (1982, p. 162) regards this issue as essentially explained by the fact that some families have an effective economic tradition while others have a "less developed tradition." Specifically, the unequal circumstances of blacks and whites can be explained by differences in black and white Protestantism. Blacks are simply practicing the wrong form of Calvinism. Among some black American Protestants, there is a higher emphasis on emotion, rhetorical pitch, and "sense of dream." According to Novak (1982), this distinctive form of Calvinism possibly has different economic and political effects. Also, among blacks, variations in their cultural past create different social profiles and rates of success (p. 219). As with many of Novak's assertions about blacks, we are given no empirical evidence to support his contention and are referred instead to the authority of Thomas Sowell.

Novak insists that cultures differ in the mental and emotional discipline taught to their children, their economic inclinations, and other factors that affect political and economic competition. Rather than assisting the poor, social welfare measures reinforce dependency among blacks (1985; 1982, p. 220). Welfare dependency affects the marital behavior of black males: Novak (1982, p. 222) cites black illegitimacy rates as evidence. The key is breaking the pattern of dependency. Once again the solution is found in promoting capital accumulation in the private sector, and any social benefit must always be a by-product. The government must focus on underwriting the costs of doing business in black communities. Presumably this does not include subsidies aimed at *black-owned* enterprises, however, since Novak insists that black communities do not at present lack the necessary capital. Novak (1982, pp. 23-224) states that it is especially necessary to change the ethos in a portion of the black community, especially citing the "irregularity and self-destructive personal habits" of black youths and the lack of "personal discipline" among the unemployables. "Ethos" is the presumed source of minority poverty and unemployment, not the economic stagnation of inner-urban areas, the regional out-migration of business and industry, the residual availability of predominantly low-wage jobs, and the impact of past and present racial discrimination (see Wilson, 1985).

Berger and Berger (1983) also emphasize a cultural basis for income differences between whites and nonwhites. They argue that Americans accept group differences only if the minority group is perceived as sharing what they term "the basic values of the bourgeois ethos, and in particular of the bourgeois family" (p. 184). They state that Americans are resistant to overcoming racial prejudice in the absence of shared allegiance to the bourgeois ethos and family. They assert that the bourgeois family is the single most important institution capable of bridging group differences (pp. 184-185). By this argument, Berger and Berger assume there are substantial differences between the values of certain minorities and the white majority, at least as concerned with family life. They ignore an immense amount of research that demonstrates the *lack* of significant differences between, for example, blacks and whites in their desires for long-lasting marriages and stable families. What *is* different is sufficient economic means to help achieve these aspirations in reality (see McAdoo, 1981).

The neoconservatives are unanimous in discerning negative consequences in the American welfare state. Berger and Berger (1983) argue that much of the welfare state legislation weakens the families of its beneficiaries. They propose that great care should be taken to prevent any more private matters from becoming "problemized" as public issues since this has led to an unnecessary crisis of the welfare state (pp. 206-207). Novak (1982, p. 218) perceives a grave crisis facing society in the form of a citizenry becoming corrupted by dependence and social welfare measures creating economic stagnation. Kristol (1983, pp. 244-245) warns that the experience of Western Europe with welfare-state politics has led to discontent, cynicism, and alienation among a potentially restless and "ungrateful" citizenry.

All are in agreement that the expansion of the government's intervention on behalf of its citizens has not made the public happier and more contented (Kristol, 1978, p. 165; Berger and Berger, 1983, p. 33; Novak, 1982, pp. 32-33). Kristol (1978, p. 220) asserts that "the welfare system encourages various social pathologies—broken families, illegitimacy, drug addiction. . . ." Transfer payments are counterproductive for all but the aged, sick, and handicapped.

Berger and Berger (1983) also say that much of the welfare state legislation weakens the families of its beneficiaries. The evidence is that in spite of the focus on social and economic issues beginning in the Great Society era, family problems have increased (p. 33). This presumably indicates that the remedies prescribed by professionals were actually "part of the disease" (p. 36). The neoconservatives assert that the growth of bureaucracies in the name of government problem solving is neither economically nor politically tolerable. They describe such activities as state interventionism, professional self-interest, and empire-building, and even cultural imperialism.

A case in point is the recent demand by women for equal pay for jobs of comparable worth. Berger and Berger (1983) flatly condemn this initiative as having a dubious relationship to the needs of families. They insist that pursuit of equal pay and other employment issues is an exercise in political futility. They urge the public to give up attempting to secure this reform because "government cannot meet all human needs" (p. 200)—women, especially, should not expect public policy to "subsidize their life plans" (p. 205).

Predictably, Brigitte Berger (1979) rejects proposals for a national program of child care on the grounds that it devalidates the family and its power over children. She decries the influence of "child care bureaucrats" and the "leviathan empire of the educationists" (pp. 8-11). Berger and Berger (1983) argue that professionals have an obvious self-interest in advocating large-scale professionally managed centers for the children of employed mothers. They suggest that children are harmed by such separations from intimate family contacts. In support of their argument they cite studies describing the negative effects on children in orphanages and under conditions of high personnel turnover (a characteristic said to be inevitable in child-care facilities), and foundling home placements (p. 155; also B. Berger, 1980, pp. 154-155). They imply that child care weakens the stable structure of the family (Berger and Berger, 1983, p. 156).

Berger and Berger (1983) assert that the demand for publicly supported child care appears hostile to children because it suggests that women want to "dump children so that mothers can pursue their selfish programs of self-realization" (p. 27). For middle-class women to enter the labor force is synonymous with "abdication" of the family's role to "the child care industry," according to Brigitte Berger (1979, p. 6). She asserts that working-class women, in contrast, experience "the pressing desire . . . to be with and care for their children" (1980, p. 154). This analysis is especially ironic in view of the failure of the profit-oriented market to provide the majority of women with genuine choices of meaningful jobs at fair compensation and affordable, quality child-care options. The implication is clear: Women with children should be exclusively concerned with child-care responsibilities. This, of course, puts mothers without employed husbands in a double bind. Not only should they be at home, but also income supports that would be clearly needed by many in order to survive nonemployment should be eliminated since, it is elsewhere argued, these measures are "antifamily."

Given Brigitte Berger's preference for parental care during early childhood and rejection of a public program of child care in the name of tax savings, her endorsement of a policy of child care "vouchers" in 1980 is especially problematic. She implies that a rich array of child-care options are readily available to the parents of young children (p. 168). She fails to recognize that the demand for affordable child care exceeds the supply, and parents suffer persistent anxiety over securing quality care—this is true even for the middle class in which greater resources make more abundant choices possible than for the poor. She makes no attempt to understand how a child-care allowance for a parent to stay at home with the child would permit a sole breadwinner or even a coprovider to withdraw from the labor force in an economy where recessions and stagnating real earnings make it difficult to sustain a family even with two (and sometimes more) earners per household. She does not appear to be proposing a child-care allowance equal to the economic contribution of employed wives (approximately one-third of a family income), much less the equivalent of the wage of an employed husband. While it is unquestionably desirable for people to have more time to devote to their family lives and friendships, a reduction in the work week and improvement in the earning capacity of jobs would be necessary to make this a genuine possibility for the majority of families.

A recurrent thesis among the neoconservatives is that professionals constitute a politically liberal "new class." They are part of a larger knowledge class composed of experts, technicians, educators, and intellectuals. They assert that the new class caused the crisis of the welfare state and is exacerbating the condition of the poor for its own self-interested purposes. Novak sees intellectuals and scholars as a new elite directly benefiting from the growing power and wealth of the state and able to dominate both the state and the economy (Novak, 1982, pp. 33, 186). Berger and Berger (1983) assert that professionals have an interest in defining social problems in a way that makes their services appear necessary. Their actions in expanding the welfare state had the unintended consequences of disrupting informal support networks in poor neighborhoods and creating a range of new problems that called for new programs to cope with them, in areas such as child care for employed mothers and treatment of juvenile crimes (p. 33). Brigitte Berger (1980) asserts that public policy is shaped mainly by organized groups based in the middle class "trying to legitimate their own interests under the guise of helping the poor and downtrodden." Actions of middle-class intellectuals often supply the state with what she calls "yet one more means of manipulating the poor" (p. 154). Kristol (1978) accuses liberal reformers of attempting to turn poverty into a "permanent provocation" (p. 217). He dismisses socioeconomic scholarship on inequality as being "shot through with disingenuousness, sophistry, and unscrupulous statistical maneuvering" (p. 176).

Recommendations for improving the well-being of families include public policies that support families in carrying out their own responsibilities for caring for their members, rather than relieving families of these tasks (Berger and Berger, 1983, p. 209). Families need to be empowered to take control of their own problems. They will find little disagreement on this general principle. However, for the neoconservatives this does not mean improving wages and family income security, despite the fact that Berger and Berger (1983, p. 210) acknowledge that "money empowers." Instead, "needy families" (in their terminology) should turn for assistance to their own subcultures, neighborhoods, churches, and voluntary associations. Aid from government agencies should be a last resort.

Commenting upon the diversity of families in American society, Brigitte Berger (1980) states her preference for the "bourgeois family." Other family types, she argues, will find it more difficult to care for the needs of children (p. 178). It is unfortunate for the coherence of her argument that she approvingly introduces Max Horkheimer (by way of a phrase she slightly misquotes from a secondary source) to emphasize the positive functions of the bourgeois family (p. 147). A further reading of the same paragraph in the original essay by Max Horkheimer (1972, p. 114) shows that Horkheimer viewed the family's positive aspects of love and caring as "not dependent on the existence of the family in its present form and, in fact, are even in danger of shrivelling up in such a milieu. . . ."

Far from celebrating the bourgeois family as a social ideal, Horkheimer (1972) saw it as an institution that persuades its dependent members to resign themselves to subordination. At times the costs of submission for individual women and children can be high: loss of happiness, despair, and material and psychic exploitation (p. 106). For society, the result is "ever new generations of people who do not question the structure of the economic and social system but accept it as natural and permanent and allow even their dissatisfaction and rebellion to be turned into effective forces for the prevailing order" (p. 108).

There is some measure of hope according to Horkheimer only insofar as individualistic motives decline as the dominant bond in relationships, and people develop a conception of society as a just community, without poverty. "Out of the suffering caused by the oppressive conditions that prevail under the sign of bourgeois authority, there can arise a new community of spouses and children, and it will not, in bourgeois fashion, form a closed community over against other families" (Horkheimer, 1972, p. 124).

THE LIMITATIONS OF INEQUALITY

Sociologists will recognize the social philosophy of the neo-conservatives as a simplified revival of the functionalist theory of inequality: Unequal distribution of life chances is necessary and inevitable. Efforts to change or alleviate the structures of inequality are wrong minded (and in any case doomed in advance) because they disrupt the otherwise harmonious interdependence among classes. Besides, differences in wealth, status, and power have beneficial consequences for society in promoting rewards for scarce abilities and specialized training.

Also, the neoconservatives explain poverty through a pared-down version of the "culture of poverty" thesis: Poverty produces people with unique individual characteristics that ensure that they remain poor. They refurbish the image of the undeserving masses, in contrast to that small segment of our society who deserve to be objects of charity as the "truly needy."

Missing from neoconservative accounts of the societal benefit derived from inequality is a recognition of the longstanding critiques of the functionalist thesis. For example, it is never clear how *much* inequality between families the neoconservatives feel is necessary to create the optimum balance of sanctions to bolster the work ethic. In addition, the uneven distribution of social rewards reflects the inheritance of status within upper-income white families and the disinheritance of status improvements among racial minorities, especially blacks. Privileged groups have long exercised advantages in power and influence over the labor market, which is very far from operating along the lines of free-market principles—otherwise, differentials in occupational rewards would decline over time, thus creating more equality instead of the reverse.

The dysfunctions of social inequality are not weighed against its presumed benefits. Inequality concentrates power in the hands of elites who then use their power to preserve the structure of unequal rewards and protect their privileges. Inequality hinders nonelites from using political influence and participating in democratic politics. Inequality intensifies racism and sexism, as these ideologies of group inferiority are used to rationalize the scarcity of opportunity in the upper ranks of society. Inequality creates conditions in our society, such as unemployment, that periodically force the talents and skills of nonelites to be underutilized. It imposes limits on the development of skills by denying training to many, including sole mothers, who would benefit from it. To the extent their self-image mirrors their social rank, the victims of inequality endure a diminished self-esteem. This among other factors adds to the difficulty of creating a movement to change the system that limits their life -chances. Likewise, inequality creates vested interests that oppose the search for alternatives that would better assure human well-being.

The neoconservative revival of the "culture of poverty" thesis is intended to account for the irony of basic human needs remaining unmet while resources stand idle. Diverse arguments contain the common thread of assuming that poverty produces people with unique personal characteristics that ensure that they remain poor. The neoconservatives ignore the critical significance of the fact that the chances of living in poverty are not randomly distributed: Racial minorities, the aged, and women who are sole mothers are more likely to be poor. Also, arguments that poverty in our society reflects the failure to expend work effort and the lack of motivation to work are irrelevant in the face of plant closures and mass unemployment. Finally, the poor are far from a homogeneous class, as the culture of poverty implies. A significant proportion of the poor are working full time at jobs whose compensation is too low to support a spouse and/or child and provide a family with a subsistence level of living.

What is most noticeably lacking in the neoconservative attempts to revive the functionalist theory of inequality is any attempt to support their arguments with a systematic application of empirical evidence. Moreover, they ignore or dismiss out-of-hand scholarship that contradicts their assertions. This may explain why neoconservative ideas have apparently failed to become accepted among intellectuals outside the narrow sphere of those who already share their convictions. They devote most of their energies to addressing their admirers in the business world and neglect to assemble the kinds of empirical support needed to persuade those who insist on weighing the evidence.

For all their scientific insufficiency and intellectual shallowness, the neoconservatives do have an important social function: Their views resonate with deeply seated tenets of an individualistic ideology. They revive the core themes of American individualism: The belief that work, thrift, and a stable family life are the route to prosperity. There are sufficient opportunities for competent and ambitious people regardless of family status or past disadvantages. People must strive for material success. Those who work hard will gain their material goals. Those who do not succeed have only themselves to blame for their failures. Thus the poor are stereotyped as deserving their fate, and the stereotypes become a further indignity to be resisted by the unemployed and other poor.

The ideology of individualism, as revived by the neoconservatives, has useful consequences for maintaining inequality. It inhibits public awareness that problems in society are shared and related to social structure. Individualism promotes a distorted view of our economic system. It ignores the ways in which the economy has been changed by technological displacement, deindustrialization, and the international flight of capital (Harrington, 1984). Uneven economic development between geographic regions of the country and separate and unequal labor markets also go unrecognized (Gordon, Edwards, and Reich, 1982). The chance of becoming unemployed during the last recession was increased by membership in a subordinate group (Majka, 1984). Economic "recovery" has had a highly uneven impact geographically, as well as socially.

Individualism focuses anxiety on the public cost of inadequate personal resources, while it obscures the public burden of expenditures having little direct benefit to families of the majority. It diverts attention away from high expenditures for the military and the use of public funds to benefit businesses, especially by way of numerous tax expenditures and subsidies. Also, it masks the extent to which the upper class has received the greater part of the income redistribution carried out by the state in the 1980s through tax cuts, massive shifts in public spending, and policy changes (Edsall, 1984, pp. 205-207).

The version of individualism promoted by the neoconservatives reinforces private consumption as a family goal and is intended to stimulate family work effort, even though it operates in the context of a dual economy that carries meager rewards for increased work effort by those in the secondary sector of low-wage jobs. At the same time, individualism weakens the awareness of class exploitation: The poor are stereotyped as lazy, even though many are employed, and a substantial number remain poor in spite of working at full-time jobs. Individualism reinforces a wage worker's economic insecurity through promoting a fear of unemployment, economic deprivation, and the shame and stigma of poverty—fears that persist even if income levels are adequate while a person is employed.

Individualism promoted by the neoconservatives serves the additional function of clouding the awareness of class interests. It attempts to convince individuals of the "necessity" of the business cycle, including mass unemployment, and directs them to shift their attention away from their own economic problems. Expressions of anger and animosity are allowed to be directed down the ranks of the class ladder rather than up. Hostility thus becomes focused upon the poor, especially those who are doubly disadvantaged, such as unemployed black youth and pregnant teenagers of all races. By treating the poor as scapegoats, the class structure is legitimated, racial and gender ideologies of inferiority are reinforced, and people become acquiescent to the worsening of social inequality that accompanies underemployment.

Dividing the working poor and other disadvantaged groups from other employed people separates them as workers and heightens competition among them over the distribution of work and the costs and benefits of government. This heightens perceptions of group differences and creates barriers against people working together collectively. It prevents them from developing a common agenda and challenging the authority structure that is a source of their distress. Individualism implies that unemployed people should cope on their own: seek work, obtain loans, use savings, and have other family members go to work. It reduces the probability that even the unemployed will hold government responsible for assisting individuals (Scholzman and Verba, 1979, p. 24).

Instead of promoting an increase in personal freedom, practices associated with individualism leave many people vulnerable and defenseless. A number of recent accounts analyze the contradictory effects of the unconstrained pursuit of private interests (Bellah et al., 1985; O'Connor, 1984; Lasch, 1977, 1983; Ehrenreich, 1983).

As social and economic conditions become more unstable and hope for political action to humanize industrial society fades, people lose confidence in themselves and the future. Personal strategies for survival sometimes take the form of an emotional retreat from the kinds of long-term commitments that presume an orderly world, and this behavior further weakens the capacity to act on behalf of oneself and others (Lasch, 1983, p. 16).

A retreat from commitment exacerbates difficulties in building relationships and making sense of one's own life in relation to others. Nevertheless, the public good cannot be realized without acknowledging interdependence and respect for diversity and the dignity of others. The ideals of democratic citizenship hold that one generation is responsible to the next. In a society with a complex division of labor, all are interdependent and owe a substantial debt to the rest of society for their personal welfare. There is both a danger and an opportunity in the fact that in a democratic society the common good cannot be realized by individuals acting alone, but instead depends on public dialogue and citizen empowerment to create more humane institutions (Bellah et al., 1985, p. 254).

RETHINKING SOCIAL POLICY

There is a very substantial unfinished agenda composed of issues and alternatives to discrimination, unemployment, and poverty that began to be considered seriously in the previous decade (Glazer et al., 1977, pp. 155-169). Policy alternatives to counter the recommendations of the neoconservatives must again become part of public political discussion. One crucial area of concern must certainly be the most appropriate means of improving the level of employment and economic security.

For some time now it has been understood that "full employment" would supply the income stability that is needed as a precondition for stable family lives and community participation. Yet full employment as a policy objective has proved to be not so much a specific program as one of several "ideal types" of solutions to persistent economic dislocations. Among those who agree that a tighter labor market is a desirable policy objective, there is substantial disagreement about what would be the best means of achieving it. The pursuit of full employment necessarily leads to choices about the distribution of social and economic resources among various groups, as well as their relative allocation between public and private objectives. The following discussion is intended to indicate some of the dilemmas underlying conventional proposals in support of full employment, and suggest a few principles and underlying assumptions needed for a genuine strategy of social reconstruction.

In an economy prone to massive dislocations in the last quarter of the twentieth century, it seems unlikely that full employment can be reached without basic changes in the nature of work. Traditionally, the terms of employment do not respond to what is required for a humane social and family life. There should be a more satisfying balance in people's lives between paid work for employers and unpaid work on behalf of families and communities. It must be recognized that a great amount of unpaid work needed by families and communities will never be satisfied in the marketplace. Accordingly, there should be an adjustment of national standards in order to shorten the hours of the work week while maintaining the existing standard of living. The goal of shortening the work week (which has been constant for 50 years) should support an increase in the numbers of jobs at every level in the occupational structure. This objective should be combined with an expansion in the availability of flexible work hours and leave time. Also, introduction of a 30-hour work week, for example, would most likely require improvements in the earning capacity of jobs at the lower-income levels.

Given many years of high unemployment and the competition for jobs, women and men have seldom been "free" to find the type of employment they prefer. Expanding the numbers of existing jobs will in itself not be sufficient to guarantee everyone who is willing and able to be employed the access to meaningful work. The content of jobs should be reevaluated. Basic changes in work roles are needed to allow employee participation in workplace planning, continual learning of new techniques of production and distribution, and to reassess the goal of constantly expanding the production of goods in view of the vulnerability of the environment.

It must be recognized that many workers have already adjusted to family needs and the scarcity of jobs by having accepted part-time work. Thus improvements in the quality of part-time work will be an important factor in future adjustments in the terms of employment. Greater status and earning capacity in part-time work has enormous potential for allowing people to pursue meaningful personal and family lives and permitting participation by both parents in the care of children. Examples of the kinds of changes needed in part-time work are the availability of career-level positions at part-time schedules with appropriate job security, pensions, full-benefit medical care, and other normal fringe benefits such as vacation and pension rights. Also, income incentives should be provided for shared jobs, and hourly wage rates should be raised substantially to reflect the fact that part-time workers are highly productive and are often expected to work with more intensity than their full-time counterparts.

Conventional proposals in favor of full employment scarcely recognize that married women in the labor force and sole mothers are in reality multiple jobholders. The failure to acknowledge housework and child care as work comes from the outdated notion that work includes only efforts that yield earnings. If employed women are not going to continue to be forced to carry a disproportionate share of housework, child care and employment without social encouragement and aid, support services to meet family needs, especially child care, are required. Also, the content of paid employment available to women should be useful and rewarding work. Women have suffered too long from underemployment in low-paying jobs without fringe benefits or long-term security. Sex equality in employment is a necessary condition for women to exercise freely the option of paid employment. This requires enforcement of equal pay policies and other practices that would end sex discrimination and sexual harassment. Because of existing levels of occupational segregation, it is also necessary to pursue equal pay for jobs of comparable worth. Finally, education and training, which would make improvements in women's employment opportunities possible, require both financial assistance and family support services. Especially important is federal financing of education that should include support for living expenses and free child care.

The cost in tax dollars of a social reconstruction that would include planning in the public sector, job creation, and family support services, especially child care, needed to make family security a reality is enormous. Yet it must be measured against the billions it costs in idle capacity and underutilized productive skills. It must also be recognized that much of the cost would represent a social investment in human capital to be realized in the future in the form of greater utilization of human abilities and more satisfying personal lives. In any case, the human cost of failing to make a financial commitment to the well-being of families is far greater.

The timing for pursuing these policy objectives is the present. That is, while we are still paying for the social and economic effects of the recessions of the 1980s, we must ensure that we do not repeat the same cycle of personal and family disruption by failing to make the changes necessary for a more humane future.

9

Person and Community: Contrasting Values in the U.S. Bishops' Pastoral on Economics and the American Culture

Margaret Hohman, SCN

The debate concerning public policy changes to assuage the economic distress of families can be joined at many levels. One requirement for effective dialogue is a consciousness of the basic assumptions that underlie one's reasoning and an awareness of their implications.

The U.S. Bishops' pastoral, *Economic Justice for All,* addresses a sweep of topics as well as the theological and ethical bases for judging economic issues. It provides a helpful context for considering some forces that affect family life either directly or indirectly.

Clearly, economic rights from the Bishops' perspective are rooted in a view of person and community that is starkly different from those of Hobbes, Locke, and others whose ideas have influenced the present economic climate.

The Enlightenment view of human nature holds that the achievement of independence is a primary goal of human life. In this view, the rights of the individual must be preserved and strongly defended from encroachment by society.

The U.S. Bishops have a radically different image of human nature as modeled in a triune God. Central to the Trinity is the total gift of Father to Son in a union of love in the Holy Spirit. Human beings created in the image of God are called to and capable of self-gift to others in community.

The relationships built in this process of giving oneself to others not only serve the growth of the person but benefit the community as a whole. Thus the Bishops can say the deprivation and powerlessness of the poor wounds the whole community. The extent of their suffering is a measure of how far we are from being a true community of persons (U.S. Bishops, 1986, p. 87). [1]

If economic distress generally, and of the family in particular, is to be understood, one place to start is to seek a greater awareness of how the present situation came about. The causes, near and remote, that contributed to past economic choices must certainly include some mention of the historical movements that produced our present cultural climate. It is helpful to examine how the church acted and reacted to these movements and the changes that have occurred in the church's understanding of its role in the world. This reflection should shed light on why the Bishops decided to issue a pastoral on economics at this time.

This chapter will contrast the Bishops' perspective on person and community with the prevailing individualism in the culture today. It will include a brief history of four cultural strains that have shaped the U.S. culture, the gradual development of the church's awareness of its role in the public dialogue on economic issues, central themes from the economic pastoral, some of the debate on family issues, and discussion of an emerging emphasis on church support for persons and families who want to participate in and influence economic choices.

PERSON AND COMMUNITY

What are the U.S. Bishops attempting to do in writing a pastoral on economics? Certainly it is paddling upstream against a strong cultural current. How will they be able to be heard by Americans whose ideas about person and community are so different from their own? The Bishops believe that

Human life is life in community [1986, p. 63].

Only active love of God and neighbor makes the fullness of community happen [1986, p. 64].

Human beings achieve self-realization not in isolation, but in interaction with others [1986, p. 65].

Human dignity, realized in community with others and with the whole of God's creation, is the norm against which every social institution must be measured [1986, p. 25].

Sustaining a common culture and a common commitment to moral values is not easy in our world. . . . Since the industrial revolution, people have had to define themselves and their work ever more narrowly to find a niche in the economy. . . . The costs are social fragmentation, a decline in seeing how one's work serves the whole community and an increased emphasis on personal goals and private interests [1986, p. 22].

The Bishops stress time and again the inseparable link between respecting the dignity of the person and solidarity in community. Needless to say, this is not a view that is widely held in our country. On the contrary, the trend is toward a pervasive individualism in our society that is either unconscious of or rejects any suggestion that the common good must be taken into account.

INDIVIDUALISM IN U.S. CULTURE

The dominance of individualism today is shown in a recently published study of American culture, *Habits of the Heart: Individualism and Commitment in America,* written by a team of five sociologists. They consider their work to be a detailed reading of and commentary on the reflections of Alexis de Tocqueville's *Democracy in America* written a century and a half ago. These authors comment that today's

American cultural traditions define personality, achievement, and the purpose of human life in ways that leave the individual suspended in glorious, but terrifying isolation. . . . What is good is what one finds rewarding. If one's preference changes, so does the nature of good. Even the deepest ethical virtues are justified as matters of personal preference. Indeed, the ultimate ethical rule is simply that individuals should be able to pursue whatever they find rewarding, constrained only by the requirements that they not interfere with the "value system" of others [Bellah et al., 1985, p. 6].

The authors see America's highest value as freedom but find many of the persons they interviewed ambivalent about or experiencing difficulty in articulating what they are free for. There seems to be little vocabulary available to describe the ends of a good life. The image of self-reliance is very strong but often in practice it becomes the ability to keep the family enclosed in self-imposed "walls" with one's own values and excludes *searching* for the good life *with* others. Even persons interviewed in the study who were engaged in organizing groups of low-income people to have more control over their lives could not articulate what a more cooperative, just, and equal social order might look like—though they considered themselves working to further that goal.

In a similar vein, Thomas Merton (1960, p. ix), in *Disputed Questions,* pointed out that the problem of the person and social organization is perhaps the most important problem of our century. Merton (1960, p. x) distinguishes between *individuals* and *persons.*

> It is individualism which has really been the apparent ideal of our western society for the past two or three hundred years. This individualism, primarily an economic concept with a pseudospiritual and moral facade, is in fact mere irresponsibility. It is, and has always been not an affirmation of genuine humane values but a flight from the obligation to love. . . . The individual. . . is a unit divided off from the other units. His freedom may not seem like an illusion when he is surrounded by the social mirage of comfort and ample opportunity. But as soon as the structure of his society begins to collapse, the individual collapses with it and he who seemed to be a person soon becomes nothing but a number.

For Merton the vocation of the *person* is to construct one's own solitude as a necessary condition for a valid encounter with other persons, for intelligent cooperation, and for communion in love.

PARTICIPATION IN THE PUBLIC SPHERE

The authors of *Habits of the Heart* are concerned that individualism could isolate Americans and undermine freedom and our democratic way of governance. Following Tocqueville, they believe that the key to survival of institutions is the relationships between private and public life, the way in which citizens do or do not participate in the public sphere (1985, p. 65).

Tocqueville (1985, p. 37) called the mores of American people "habits of the heart"—the notions, opinions, ideas that shape mental habits, the habitual practices with respect to such things as religion, political participation, and economic life. He saw these mores as a key to American success in establishing and maintaining a free republic.

The U.S. Bishops (1986, p. 77) also recognize the interconnectedness of these aspects of life and the need for them to be addressed together in pursuing improvements in the economic area. Their own Christian and human vision is grounded in the conviction that

> justice demands that social institutions be ordered in a way that guarantees all persons the ability to participate actively in the economic, political, and cultural life of society. The nation's founders took daring steps to create structures of participation, mutual accountability, and widely distributed power to ensure the political rights and freedoms of all. We believe that similar steps are needed today to expand economic participation, broaden the sharing of economic power, and make economic decisions more accountable to the common good [p. 297].

Events in our history profoundly influenced the mental habits and practices of Americans and produced the present culture that is predominantly individualistic. The economic distress of families today has been a long time in the making and is the result of many factors, economic and otherwise. Examining briefly some of these historic trends will provide the context in which to place the reflections of the U.S. Bishops and their calls for a greater sense of Christian commitment and change in public policy.

U.S. CULTURAL ROOTS

Four cultural strains were evident in the early days of the republic. Bellah et al. (1985) typify them using four prominent persons from our early history.

John Winthrop (1588-1649), first governor of the Massachusetts Bay Colony, illustrated the *biblical* strain in American culture. He believed very much in a community bound together in mutual respect. The Puritans' fundamental criterion of success was not material wealth but rather the creation of a community in which a genuinely ethical and spiritual life could be lived.

The *republican* strain in American culture was exemplified by Thomas Jefferson (1743-1826). Jefferson believed in a self-governing society of relative equals in which all participate. He feared that "our rulers will become corrupt, our people careless." If people forgot themselves "in the sole faculty of making money," the future of the republic would be bleak and tyranny would not be far away.

The *utilitarian individualist* was exemplified by Ben Franklin (1706-1790), the poor boy who made good. For him, the most important thing about the freedom America afforded was the choice for the individual to get ahead on his own initiative. Many today believe that in a society where each one's own interest is vigorously pursued, the social good of all will automatically emerge. This is utilitarian individualism in pure form. Franklin did not believe this, but his image and sayings such as, "God helps those who help themselves," contributed to this impression.

Walt Whitman (1819-1892) was the prototype of the *expressive individualist*. Whitman perceived the successful life to be one rich in experience, open to all kinds of people, luxuriating in the sensual as well as the intellectual. The ultimate use of America's independence was in cultivating and expressing the self and exploring its vast social and cosmic identities (Bellah et al., 1985, pp. 30-35).

During this early period of U.S. history, the strongest symbol of American culture was the independent citizen, a self-reliant, righteous, small farmer or craftsperson whose spirit was the idealized ethos of the township.

By the end of the nineteenth century, a very different situation prevailed. There was rapid expansion westward and industrial growth after the Civil War until World War I. A profound transformation occurred. The semiautonomous local societies were pulled into a vast national market guided largely by wealthy private citizens and financial groups. Local institutions could not deal with the problems that were increasingly national in scope. It was a time of a new industrial order, factories, ward bosses, immigrants, slums, political parties that changed in the stormy political conflict. There was an emancipation from small town morality that released an untrammeled pursuit of wealth without regard to the demands of social justice and the effects on the social fabric of a democratic society.

The competitive forces in the marketplace forced a division of life into various sectors, for example, workplace and home, in order to contain potential conflicts. There was a split between utilitarian individualism in the marketplace and expressive individualism in the family. The goal of living became some combination of occupation and lifestyle that is economically possible and psychically tolerable. During this time, the biblical and republican cultural strains grew weaker while individualist ones grew stronger (Bellah et al., 1985, pp. 40-46).

In this context, the sense of work as a *calling* performing a definite function in a community as a part of the civic and civil order of that community became changed to work as a *career,* a profession that offers personal advancement or honor and is unrelated to service in a particular community setting.

A NEW UNDERSTANDING
OF CHURCH MINISTRY

During this period, the American Catholic Church was primarily concerned with ministry to its own immigrant people, providing them with educational opportunities and especially supporting the struggle of the workers. The mainstream Catholic social thought that developed during this time and has continued to the present was liberal in orientation, emphasizing social justice, cooperation with non-Catholics, and rapid Americanization of the immigrants. Spokespersons for Roman Catholics felt they had to prove there was no incompatibility between their faith and their Americanism to the native Protestants who viewed with suspicion these immigrant persons speaking in foreign tongues and owing allegiance to a foreign ruler. At the same time, Catholic liberals had to struggle with misunderstandings of conservative Catholic Europeans whose experience was so different. American Catholics were dealing with non-Catholics in a pluralistic society about common social concerns. Several persons were especially influential in giving direction to Catholic social justice efforts. Through the influence of Cardinal Gibbons, the American Catholic Church strongly defended the Knights of Labor, a nondenominational organization, in their efforts to obtain justice.

In February 1919, the U.S. Bishops' Administrative Committee of the National Catholic War Council issued a forward-looking document that was very much in tune with the progressive, reforming element in American society during the first two decades of the twentieth century. It was a gradualist, reform-minded document that called for short-range and long-range efforts dealing with unemployment, a living wage, labor's right to organize, housing for the working class, a legal minimum wage, provision for state insurance against illness, unemployment, old age and other disabilities, labor participation in industrial management, vocational training, laws against child labor, cooperation, copartnership, and the call for the majority of the workers to become owners, at least in part, of the means of production.

The author of the document was Monsignor John A. Ryan, an economist, a professor at Catholic University, and Director of the Social Action Department of the National Catholic Welfare Conference from 1920 to his death in 1945. His theoretical writings were rooted in Catholic natural law theory that emphasizes order and harmony and an appeal based on reason and persuasion. This approach sees relationships not in terms of hostility, opposition, and conflict, but rather proposes that all are called to work together harmoniously for the common good that then rebounds to the good of the individual. Ryan maintained that the end of the state is to promote the welfare of its citizens—as a whole, as members of families, and as members of social classes. The goods of creation exist for all human beings, so the natural right of ownership is always qualified by the higher common right of use. A human person's need gives the primary title to property (Curran, 1977, pp. 50-58).

Another person who powerfully influenced the direction of Catholic social thought was Jesuit John Courtney Murray. His distinctively American contributions on religious freedom changed the course of the Vatican II document on this issue. This, along with the John Kennedy presidency, was a kind of coming of age for American Catholics, the culmination of a long struggle to prove that Catholicism, an immigrant and minority religion, is at home in the American ethos. Murray, in his book *We Hold These Truths,* points out that Catholic participation in the American consensus has been full and free, unreserved and unembarrassed, because the contents of this consensus—the ethical and political principles drawn from the tradition of natural law—approve themselves to the Catholic intelligence and conscience (Murray, 1960, p. 47).

The recent pastorals of the U.S. Bishops, *The Challenge of Peace* and *Economic Justice for All,* illustrate another development in Catholic social thought. Vatican II documents recognized the need to overcome the dichotomy between the natural and supernatural, to place the scriptures at the heart of all theology, and to make belief in the kingdom of God more relevant to daily life. Following that lead, the Bishops in these two documents have very explicitly based their calls for action on both scriptural and ethical considerations. Both Judeo-Christian faith and appeals to reason are given as motivations for living a just life and working for a just society.

CENTRAL THEMES IN
THE ECONOMIC PASTORAL

Three biblical themes, creation, covenant, and community, are the basis of the Bishops' faith convictions on economic justice. These themes highlight the relationship between person and community.

At the summit of creation stands the creation of man and woman, made in God's image [Gn. 1:26-27]. *As such every human being possesses an inalienable dignity that stamps human existence prior to any division into races or nations and prior to human labor and human achievement* [1986, p. 32].

Sin simultaneously alienates human beings from God and shatters the solidarity of the human community [1986, p. 33].

Being free and being a coresponsible community are God's intent for us [1986, p. 36].

Central to the biblical presentation of justice is that the justice of a community is measured by its treatment of the powerless in a society, most often described as the widow, the orphan, the poor and the stranger (non-Israelite) in the land [1986, p. 38].

The biblical emphasis on covenant and community also shows that human dignity can only be realized and protected in solidarity with others. . . . Respect for human rights and a strong sense of both person and community responsibility are linked, not opposed. . . . These rights are bestowed on human beings by God and grounded in the nature and dignity of human persons. They are not created by society. Indeed, society has a duty to secure and protect them [1986, p. 79].

The response to these biblical themes must be both personal and corporate, involving one's own personal conversion as well as the change of social structures that are harmful to persons and community.

The Bishops (1986) spell out some basic minimum conditions for life in community. They should include:

(1) Work that is self-fulfilling, allowing everyone to meet basic material needs and make a contribution to unity within the family, the nation, and the world community.
(2) Basic minimum levels of food, clothing, shelter, rest, and medical care should be available to all.

(3) The right to work in health and human dignity must be respected with a wage that protects the family and prevents exploitation.

(4) Justice demands the establishment of minimum levels of participation in economic decisions just as we have protected civil and political rights of persons and communities.

(5) Although equal distribution of resources to persons and groups is not possible and many factors contribute to an unequal sharing of economic benefits, still the great disparity in income and wealth in the world today is morally unacceptable.

Among these conditions listed, the Bishops would make meeting the basic needs of the poor and increasing economic participation for the marginalized priority items in the investment of wealth, talent, and human energy. Economic decisions must always be evaluated in the light of their impact on the poor and economic rights and responsibilities must find expression in the institutional order of society (1986, pp. 84-94).

The specific policy recommendations made by the Bishops in the areas of employment, poverty, food and agriculture, collaboration in shaping the U.S. economy, and interdependence of worldwide economic relationships all flow from the oft-repeated teachings of the church on the dignity of the human person, the unity of the human family, the universally beneficial purpose of the goods of the earth, the need to pursue the international common good, and the intensifying imperative of distributive justice in a world more sharply divided between rich and poor.

The Bishops' economic pastoral has been greeted with mixed reactions. Haynes Johnson, for example, on PBS's *Washington Week in Review,* characterized it as "old-fashioned." What ever that meant to him, the document is certainly not fashionable. Such reactions should not be surprising. Is it not the role of the church to call both its own people and all persons of good will to the demanding task of including the moral dimension in any examination of public policy?

ECONOMIC DISTRESS OF FAMILIES DEBATED

The present debate over social policy, especially the effectiveness of many previously enacted social programs, is stirring strong, conflicting opinions. Senator Daniel Moynihan in the Godkin lectures at Harvard University in April 1985 calls, as he did in 1965, for a National Family Policy that, through a variety of approaches, should be directed to the quality and stability of the American family. In 1965, he illustrated how American social policy had been directed primarily toward the individual and not toward the family as a unit (Moynihan, 1986).

Speaking for the opposition, Charles Murray's *Losing Ground, American Social Policy, 1950-80,* published in 1984, has become the bible of those who believe that government efforts only make matters worse. Murray would scrap the entire federal welfare and income support structure for working-aged persons, including AFDC, Medicaid, Food Stamps, Unemployment Insurance, Worker's Compensation, subsidized housing, disability insurance, and the rest. His argument is that we have only made the poor dependent by these types of programs (Moynihan, 1986).

Moynihan counters Murray's claims, which he calls unsubstantiated, by pointing out the near abolition of poverty among the aged as a result almost exclusively of social policy. In 1983, for example, the rate of poverty among the very young was nearly six times as great as among the old. Moynihan points out that indeed a welfare explosion did take place in the 1960s, but it was in social insurance programs that touch the poor least. It was not AFDC payments that caused family breakdowns, as some critics imply. Moynihan (1986, pp. 130-131) cites a study of David Ellwood and Lawrence Summers of Harvard that states:

> Since 1972, the fraction of all children who were living in a female-headed household jumped quite dramatically from 14% to almost 20%. During that same period, the fraction of all children who were in homes collecting AFDC held almost constant at 12%. . . . If AFDC were pulling families apart and encouraging the formation of single-parent families, it is hard to understand why the number of children on the program would remain constant throughout the period in our history when family structures changed the most.

Where then are we to look for the reasons behind the growing number of single-parent families? Moynihan believes Murray's work is concerned primarily with the growth of an urban minority underclass that Moynihan predicted in 1965 before the Great Society started and that has continued as if the Great Society programs had never happened. The family policy debate is a variation of the social question of the nineteenth century. According to Moynihan, no satisfactory explanation exists for the growth of single-parent families, and no approaches exist that promise a large-scale solution. However, a credible family policy will insist that responsibility begins with the individual, then the family, and only then the community and in the first instance the smaller and nearer rather than the greater and more distant community (Moynihan, 1986).

Another study by David Ellwood and Mary Jo Bane has found that largely unmeasurable differences in culture, attitudes, or expectations seem to account for most of the differences in various states in birth rates to unmarried women and in divorce and separation patterns among families with children. Only one dramatic impact of the size of AFDC payment benefits in various states was shown by the study. In low-benefit states, a young mother not living with a husband is very likely to live in the home of a parent. In high-benefit states, such women are more likely to live independently (Moynihan, 1986).

Moynihan points out that some aspects of past tax decisions have worsened the relative tax burden of poor families. In 1948, more than three-fourths of median family income was exempt from federal tax. By 1983, less than one-third of median family income was exempt. This was largely due to the fact that the personal exemption was not indexed for income growth or increases in the Consumer Price Index. If you include both social security and federal income taxes paid, an American family of median income in 1948 paid 4.4% of its income to the federal government. By 1982, they were paying 18%. Moreover, in the 1960s and 1970s, all the entitlement programs of the federal government were indexed against price inflation, with the single exception of the entitlements of children. The consequence is that indigence all but disappeared among the aged, while it significantly increased among the young (Moynihan, 1986).

REVERSING THE SLIDE
TOWARD THE ABYSS

Bellah et al. (1985) describe America's present state as "a slide toward the abyss" but do have some suggestions for reversing the trend. The litmus test for a healthy society in both the biblical and republican cultural traditions is how that society deals with the problem of wealth and poverty. The transformation of our society, these authors suggest, must happen at a number of levels. It cannot come only from state initiative that might be tyrannical. Personal transformation among large numbers is essential, and must involve not only a raised consciousness but action as well.

A social movement born out of existing groups and organizations, something like the civil rights movement, might lead to changes in the relationship between our government and the economy. This would certainly include new initiatives in economic democracy and social responsibility and a greater involvement and efforts to restore the political process to dignity and legitimacy. With a more explicit understanding and articulation of those goals we have in common and those goals we seek to attain together, our differences might not threaten us so much. The effort to link interests with the conception and search for the common good would certainly require a deepening of the public political discourse so that the fundamental problems are addressed rather than obscured. In the world of work, if we reduce the inordinate rewards of ambition and our inordinate fears of ending up losers, we would have a possibility of a great change in the meaning of work. It would become part of the ethos of work to be aware of our intricate connectedness and interdependence (Bellah et al., 1985, pp. 284-295).

THE CHURCH: A
COMMUNITY OF DISCIPLES

The U.S. Bishops speak with very similar emphasis. They especially urge Christian communities to commit themselves in solidarity with the suffering and to confront the sinful structures that institutionalize injustice while experiencing the power and presence of Christ.

In pursuit of concrete solutions, all members of the Christian community are called to an even finer discernment of the hurts and opportunities in the world around them, in order to respond to the most pressing needs and thus build up a more just society. This is a communal task calling for dialogue, experimentation, and imagination. It also calls for deep faith and courageous love [1986, p. 328].

To worship and pray to the God of the universe is to acknowledge that the healing love of God extends to all persons and to every part of existence, including work, leisure, money, economics, and to all those practical policies that either lead to justice or impede it [1986, p. 329].

To weigh political options according to criteria that go beyond efficiency and expediency requires prayer, reflection, and dialogue on all the ethical norms involved. Holiness for the laity will involve all the sacrifices needed to lead such a life of prayer and reflection within a worshiping and supporting faith community [1986, p. 336].

The Bishops' call for integration of work, life, and worship and the sociologists' suggestion that we need a social movement to return to biblical and republican traditions gives us a vision of where we might want to go. They do not address the important aspect of how that might be accomplished. What is being asked for is a monumental turn around that will require not only a clear understanding of the direction that is sought but an appreciation as well of the dynamics of social change, the patience and perseverance that will be needed in such a difficult transformation, and the determined leadership required to initiate and prod the process along.

A number of groups have the capacity to contribute to such a movement. The Catholic Church, for example, by its institutional structure has a presence in the world that few institutions have. It is at the same time a transnational, national, and local community. It touches groups across the spectrum from widely dispersed, small local groups in parishes through diocesan, national and international bodies. No other corporate groups have this potential—not even IBM or the U.S. Post Office.

The Bishops, however, cannot wave a magic wand or "electrify" the faithful like so many little grains of iron filings to point in the right direction! One irony associated with the church's success in mainstreaming U.S. Catholics is that they are largely indistinguishable (if you exclude the newest Hispanic influx to America) from their individualistic compatriots.

Instead of a ministry to poor immigrants in a foreign land, the church must preach and practice a theology of letting go, of sharing the gifts and resources we have been given, of stewardship and contributing to the common good out of our substance. The church will have to help its largely middle-class members to live in such a way that they can become oppositional, truly a sign of the already not-yet kingdom in an environment where the focus is on the competitive pursuit of this world's goods.

Vatican II has stimulated much change and one hopes some beginnings of renewal among Catholics. The church enters the social and political arena precisely as a religious community, a religious institution whose very work cannot be carried out unless it is engaged in protecting human dignity, promoting human rights and fostering the peace of the human family. Thus, in the public policy arena, religious groups are voluntary associations, like political parties, or labor unions, or other interest groups, with a specifically moral, religious angle of vision on the political process (Vatican II, 1965, pp. 40, 42, 76).

In 1971, a World Synod of Bishops (1971, p. 6) made it even more explicit that essential to being a church is to work for justice in the world.

> The work of justice and the transformation of the world fully appear to us to be a constitutive dimension of the preaching of the gospel, or, in other words, of the church's mission for the redemption of the human race and its liberation from every oppressive situation.

THE GROWTH OF CHRISTIAN COMMUNITIES

There is evidence of a growing realization that being a part of a small faith community that is willing to engage itself in building a more just world is one important way of being a People of God. Jim Wallis of *Sojourners* believes that in the churches our communion with God and with one another is so frail and limited that we simply have not the resources and strength to live by what we say. The tremendous gap of credibility between the confession of the church and the daily life evidenced among Christians is the principal cause of unbelief in our time and the primary reason for our political conformity and spiritual lukewarmness (Wallis, 1980, p. 11).

The term *basic ecclesial communities* (CEB) appeared in Latin America in the 1950s (particularly in Brazil, Chile, and Panama). The name reflects the influence of the "grassroots education movement" taking place in these countries. The Brazilian Bishops' plan for overall pastoral care (1962-1965) supported the concept. The Latin American Bishops' meeting at Medellin in 1968 mentioned them in twenty-three different paragraphs, describing them as essentially dynamic, varied, and novel (Kerkhofs, Mendoza, and Hartsens, 1976, pp. 6-7). Priests were encouraged to form CEBs and were asked to give special consideration to the formation of lay leaders. In the 1979 Puebla Conference, despite opposition by some conservative foes, the CEBs again received strong episcopal support (Eagleson and Scharper, 1979, p. 211). The CEBs mushroomed all over Latin America and spread rapidly in Africa with episcopal support.

In these and other areas of the Third World, it has largely been a movement where the participants have been low-income and oppressed people. Transposing this into the U.S. culture will take a creative effort to adjust the approach to our middle-class people. Efforts to create an American version of the base communities is still only in the early stages, but some good models have been given us by the New Jerusalem Community in Cincinnati, the Church of the Savior in Washington, D.C., Sojourners, the Paulist Center in Boston, and a number of others. Renewal efforts such as "Christ Renews His Parish" and the "RENEW" program, where they have been used, are helpful in preparing people for working to become faith communities in mission.

Basic Christian communities will have to find the means of carrying out their two-fold function: of nurturing the community members in their personal and spiritual growth, and at the same time becoming aware and taking action on some social and political issues to which they are drawn. Both dimensions must be a part of the life of the community. Experience with base communities in Latin America has shown that developing one dimension to the neglect of the other has not resulted in long-lasting, committed communities.

A life according to the Gospel has no meaning if it is not related to the needs and problems we face today, in a context that is real. It is important to give witness through a committed life in a group, the witness of a community, tackling the societal tasks facing the group and committing itself on the political or social level for reasons inspired by faith.

Growing or evolving to the point of becoming a basic Christian community takes quite a long time. Two or three years of praying together, experiencing, and sharing with each other may be necessary before a group would be ready to even desire to work to become the reality of a local church. Persons alienated by present church structure and practice most probably will need an "incubation" period that would allow the talking out of much anger, frustration, alienation that is now felt and a gradual growth in the group of the idea that they themselves are called by the Spirit to take responsibility for the creation of their local community of the larger church and for its role in mission to the world.

The Dayton Office of Social Action and World Peace has made a very modest effort at preparing the way for forming a variant on the base Christian community in the northern area of the Archdiocese. During the 1984-1985 school year, a group of ten persons from various parishes met regularly to experience being a faith community. The emphasis was on development of parish leaders who could go back to their own parishes and begin similar justice and peace committees that would be in ministry to their respective parishes. During the 1985-1986 year, the group continued with a seminarlike practicum dealing with their needs and experiences in forming the parish justice and peace committees. In the same year another basic group was begun. The group experienced various prayer forms, personal and communal, told their personal stories, shared their Myers-Briggs personality profiles, practiced active listening skills, studied several social issues, learned about the power cycle and the steps in effective planning and working with groups, and discerned together over decisions in a communal way.

Though one cannot predict what style the basic Christian communities will take here in the American culture, some form of small local community is surely in the future of the church. The effort now should be primarily focused on developing ways to prepare people to be leaders in such groups. Since the publication of the U.S. Bishops' pastorals, *The Challenge of Peace* and *Economic Justice for All,* an increased interest among Catholic people in social and political issues has been evidenced. Whether this will contribute to the social movement that Bellah and others are calling for, and whether all of this will help the structure of the family has yet to be determined.

NOTE

1. Papal texts and pastoral letters of Bishops are referred to by author, date, and paragraph number in the text, therefore the abbreviation "p." in citations of pastorals and encyclicals means "paragraph."

10

Rethinking Responses to Economic Distress: A Critique of Full Employment

Fred Block

In contemporary American politics, one must be able to formulate a political program in language succinct enough to fit on a bumper sticker. During the past ten or fifteen years of economic distress, "full employment" has been the centerpiece of the bumper stickers of those who have sought to protect families from economic distress. (Recent examples include Bowles, Gordon, and Weisskopf, 1983; Schor, 1985; Mandle and Ferleger, 1985.) Yet this slogan has failed to hold its own against the slogans of the right—tax relief, get the government off the back of the people, and so on. While the electoral victories of the political right have a variety of sources, this chapter will argue that the failures of liberals and the left to rethink their strategies is an important source of their recent political failures (Block et al., 1986). The argument, in brief, is that the "full employment" slogan is the wrong message for the bumper sticker.

The appeal of the full employment slogan is relatively obvious. Much of the economic distress of families can be traced either to high un-

AUTHOR'S NOTE: I am grateful to Richard Cloward, Barbara Ehrenreich, and Frances Fox Piven who contributed to the development of the ideas in this essay.

employment levels or to the unsatisfactorily low wages associated with the jobs that are available. Full employment would solve both of these problems. First, those who are unable to find work would be able to work in a full employment economy. Second, full employment would improve the bargaining power of all workers making it possible for low-wage workers to improve their standard of living. Moreover, since full employment would benefit both unionized employees and poorer workers who are disproportionately women and minorities, a full employment strategy promises to harmonize the interests of different sectors of the population that have often been in conflict.

The full employment slogan also represents a response to the deep suspicion in American culture toward welfare payments that provide "something for nothing" (Schor, 1985). It is assumed that a successful full employment strategy would make it possible to keep nonwork-related welfare transfers to a minimal level because most families would derive enough income from work to meet their needs. In short, full employment holds out the promise of alleviating the economic distress of families without extensive welfare provision except in the case of the aged and the disabled.

Finally, the full employment strategy draws on the positive idea that everyone should have the opportunity to participate in meaningful work activity. Since it is clear that work plays a key role in adult development (Veroff, Douvan, and Kulka, 1981, chap. 6), the full employment demand insists on the universal entitlement to that experience.

Yet despite these apparent advantages, the irony is that the strategy and rhetoric of full employment have actually made it harder to progress toward a society with tighter labor markets where there is a universal entitlement to meaningful work activity. The pursuit of full employment has been a diversion from the development of more adequate responses to economic distress.

THE PROBLEM OF
THE QUICK FIX

The most serious problem with the full employment demand results from the political strategy that has been linked to full employment over the past fifty years. Twice in that period—in the 1940s and again in the 1970s—supporters of full employment, centering on the trade unions, have waged struggles to pass national legislation that would assure full employment by making the government act as employer of last resort.

On both occasions, the outcome was the same—a piece of legislation was passed that contained a commitment to full employment without the provisions for actually achieving the goal. In the give and take of politics, the bills were gutted, and the idea of the government having an obligation to provide employment for all who need it was eliminated. (The classic account of the 1946 act is Bailey, 1950; on the later episode, see Ginsburg, 1983, pp. 63-84.)

This repeated outcome is hardly surprising. The proponents of full employment argue for it on the grounds that it will improve the bargaining position of both unionized and nonunionized employees. This means, quite obviously, that it would damage the immediate interests of virtually all employers in the country who would face a labor force with expanded options and reduced fear of being fired. It is hard to overstate the significance of such a transformation in the United States where employer power at the workplace is often unrestrained (Brody, 1980; Atleson, 1983). Hence it is hardly surprising that the business community employs its formidable lobbying power with rare unanimity so that Congress ends up passing legislation with nothing more than symbolic concessions to working people.

The only scenario under which such an outcome would not be inevitable is if the lobbying power of business were to be counteracted by an extraordinary mobilization of poor and working people in support of this kind of legislation. This would involve not just some letter writing and a few big demonstrations, but marches and rallies that involved tens of millions of people. Even then, the legislative outcome would be far from certain. But even if we assume that this mobilization produced legislative success, there is still the problem of implementation. The business community would continue to press its opposition through all available channels and continuing political pressure would be necessary to offset these efforts. But the most serious challenge would occur once the government began to implement the legislation by stimulating the economy and by hiring enough people so that unemployment levels actually began to decline significantly. At this point, we could expect the business community to engage in an investment strike as a form of protest. Since any steps to achieve full employment would most probably be accompanied by wage and price controls that were designed to prevent a surge of inflation (Mandle and Ferleger, 1985, pp. 83-85), the withholding of investment would be explained in terms of the inadequate profit levels that resulted from the price controls. The result of the investment strike would be a sharp economic slowdown (Block, 1977). The government would be faced with a stark choice. Either it would back down and retreat on the implementation of full employment, or it would have to challenge the business community directly by attempting to coerce employers into keeping their workplaces open. Since the latter choice has never been successfully pursued within a capitalist democracy, it seems far fetched to imagine that it would happen in the United States.

In a word, it is difficult to imagine the success of a legislative full employment strategy in the United States in the absence of a mass popular movement that was willing to contemplate a transition to socialism. If such a movement existed and had broad support, then employers might well be willing to concede full employment as the lesser of two evils. This was more or less the situation in Sweden where full employment capitalism appeared to be the only practical alternative to socialism (Esping-Andersen, 1986). But it is obvious that we are very far from that situation in the United States today. [1]

In some political struggles, it is not necessarily important whether the final legislative goal is reached. It has been argued, for example, that while feminists lost the battle for the Equal Rights Amendment, they won the war to redefine the position of American women. In short, the struggle over legislation can serve as the backdrop for widespread agitation that changes deeply held values and established institutional practices. But this logic does not apply to the fight for full employment since the only thing that changes the basic reality for the families of poor and working people is the actual implementation of a full employment policy. While some people are obviously better off with 6% unemployment rather than 7% unemployment, and 5% rather than 6%, it is only when you get close to the situation where everyone who wants a job can have one that there will be significant changes for those without work and those working at or near the minimum wage. In that sense, full employment has the quality of an all or nothing demand for many of the intended beneficiaries.

This suggests that when full employment is pursued through the national legislative route, some of the unifying quality of the demand is illusory. In the long period of agitation until the legislation is actually implemented, most of those people who are unemployed or in low-wage jobs—a population that is disproportionately composed of women and minorities—get no actual relief. And since, as we have seen, the prospects of successful implementation are chimerical, there is little long-term relief either. On the other hand, one would expect that as the pressure for full employment legislation intensifies, the government would be more active in trying to keep unemployment levels lower on the theory that high unemployment increases the pressure for legislation. Hence the agitation might actually succeed in reducing the unemployment level by a couple of points that would probably provide some immediate relief, particularly for unionized employees in manufacturing. In short, rather than unifying diverse constituencies, this strategy actually provides some benefits for organized and less marginal employees while doing nothing for those most in need of relief.

But probably the most telling critique of the legislative full employment strategy is that those who have pursued it have done so with only minimal efforts at the kind of popular mobilization that would be necessary to avoid legislative defeat or to assure effective implementation (Ginsburg, 1983, pp. 77-78). It has only been since the 1980 Reagan victory that the AFL-CIO has even launched efforts at political education among its own rank and file. An organization that has been reluctant to carry out political education for electoral purposes among its membership can hardly be expected to encourage serious mass extraparliamentary mobilizations. [2]

It is in this sense that the legislative full employment strategy has always represented a kind of quick fix for the problems of labor and the poor. The idea is that by somehow getting this legislation through Congress, a relatively weak trade union movement will suddenly find itself in a situation where its economic leverage is greatly magnified. Instead of working to strengthen the base of the union movement through mobilizing the organized and organizing the unorganized, full employment legislation has represented a shortcut to the kind of more politically effective working class that exists in other capitalist democracies.

The strategy also represents a quick fix for the often problematic relationship between white male trade unionists and minority and women employees. Instead of gradually building trust and cooperation through mutual concessions and joint action, the idea is that the conflicts of interest can be effectively eliminated through one legislative victory.

There are times, of course, when quick fixes are politically popular. Reagan's "Supply-Side Tax Cut" was a quick fix that helped contribute to his electoral successes—even in 1984 when it was transparent that the quick fix had not achieved a number of promised results. But it must be remembered that Reagan's tax cuts shifted billions in resources to the rich and powerful. Measures that cut against the interests of the rich and powerful—such as mandated full employment—can never succeed on the enthusiasm of the moment: There are no successful quick fixes on the left—only carefully worked out ideas and effective popular mobilization.

THE TRANSFORMATION
OF THE ECONOMY

Above and beyond the formidable political difficulties in implementing a full employment strategy is the fact that such a strategy runs against the grain of current economic transformations. Part of the problem is simply that ongoing technological change is likely to reduce further the total demand for labor with the result of even more unemployment (Block, 1984a, 1984c). But the deeper part of the problem is that the structure of employment is changing and the full employment demand represents a diversion from the kind of policies that are necessary to promote economic justice and equality. To understand this latter argument, it is necessary to look both at trends in aggregate employment and trends in labor force participation.

There is an old debate about the impact of technological change on employment levels that has been rekindled in recent years by the new wave of technological advances associated with microelectronics. (See Block, 1984c, for references.) Generally this debate has been fought out over the question of the number of jobs available in the economy. However, the content of a job in the total annual hours of work has changed significantly over time. If one looks at the total hours of paid employment per capita, it is clear that this figure has declined sharply across the twentieth century in the major Western capitalist nations. In short, technological change has made it possible to produce an expanded flow of goods and services with a declining amount of work per man, woman, and child (Kuznets, 1971, pp. 52-61).

There have been exceptions to this tendency, however, such as the period from 1963-1979 in the United States. In this period, hours of work per capita actually increased as a result of dramatic employment gains in the service sector at the same time that manufacturing and the public sector were also adding additional employment. The trends in the United States during these years are quite unusual since other developed capitalist nations have seen marked declines in per capita hours of labor during the same period.

The big question is whether this recent period of U.S. history was a short-term aberration or whether it represents the wave of the future in which service sector employment will grow so rapidly as to keep per capita hours from falling. There is no way yet to provide a definitive answer to this question. It is the case that the growth of service employment was very rapid during the Reagan recovery of the period 1983-1984, but those employment gains have not been sustained at the same rates since then, and they did come after the long period of recession from 1980 to 1982. Moreover, there is good reason to believe that the impact of new technologies will have a significant negative impact on clerical and sales employment, which have been key areas of employment growth in recent years (Leontief and Duchin, 1986, chap. 3). Furthermore, the evidence is strong that manufacturing will make only a negative contribution to total employment over the next ten years. Manufacturing hours were still well below their 1979 peak in 1986 (*Survey of Current Business*) and the continuing process of technological advances in heavy industry that have traditionally employed a high percentage of the labor force suggests a continuing contraction (Block, 1984a).

In short, for total employment hours per capita to continue to expand in the second half of the 1980s will require that the extremely rapid rates of service-sector employment growth of the 1970s actually quicken, since manufacturing that contributed to overall employment growth in the 1970s can be expected to contract in the 1980s. Such a development is possible, but it does not seem likely.

One of the key mechanisms for handling reductions in per capita hours of labor has been to shrink the percentage of the population that is economically active. Historically, this has occurred through requiring school attendance of young people, facilitating retirement for older workers, and by defining the housewife role as proper for married women. Through these devices, the percentage of the population that was economically active declined through the first half of the century.[3] In recent years, however, along with the sharp upturn in labor force participation of married women has come increased rates of participation among both high school and college students (*Handbook of Labor Statistics*). At the same time, there is evidence that many of the "retired" are reentering the labor force, and the exit of older workers from the labor force has begun to slow. All of these trends have produced sharp upturns in the United States in the percentage of the population that is in the labor force. By 1986, 65% of people 16 and over were in the labor force as compared to rates below 60% in the early 1960s; this increase added 9 million people to the labor force.[4]

It seems likely that his upward trend will continue in the future. Wives, young people, and older people will continue to claim access to paid employment in increasing numbers for the same reasons—the search for both the prestige and the income that comes from paid employment. However, even when aggregate hours per capita were rising, as between 1963 and 1979, the hours per member of the labor force were contracting. If hours per capita stabilizes or returns to its historical downward trend, while labor force participation rates continue to rise, there will be far sharper reductions in the hours per member of the labor force.

There are basically three ways of accomplishing a reduction in the hours per member of the labor force. The first is to reduce the hourly content of a full-time job by shortening the work week and the work year. The second is by increasing the amount of part-time work and the third is an increase in the unemployment rate. In the United States, reliance has been entirely on the second and third mechanisms since the full-time work year has remained quite stable.

The result is a pattern that creates a widening gap between well-paid full-time jobs and poorly paid and marginal part-time employment. The gap is intensified by the lack of entitlement of most part-time workers to the various employment benefits that many full-time employees have gained. Obviously, prime age white males are most likely to be in full-time employment, and it is women, minorities, and young people who are more likely to be part timers or unemployed.

If the hypothesis is correct that aggregate hours per capita are unlikely to grow while labor force participation continues to rise, then there will be growing conflicts over access to the available employment hours. Without appropriate policy responses, these conflicts are likely to intensify racial, gender, and age divisions within the labor force and lead to a further worsening of the position of organized workers.

The appropriate policy response to this new historical situation in which most people 16 and over want to be in paid employment is to begin to narrow the gap between full-time and part-time work. The first step is to reduce the number of hours of a full-time job to the 25 to 30 hour per week range. [5] The second step is to upgrade the pay levels and benefits of part-time workers. [6] By narrowing the gap, individuals would then have much more freedom to move back and forth between part-time and full-time employment without sacrificing access to well-paid work. It would then be possible for individuals to alter their work commitments to fit with different life course situations such as the need for more education, the desire for more time for child rearing, or a preference for a less rigorous work schedule in old age. Together, these two measures would contribute to a more equitable distribution of work opportunities, and they would help to diminish the income gap between women and men employees and between minority and white employees.

To be sure, a shortening of the work week is not a panacea for the problems of the labor market; some advocates of a shorter work week have also slipped into the quick fix approach. The reality is that shortening the work week is unlikely to produce as much new employment as its advocates tend to suggest. Other initiatives such as sabbaticals and educational leaves that would periodically remove many prime-age individuals from the labor force (Sirianni and Eayrs, n.d.), increased public sector employment, and expanded support for small business and cooperative enterprises would also be necessary to help tighten the labor market. The point, however, is that full employment rhetoric tends to obscure the pressing need to renew the labor movement's historic fight for a shortening of the work week. Such a fight would contribute to a more equitable redistribution of the workload, which is a pressing necessity in a society in which prime-age, white men have ceased to be the majority of the labor force. Full employment rhetoric also draws attention away from the need for measures to improve the work situation of part-time employees.

To be sure, reforms such as a shortening of the full-time work week and an upgrading of part-time employment are also not easily won. But these struggles are more promising than the fight for legislation to mandate full employment for several reasons. First, these are demands that can be fought for effectively in a variety of different arenas—at the workplace, at the state and local level, and at the national level. It was precisely such diversified efforts that contributed to earlier legislative successes in reducing the length of the working day. Second, these demands create less automatic unity among business interests; some businesses benefit from increased leisure time and others hire relatively few part timers. With a less unified opposition, it is easier to win meaningful reforms.

FALSE NECESSITY

At the moment, there is little agitation either for a shorter work week or for the upgrading of part-time employment because we are living under the tyranny of "false necessity." False necessity refers to the economic ideas that are used to justify assaults on civilian spending, on government regulation of business, and on trade unions. We often hear, for example, that we cannot as a nation afford more generous wage levels or decent social spending because that will interfere with our capacity to compete in international trade. Another equally important claim is that the recent redistribution of income toward the rich was necessary in order to encourage high levels of investment that are indispensable for economic growth.

A critique of all these claims is well beyond the scope of this chapter (see Kuttner, 1984; Block, 1985). Suffice it to say that there is a remarkable lack of evidence for any of these claims and they all rest on problematic assumptions about economic life. But despite their falseness, these claims still dominate our political life. They are the single most powerful force in making progressive proposals appear irrational and irresponsible, and as long as doctrines of false necessity keep their hold on the popular imagination, reformers will be continually in the position of fighting defensive struggles against right-wing initiatives. Hence the most urgent task is to develop a political strategy and a political discourse that can effectively challenge false necessity. It is here, however, that full employment rhetoric is particularly inadequate.

Part of the very appeal of full employment rhetoric is that it taps into the traditional Protestant work ethic with its belief that hard work is uplifting. This work ethic is also the source of the widespread hostility to those who receive unearned income—that is, welfare—since those who live by the sweat of their brow are deserving and those who do not are sinners. In this complex of ideas, it is an absolute obligation to work— both to save the individual from sin and to save the society from economic disaster.

In fact, one important source of rhetorical support for the idea of full employment is that those who embrace the work ethic need to believe that the undeserving poor have a chance to redeem themselves through hard work. Hence even many deeply conservative citizens will express support for the idea that everyone who wants a job should have one. [7] However, what advocates of full employment gain in rhetorical support from some conservatives is more than offset by their decreased ability to challenge false necessity.

As was argued above, developed capitalist societies have produced an ever expanding flow of goods and services while reducing the amount of labor per capita. Hence the notion that increased labor effort is necessary for economic growth is patently false; on the contrary, economic development has progressed with dramatic increases in the availability of leisure time. Yet the idea that a society must maintain a high level of work effort is a fundamental premise of both false necessity and the work ethic. However, full employment advocates are reluctant to challenge this premise for fear that they will lose support from those committed to the work ethic. Hence full employment rhetoric slides back and forth between the argument that everyone has a right to employment and the argument that everyone needs employment. [8] But the latter argument serves to reinforce claims of false necessity.

While there is no proven way to challenge false necessity, our recent history suggests some powerful lessons. The strength of the left in the 1960s was linked to the widespread belief that the United States was an affluent society that was misusing its great wealth. This belief created a space for the emergence of radical movements and for serious efforts at social reform. Conversely, as Americans became persuaded during the 1970s of the seriousness of the economic crisis, claims of false necessity overwhelmed any reformist intentions. Despite the left's insistence that the economic crisis proved the irrationality of capitalism, the actual consequence of the crisis was the dramatic strengthening of the political right.

This interpretation suggests the importance of reminding people of the enormous wealth of this society and of challenging the prevailing views of our economic difficulties. Instead of the accepted view that our economy is having trouble producing enough, the argument should be that our productive capacity remains extraordinary, but that institutional reforms—in the distribution of income, in the role of government, and in the management of the workplace—are needed to take advantage of the expanded productive potential. By pointing to the actual reality of "science fiction" advances in productive technology—robotics, computer-aided manufacturing, and so on—it is possible to convince people that our inherited institutional arrangements and economic assumptions are dangerously obsolete. False necessity can be effectively challenged by asking why it is that despite these fantastic advances in productive technology, real hourly wages are declining and more people have to suffer economic marginalization.

This is the strongest reason for jettisoning the full employment slogan. The attack on false necessity and on deeply held popular attitudes must begin with an emphasis on historical discontinuity. The argument must be that attempts to deal with these new realities through familiar techniques and rhetoric will be doomed to failure. If people can be persuaded that we are in a new historical situation in which accepted beliefs no longer provide adequate guidance, then the political space can be opened up for the reemergence of radical social movements and for a new period of social reform.

To be sure, this process of persuasion will not occur simply through people giving papers at academic conferences. This rhetoric has to be linked to concrete struggles, especially those waged by groups that are paying the heaviest price for technological advance. These groups have to find ways to challenge directly the claims of false necessity, first, by emphasizing that with the society's extraordinary wealth, there is no reason for the current suffering, and, second, that the development of more humane social policies is consistent with continued economic advance within this new political-economic situation.

THE INSTRUMENTALIZATION OF SOCIAL LIFE

When advocates of full employment are pressed to address the question of what kinds of jobs will be available as technological advance reduces the need for human labor in a wide variety of traditional activities, they usually answer that there will always be a great deal of work to be done in the human services—such as caring for small children and the elderly. In fact, one recent advocate of full employment explicitly argues that women's labor in the home should be recognized as employment and granted a wage (Schor, 1985). While this argument is motivated by a desire to improve the social and economic position of housewives, it follows a logic that is implicit in the full employment ideal—that all valued human activity should be recognized as employment and granted a wage.

The problem with this is that it is also the basic logic of capitalist society—that individuals should only do things for which there is a direct economic gain. But as innumerable commentators have pointed out, such a logic is subversive of the very fabric of a human community that depends on the willingness of individuals to do things for others even when there is no possibility of economic gain (Titmuss, 1971). In short, full employment advocates are thrown into the uncomfortable situation of supporting the tendency in capitalist society continually to replace familial or voluntaristic activity with paid employment.

There are difficult issues in this discussion since it has been part of women's subordination that they have had disproportionate responsibility to do familial and voluntary labors that have not been economically rewarded. However, there is an alternative to the capitalist logic that instrumentalizes all of social life. The alternative is to reduce the time demands of paid employment on both men and women so as to increase the amount of time available for familial, voluntary, and communal activity. There should also be ample opportunities for both men and women to devote themselves for periods of time to work that is not remunerated. But along with increased opportunity to engage in these uncompensated activities, there will also have to be a cultural reversal that increases the value and legitimacy of uncompensated activities. While such a cultural reversal will be difficult to accomplish, it is hard to imagine any progress toward a good society without a dramatic reduction in the instrumentalization talizationtalizationof social life.

In a word, the idea of full employment prefigures a society in which individuals are primarily responsive to economic rewards in shaping their social life. The more desirable alternative is to prefigure a society in which there is a rebirth of voluntary and communal efforts, and one does this by shrinking the dominion of paid employment over human existence.

ALTERNATIVE DIRECTIONS

This chapter cannot offer either a bumper sticker or a coherent political program as an alternative to full employment. There are, however, several key points that follow from the critique of full employment that are particularly important for the construction of an alternative response to economic distress.

The first point is to realize that there is no legislative shortcut to the effective mobilization of a powerful grassroots social movement in favor of reforms that will aid those in economic distress. Such grassroots movement must be able to press for a wide range of intermediate reforms—changes that make real immediate differences for some of those in need, but that fall short of fundamental social change. Those intermediate demands, as social movement theory tells us (Piven and Cloward, 1977), will help persuade people that political struggle is not futile. And such intermediate demands—as, for example, for federal legislation to facilitate worker buyouts of factories scheduled to close—are winnable because they are not as immediately threatening to business as full employment legislation. When fighting for these kinds of intermediate demands, it is possible to get concrete concessions that actually help people rather than the rhetorical concessions that have been the results of the full employment struggle.

Second, in putting together coalitions to fight for reforms, there are new opportunities because one no longer faces the restrictions that were built into full employment politics. Full employment coalitions almost always place trade unions at the center, so that other groups are asked to join in alliance with the unions. This pattern has given the trade union leadership a kind of veto over the politics of the coalition; if the environmentalists or peace activists insist on their demands being made part of the struggle, the trade unions are in a position to say no. The result is often a weak and narrow coalition. The alternative is to put together the concerns of a broad range of constituencies—the poor, women, minorities, peace activists, environmentalists, public sector employees, as well as traditional unions. Instead of assuming that unions are the core group, one would make an active effort to encourage unionists to join a broader coalition in which no single group has veto power. [9]

Third, abandoning full employment rhetoric provides the opportunity to press the idea that economic transfers to the nonworking population—welfare programs—are legitimate. Once one rejects the full employment utopia in which everybody is working for a wage, it is possible to show people that technological change is reducing the weight of paid employment in the individual life course. If the average individual works the equivalent of 30 years of full-time work out of an 80-year life course, it is clear that there are many years of life in which individual income is not directly linked to the individual's effort. Once the society fully recognizes this new reality, it becomes clear that providing income that is not connected with work is absolutely essential to bolster economic demand, and to make possible a rational organization of adult life in which individuals have the opportunity to combine employment with child rearing, education, and various voluntary and community activities. This legitimation of welfare could also facilitate the most effective immediate response to the economic distress of families—improving and destigmatizing the benefits of current welfare programs.

Fourth, the struggle for these intermediate reforms should stress the themes of social justice *and* economic efficiency. One can challenge false necessity most effectively by seizing control of the efficiency argument and using it for progressive ends. For example, improved levels of income support for the poor—through tax reform and improved welfare payments—can be defended on the grounds that the present skewed distribution of income weakens consumer demand and makes the economy more dependent on highly wasteful military spending. As in the 1930s, measures that redistribute income to the poor will strengthen consumer demand and create conditions for economic growth based on an efficient use of resources. It is also the case that current social policies that basically write off a generation of inner-city youths are penny-wise, pound foolish. Whatever money is saved in the short term through "benign neglect" will be dwarfed by the long-term costs of law enforcement and incarceration. One can also argue that providing greater economic security for workers will also contribute to economic efficiency by diminishing fears of technological displacement and creating a climate in which workers see technological advance as something that will contribute to their own welfare.

In the process, it is also important to redefine the concept of efficiency away from the corporate balance sheet. It is hardly efficient to let corporations raise their profits by being careless in disposing of toxic wastes, when the society as a whole will be forced to pay billions to clean up the consequences. And ultimately, the concept of efficiency can be used to rethink our ideas about what constitute social goods. Capitalist efficiency tends to focus on how we can maximize the output of GNP with existing inputs of labor, capital, and raw materials. But if we decide that we want to also place a high value on such other goals as living in harmony with the environment and assuring that all people have the opportunity for self-development and self-fulfillment, then the concept of efficiency can be useful in helping us figure out how we can best reshape our institutions to achieve those goals with our available resources.

NOTES

1. Even in countries like France, West Germany, and the United Kingdom with strong union movements and a more vital socialist tradition, there has been a full-scale retreat from the pursuit of full employment over the past ten years. In France, a socialist government was forced to live with high levels of unemployment throughout its term of office.

2. For a recent account that gives anecdotal evidence about the conservatism of the National Committee for Full Employment, the leadership organization that has dominated full employment politics in recent years, see Grossman (1985).

3. This trend is not apparent from the U.S. data because women who were economically active in agriculture and other activities were rarely counted as such by the census takers. For revised data, see Ciancanelli (1983).

4. While official unemployment rates are based on the number of people who are actually in the labor force, there is considerable evidence that many people who are not currently in the labor force would join it if there were a reasonable prospect of finding a job

(Ginsberg, 1977). The large size of this "labor market overhang" further complicates the prospects of full employment.

5. This could be done in a number of stages to avoid reductions in full-time wage levels. Earlier reductions in the full-time work week led to significant productivity gains since employees worked more intensively in the shorter period. In addition, employees would have to sacrifice gains in real wages for shorter hours. Their reward for this sacrifice, however, would be greater employment security.

6. Such upgrading will encounter stiff resistance from employers, but the principle of nondiscrimination can be used to press demands that part-time employees be given at least a proportionate share of the employee benefits available to full-time employees. Moreover, as the full-time work week declines toward 25 hours, some of those currently trapped in part-time jobs because of other obligations would be able to make the shift to full-time employment. The more that this happened, the more employers would be forced to improve compensation to hold on to part timers.

7. Actually, this rhetorical support is deceptive. Since these deeply conservative voters believe in both full employment and a limited governmental role in society, they will not actually support strong governmental action to achieve full employment. For evidence that religious conservatives oppose government spending on social programs, see Wuthnow (1985).

8. It is precisely this slippage that makes it very difficult to resist the increasingly strident conservative demands for coercive workfare schemes that promise to put all able-bodied welfare recipients to work. Since advocates of full employment appear to believe that everyone should work, it is difficult for them to oppose the logic of workfare.

9. This point is closely linked to the issue of rhetoric. In an earlier statement, I wrote that "the left says, 'We want full employment *and* we want those jobs to be jobs at decent union wages with decent working conditions. We want full employment *and* we want a thirty-hour week.' The problem is that people hear the first part of the statement and their belief in the necessity of scarcity is reinforced and they don't hear the second part, or when they hear the second part they say, 'That sounds nice but we can't afford it.' In effect we undermine our own programs when we put the demand for full employment first" (Block, 1984c, pp. 27-28).

PART V

Sources and Impact of Federal Policy

This section emphasizes the effects of economic dislocations on structured social inequality. In the 1980s, recessions have had different impacts on individuals because of their membership in different social groups. Especially vulnerable have been women heads of households, children, racial minorities, and workers in mass production or "smokestack" industries.

Many policy actions during the 1980s recessions not only failed to relieve the economic distress of families but in fact exacerbated it. Cuts in social welfare spending occurred when adequate income through paid employment was more difficult to secure as the recessions generated underemployment and high rates of unemployment. Family support services needed to cope with sudden hardship were cut as budgets were reduced and staff was laid off. Tax reductions were aimed at privileged groups and wealthy corporations while the poor paid increasing proportions of their real income in taxes. As individuals in public and private life pursued their own personal interests during the recessions, entire groups or classes were harmed. In many instances, gains resulted for privileged groups, but the victims received minimal help to cope with their impossible circumstances and disrupted lives.

The chapters in this section assume that government can and should create a buffer between families and economic distress. Arguments supporting the protection of families from the harsher effects of economic change are based on a recognition that personal suffering and the deterioration of relationships due to economic hardships are preventable. As these and previous chapters show, the breakdown of family material and emotional security through economic decline has costs that cannot be measured simply by dollar amounts and the negative experiences are not limited to a brief time span.

This section explores policy alternatives that can provide a buffer between families and economic dislocations. The diverse recommendations of these chapters have several unifying themes. The authors assume that social goals should be at least as important as growth in the private economy. The greatest emphasis should be given to family well-being, equality, community stability, and democratic participation. The chapter by Rosemary Sarri recommends enhanced public services, including welfare, in a new welfare state built upon a thoroughgoing analysis and revision of the most basic elements. Andrew Winnick emphasizes the importance of sufficient numbers of jobs at adequate wages and measures to overcome racial and gender inequality. He believes these reforms cannot be realized without changing the balance between military and domestic spending. Robert Kelly emphasizes the importance of social ingenuity and experimentation to devise successful models for solving employment problems while building self-determination and economic justice.

Economic agendas ought to be evaluated in terms of their social usefulness, not dollar costs alone. Some of the expense of protecting families and individuals from the worst impact of economic forces is in fact an investment in their social and economic futures. If some of the irrationalities of other social institutions could be prevented, the welfare state would have to devote fewer resources to their consequences, such as joblessness, family disruption, and community disintegration.

To make the kinds of economic changes necessary for family well-being will almost certainly require greater citizen participation in political life. Vulnerable groups cannot be made less vulnerable except by organizing to ensure that policymakers are responsive to the public investment and citizen involvement in these investment decisions. Only by mobilizing for a more humane economic future can we be sure that we are going to live in a society that is *worth* living in.

11

The Impact of Federal Policy Change on the Well-Being of Poor Women and Children

Rosemary C. Sarri

The economic well-being of women who head families with minor children has long been problematic and an issue of social debate in the United States. In the late nineteenth century, women who were widowed and heads of families encountered some of the same difficulties that single mothers experience today a century later, although we now like to think that widows were treated more benignly than are divorcees or never-married women today. However, since the mid-1970s there has been a dramatic increase in the numbers of single mothers accompanied by a serious deterioration in their economic status. This situation has resulted from a variety of factors: divorce, lack of child support by fathers, low wages of women in the labor force, and last but not least, since 1980, new federal policies that have exacerbated the impoverishment of these families. In 1986, more than 26.3% of the 33.4 million families with children had only one parent, an increase from 12.9% in 1970 (U.S. Department of Commerce, Bureau of the Census, 1986). More than nine out of ten of these families are headed by women with minority group families most often headed by women. What is particularly problematic about these families is the fact that more than half are trying to live with incomes below the poverty level and with far fewer work-related or social benefits than are obtained by male workers. Since more than half of all poor children reside in these households, the long-term consequences for societal well-being are placed in jeopardy. This chapter reports on what happened to a sample of single mothers in Michigan and Georgia who were terminated from Aid to Families with Dependent Children (AFDC) in 1982—how they coped with reduced income, lack of Medicaid, Food Stamps, child care, and other work-related benefits. By the mid-1980s, major proposals for welfare reform at national and state levels centered on various efforts to require that women receiving AFDC work outside the home. These proposals, commonly called "workfare," are being implemented in most states; therefore, it is important to consider how single mothers attempt to cope with the dual roles of parenting and employment.

FEDERAL POLICY CHANGE UNDER OBRA

In 1981, at the request of the Reagan administration, Congress passed the Omnibus Budget Reconciliation Act (hereafter referred to as OBRA), which eliminated cash supplements, Food Stamps, Medicaid insurance, and eligibility for child care, housing, emergency assistance, and work-related expenses for many working women with children who were recipients of AFDC. Since 1967, low-income working women had been eligible for AFDC supplements when their income was below 150% of the poverty level, and others with lower incomes were permitted to disregard some of their earned income in determining their eligibility. OBRA required that all AFDC heads of households who were working and earning income above certain specified minimum levels be terminated from all benefits linked to AFDC status. This statute represented a substantial reversal of federal policies that had been developed since 1935 to provide more comprehensive benefits and work incentives to low-income, single-parent families with working mothers (Bell, 1965; Palmer and Sawhill, 1982).

Nationally, more than 442,000 families with 1.3 million children lost their benefits as a consequence of this legislation (GAO, 1985). From the numerous evaluations that have been completed about the impact of OBRA, it is quite clear that the federal government and many state governments realized substantial savings even though AFDC is one of the smaller federal welfare programs—almost minuscule in comparison to Social Security for retirees. The General Accounting Office (1985) estimated that as of June 1984, approximately six billion dollars had been saved since 1981. However, other research by the Congressional Research Service (U.S. Committee on Ways and Means, 1984) indicates that over 550,000 persons were thrust into poverty because of the policy changes, and these persons were disproportionately single-parent families headed by women. Between 1981 and 1985, programs serving needy families sustained 30% of all budget cuts, although they constituted less than 10% of all federal expenditures. In addition, tax reforms added an additional burden while they provided large benefits for middle- and upper-class citizens. Despite the economic recovery in 1984 through 1985, this population of working poor women has remained in poverty. Poverty statistics in 1985 indicated that the poverty rate declined for white males and for two-parent families, but not for minorities or for female single parents with children (U.S. Department of Commerce, 1986). In fact, the poverty gap has continued to widen between high- and low-income families in recent years as Ehrenreich (1986) and others have noted.

Why then was this population of working single parents and their children targeted for benefit reduction? Resistance to welfare support for low-income women and children is longstanding in the United States. Pearce (1982) points out that differentiating the "deserving" from the "undeserving" poor was the most consistent theme of the many policy and program changes that occurred in federal and state legislation in this century. Moreover, the Reagan administration espoused philosophies that were antithetical to support for these families.

The writings of Martin Anderson (1978) and George Gilder (1981) provided the ideological underpinnings for the changes that were implemented in the OBRA legislation. Anderson argued that poverty in the United States had been virtually eliminated and that existing social programs were more than adequate for those truly in need—that the best welfare reform was work because guaranteed income would only reduce work effort. In turn, Gilder asserted that working-age, able-bodied poor people (especially women) should be weaned away from the welfare programs, because of the "moral hazard of liberalism." He further argued that welfare programs "promote the value of being 'poor' and perpetuate poverty."

Despite the compelling data to the contrary, and perhaps because of strongly held ideologies, policymakers in the Reagan administration accepted the thesis about the dangers of welfare dependency and implemented changes whereby working-age, able-bodied poor women were terminated from AFDC and other income supports. No consideration was given to environmental factors such as economic recessions, double-digit unemployment, sex discrimination in employment—all of which would make it impossible for many women to earn the income needed for basic survival by their families. Also ignored was the fact that 40% of all AFDC recipients who leave AFDC have incomes below the poverty level in the years following receipt of AFDC support (Bane and Ellwood, 1983).

OBRA, a radical redirection of federal welfare policy, has sparked an intense debate, particularly since the publication of the major critique of welfare programs for the poor by Charles Murray (1984) who argued that the programs themselves exacerbated the problems of poor men and women. Federal administration officials claim that the Reagan reforms preserved the AFDC safety net by targeting resources on those who genuinely needed assistance, and that those beneficiaries who were cut as a result of the reforms were "families with enough income to support themselves." On the other hand, critics contend that the cutbacks in federal benefits between 1981 through 1983 disproportionately affected households with annual incomes below $10,000 and especially hurt poor working families whose work efforts are being undermined, rather than supported by public policy. This debate accelerated in 1986 with the passage of numerous workfare-type programs by the states, and with the introduction of legislation by Senators Evans and Durenberger, and Representative Downey, in both the Senate and the House, to establish national minimum AFDC benefit levels with dramatically increased federal fiscal responsibility (U.S. Senate, 1986). However, seldom heard in these debates have been the voices of the families themselves, working mothers and their children, whose present and future economic well-being and quality of life have been dramatically changed. The research reported here provides the opportunity to hear directly from those who experienced the impact of federal policy changes.

CONCEPTUAL FRAMEWORK

This study examined the impact of OBRA policies on working women and sought to determine how these women coped and attempted to maintain individual and family well-being when confronted with loss of AFDC benefits, cash income, Food Stamps, and/or Medicaid insurance, as well as housing, energy, child care, or school lunch allowances in some special circumstances. Our guiding hypothesis was that both objective (e.g., economic need) and subjective factors (e.g., perceived stress) would influence the respondent's coping behavior, but that responses would be mediated by informal (e.g., kin, friends, and neighbors) and formal (e.g., social agencies) social networks and by the availability of resources such as health insurance associated with employment. We expected that coping behavior might be adaptive or maladaptive in terms of the family's subsequent well-being.

Crisis and stress theories have long recognized that the same objective event may have different functional effects depending upon (1) how it is perceived, (2) the decision-making and problem-solving strategies subsequently implemented, and (3) the response of the family, work, and community to those strategies (Catalano and Dooley, 1980; Cobb, 1974; Kessler, 1979; Hill, 1974; Gore, 1978). The perception of an event as a crisis is further conditioned by both individual sociopsychological factors and by the situational context within which it occurs (Dill et al., 1980). Thus when confronted by changes in AFDC policy that reduced incentives to work—how did women conceive their options? What steps, if any, did they take to overcome the impact of their loss of income so as to restore their family's well-being? How important in a woman's decision making was her need for Medicaid protection? Until now most research has focused on economic and social-psychological attributes of the recipient; almost no attention was directed to the consequences of the policy change for the qualities of these families' lives. We, therefore, sought to ascertain how women responded to these crises and negative conditions and then to examine their relationship to health and well-being.

Following a woman's initial decision to work, it is important to detail the various strategies that women employ to master their problems in balancing work, income, and family needs. As Belle, Dill, and their colleagues (1980) observed in the Boston study of AFDC families and stress, the environment of low-income women frequently opposes their efforts to master problematic situations. Strategies that would be effective in more hospitable social contexts may fail to produce desired results for this sample of working AFDC recipients.

METHODOLOGY

Terminated recipients in Michigan and Georgia were identified with the cooperation and assistance of the state departments of social services, and random samples were drawn in selected counties, although sampling procedures differed in the two states. In Michigan, six counties were selected that had unemployment rates ranging from 9% to 20% in 1982. Three counties had low rates of unemployment and three had rates at the upper end of the range. Variation in unemployment rate was selected as a critical sampling variable because of the wide range among Michigan counties and because it is an important indicator of relative opportunity for employment. A total of 356 completed interviews were obtained from an initial sample of 400. Some cases were found to be ineligible and other persons could not be located. This report includes only those who were single parents with minor children (N = 279), and for some analysis, an additional 37 cases were included who had been terminated because they fell under the ruling pertaining to presumed stepfather responsibility for care of children.

In Georgia, a sample of 207 single-parent families from 27 rural and urban counties was selected, but county unemployment rate was not considered in the sampling. In both states the county was selected as the unit for sampling because services are administered at the county level. However, there were marked differences between the two states in how OBRA was implemented and in benefit levels before termination. Michigan had an average benefit level in January 1981 of $462 per month while in Georgia the comparable figure was $164. OBRA was quickly and fully implemented in Michigan, partly because the state experienced a serious economic recession and high unemployment in 1982. AFDC caseloads rose rapidly despite the efforts of state officials to limit them. In contrast, state officials in Georgia sought to slow terminations by raising the level of the standard of need that is the basic eligibility criterion. They recognized that benefits were extremely low and without such action many would have been thrown into desperate poverty.

Respondents were contacted by mail to obtain their consent for participation in the study. All of the interviews were completed in the respondents' homes. The surveys were completed by two different research groups, but the instruments utilized were identical for 60% of the schedule items. Information was obtained about welfare experience and attitudes, health, household composition and mobility, income and expenses, employment, education, marital and family background, parenting and child care, social supports, and coping behavior. The mother was the only person interviewed, but she provided information about all other members of the household.

Women were interviewed between 12 and 15 months after termination so as to obtain information about coping and crises over a more extended period. This resulted in some loss of the original sample because persons could not be located despite our diligent search. It is probable that some of those we were unable to locate were persons who had become homeless and were in the most difficult circumstances.

FINDINGS

Personal and Social Characteristics

There were a total of 1,821 individuals residing in 466 households reported on here—849 in Georgia and 1,132 in Michigan. Of that total, 68% in Georgia and 62% in Michigan were children under the age of 21. The median household size was four persons.

The median age of the respondents was 29 in Georgia and 33 in Michigan, as Table 11.1 indicates; 37% were nonwhite in Michigan compared to 79% in Georgia. The median school grade completed was 11 in Georgia and 12 in Michigan. In total, 80% had completed high school or its equivalent in Michigan and 27% had some postsecondary education; 12% were enrolled in school at the time of the interview. In Georgia, 47% had completed high school requirements, and none was enrolled in school when interviewed. Overall, Michigan women had substantially more education.

At the time of the interview, 80% in Michigan and 90% in Georgia identified themselves as single parents, but there were further differences between the two samples. In total, 48% in Georgia and 26% in Michigan were never married. There were more women married, separated, and divorced in the Michigan sample (56%) than in Georgia (43%). Michigan had provisions for supporting children in stepparent families prior to OBRA whereas Georgia did not.

While there was almost no difference in the number of children in the household size in the two samples, children in Georgia were younger than those in Michigan, not surprising given the difference in mothers' ages. Moreover, Michigan women were more likely to go on AFDC at an older age (24) and primarily because of divorce, domestic violence, and/or child abuse, whereas in Georgia women first received AFDC at a median age of 20, primarily because of pregnancy or job loss.

Questions about household mobility, asked only in Michigan, revealed considerable mobility subsequent to loss of AFDC benefits. Nearly one-quarter moved at least once and 7% moved two or more times during 1982 after termination. Other households had persons move out (23%) and persons move in (29%). In sum, 53% of the households expe-

TABLE 11.1
Personal and Social Characteristics of Working
Former AFDC Recipients

	Michigan *N = 279*	*Georgia* *N = 207*
Median Age in Years	33	29
% Nonwhite	37	79
Education		
Less than Grade 12	22%	33%
High School Grad or GED	78%	47%
Some postsecondary	27%	10%
Currently enrolled	12%	0
Average No. of Children		
In household	2.1	2.0
In AFDC Unit	1.8	2.0
Median Age of Children	12	9
Marital Status		
Median age at first marriage	19	19
% Currently married	23	9
% Married one or more times	49	43
% Never married	26	48
AFDC Experience		
Age at first grant	24	20
No. of times on AFDC	2.21	1.8
Household Mobility in 1982		
% Moved 1 or more times	23	N.A.
% Households with persons moving out	23	N.A.
% Households with persons moving in	29	N.A.
% Households with 1 or more mobility indicators	53	N.A.
Household Composition		
% Mothers and children only	84	48
% Mothers, children and other adults	16	52

rienced one or more of the mobility indicators while 34% experienced
two or more mobility indicators. When households were recomposed,
women most frequently moved in with relatives (parents, grandparents,
or other siblings). Where such were not available, women moved in with
friends or sought help from social agencies.

Intrafamilial conflict was overwhelmingly the major factor that led to marital disruption, separation, and/or divorce and then to application for AFDC. No one stated that the availability of welfare was a factor in his or her decision. For many the conflict was serious and longstanding; 45% in Michigan reported that their spouse had been repeatedly violent toward them or their children or both; and 55% reported that there was serious general conflict in the family. Several respondents reported still being in fear of battering, but few had access to or had ever received any services from a domestic violence program. At some point in the cycle of violence, each of these women decided to leave home with children and applied for AFDC.

Bane and Ellwood (1983) reported that the single largest cause of movement into poverty was decline in the household head's income—overall 37%, but 60% for male heads and 14% for female heads, indicating that for female-headed households job loss is not a strong predictor of poverty. Instead, the poverty "spells" begin when a woman becomes a female head, especially if she has young children, and they last far longer for her. In the Michigan survey, 74% reported that they applied for AFDC when their marriage or partnership broke up, clearly similar to the findings of Bane and Ellwood.

Welfare Use and Experience

Some researchers and policymakers argued that AFDC earner families would not attempt to return to the rolls once they were terminated, although others argued just the opposite (Stockman, 1983; Joe and Farrow, 1982). The former stated that women would obtain adequate income through full-time employment and seemed unaware that they would encounter any problems in meeting the cost of child care or health insurance since many were employed in uncovered industries. They also failed to note that many AFDC recipients eligible for termination were already employed full time, but could not earn sufficient income given the types of jobs and compensation typically available to low-income working women.

The overall return rate for women to AFDC, Medicaid and/or Food Stamps in this Michigan sample was 55.9% over an eighteen-month interval, as the results in Table 11.2 indicate. County differences were pronounced with higher rates in the counties with high unemployment, as had been predicted.

TABLE 11.2
Welfare Support After Termination in Michigan (N = 279)

	AFDC	Medicaid Only	Food Stamps Only	One or More Programs
Percentage received assistance for at least one month between termination and interview	24.0	31.9	43.0	55.9
Percentage on Medicaid or Food Stamps at interview	—	21.9	12.0	27.7
Percentage returned to AFDC after termination and following reapplication	24.0	10.0	33.0	39.8

NOTE: This sample includes only those cases fully meeting all OBRA criteria for termination in 1982—but excluding those terminated because of the stepfather rule since their situations tend to vary substantially from this sample.

Higher numbers of women received Food Stamps after having been terminated (43%); and Medicaid (31.9%). The terminations were implemented beginning October 1, 1981, and by December 1981, 70% of this sample had been terminated—primarily because of having too high income rather than other criteria applicable in OBRA. Among the 24% in Michigan and 38% in Georgia who reapplied and were successful in their reapplication, their average benefit at the time of the interview was $116 higher in Michigan and $100 higher in Georgia than it had been when they were terminated. State benefits were not increased, but these women who returned were not working and therefore became eligible for the larger amount and also for increased Food Stamps. Thus the state experienced greater cost when the women had to return to AFDC. In Georgia it was estimated that one returnee received an amount equivalent to that received by four recipients before OBRA.

Less than 10% of the respondents understood the details of the policy decision, knew how much income they would have, or how much property they could have before they would be terminated. Only 7% ever appealed a decision of the Department of Social Services, but among those who did, 61% were successful with their grievance. Only 36% reported that they were informed that they might continue to be eligible for Food Stamps after termination.

TABLE 11.3
Income Before and After OBRA

	Michigan (N = 215)		Georgia (N = 191)	
	Average Monthly Income of Household	Respondent's Job Earnings	Average Monthly Income of Household	Respondent's Job Earnings
1981	$822	$609	$609	$451
1982	$748	$687	$554	$446

In total, 44% reapplied for welfare after being terminated, and an additional 37% said that they wanted or needed to reapply—for an overall total of 73%. More than half visited the local social services office an average of three times to inquire about or reapply for benefits. Among the 41% who did not reapply, 69% said they did not do so because they thought they were ineligible. Need for health insurance was the most frequently stated need (39%), and that was not surprising because 37% did not have health insurance coverage for their children.

Economic Well-Being

When OBRA took effect, all the women in the survey had their AFDC benefits terminated, and most also lost Food Stamps and Medicaid. What did that mean in terms of income? At the time of the OBRA cut, the average recipient received $173 per month in Michigan and $64 in Georgia; their average job earnings equaled $609 in Michigan and $451 in Georgia. Therefore, 74% of their total income was obtained through the respondent's employment. Correspondingly, in Georgia the average grant at termination was $64 accompanied by an average Food Stamp grant of $84; and the averaged earned monthly was $451, as Table 11.3 indicates.

Employment earnings were of overriding importance in determining economic well-being. However, an irony in OBRA as well as in other welfare-related legislation is that when women who are working get a small portion of their income from AFDC, their overarching role becomes that of "welfare recipient." They are no longer considered as employees even though they work full time, nor are they considered among the

TABLE 11.4

Percentage Distribution of Respondents' Current or, if not
Working at the Time of the Interview, Most Recent Job, and
Women Workers in United States (1982), by Occupation

| | Respondents | | U.S. |
| | Michigan | Georgia | (female) |
Occupation	(N = 279)	(N = 207)	(N = 43, 256,000)
Professional	2	1	17.7
Managerial	2	2	7.4
Sales	7	0	6.9
Clerical	33	19	34.4
Crafts	1	1	2.0
Operatives	11	20	8.9
Transportation Operatives	2	0	0.7
Laborers	1	1	1.2
Service	41	56	19.7
Farm Workers	0	0	1.1
	100	100	100

SOURCE: Table No. 693, *Statistical Abstract of the United States: 1984*, (104th Ed.) (Washington, DC, 1983). Detailed data not available for 1982.
NOTE: Question: "What type of work do (did) you do?"

"deserving" poor. Subsequent to OBRA, Michigan women were more successful than those in Georgia in securing additional earned income by increasing their hours of work or hourly wage. In Georgia women actually experienced a decline in earned income from $451 to $446 per month, largely due to the effects of part-time and unstable employment as well as their low wages.

Nationally, the number of women in the labor force raising children alone doubled between 1970 and 1980. As of 1985, 70% of all women with school-aged children were in the labor force; among single mothers the percentage exceeded 80% (USDOL, 1985). Even 48% of mothers of infants worked outside the home. Obviously, it is not work effort that explains why women are poor, but rather it is the low wages that they are paid.

The type of employment that these women had explains why they depended upon AFDC to support their low earnings and lack of medical benefits. Their jobs were located in two sectors: clerical and service, as the findings in Table 11.4 reveal. Their average hourly wage was $5.13 in Michigan and $2.58 in Georgia. Only 29% of the Georgia workers earned more than minimum wage while 95% in Michigan exceeded the minimum. Michigan is a more unionized state with higher wage levels that benefit all workers, but women receive far less than men even when unionized.

When women in this sample are compared with women workers nationally, far fewer are employed in professional occupations than would be expected. They are also underrepresented in clerical and sales occupations in Georgia, perhaps a result of racial discrimination in these industries. These women had very stable employment patterns for 90% working at the time of the interview had the same job they had at termination 12-15 months earlier.

When earned income is low, as it was for these women, even a small amount of additional income can be a high proportion of total income and make a substantial contribution to well-being. On the average, when these women lost their AFDC benefits, they lost 21% of their income with one month or less notice. In addition, the loss of Medicaid, Food Stamps, and child-care transfers took on a great importance for many who had few or no benefits in their employment.

Expenses for these families did not fall when their incomes plummeted. In fact, these continued to rise because of inflation, especially in utilities and housing costs. Respondents reported that expenses for housing, utilities, food, child care, transportation, medical care, and clothing exceeded their monthly household income by 105% in Michigan and 110% in Georgia, leaving almost nothing for school and other necessary expenses.

Those shaping OBRA determined that working women should be independent of the welfare system. They argued that receiving supplementary welfare benefits was disruptive of families and/or psychologically damaging (Stockman, 1983). No consideration was given to the fundamental problems being experienced in this deindustrializing society by female single heads of household who had limited access to high-paying positions or even to jobs that had social benefits that middle-class persons take for granted as a basic job provision. As Sandra Danziger (1985) has noted, the rate of working for welfare mothers rose more steeply between 1965 and 1978 than for all other groups of single mothers. Thus clearly they evidenced high levels of commitment to labor force participation, contrary to the assertions of Anderson, Gilder, Murray, and Stockman.

Regardless of the rationale offered by the federal policymakers in 1981, the fact is that many mothers with low incomes suffered a substantial loss of income as a result of the policy changes included in OBRA. At the time of the OBRA cuts, 18% of the Michigan families and 70% of those in Georgia had incomes below the poverty level, but by the end of 1982 more fell below the poverty level (42% in Michigan versus 89% in Georgia). Clearly, federal policy substantially contributed to their increased poverty—whether it was intended to do so or not.

Constraints on Well-Being

Health. When women in this study were removed from AFDC, they were presumed able to provide for themselves and their children, but removal from AFDC also meant loss of entitlement for Medicaid. Even though most worked full time, one-third had no health benefits for themselves or their children. Because eligibility for AFDC disregards morbidity, single-mother families who are removed from AFDC on the basis of income and assets, and who also have high morbidity, confront critical questions about whether to seek medical care and how to pay for it. While technically, Medicaid can be obtained by "medically needy" families, based on high medical expenses and low income, this program in actuality is available to very few of the working non-welfare poor population.

The health conditions presented in Table 11.5 report the percentages of women and children responding affirmatively to each measure. It indicates that 10%-35% of the women report incidences of arthritis/rheumatism, gynecology or kidney problems, hypertension, repeated respiratory infections, and ulcers or stomach pains. Additionally, 4%-26.6% report having asthma or allergies, blood circulation or heart problems, repeated ear infections, and tonsillitis. The leading morbidity conditions for children were asthma and allergies (21.9%), repeated colds (28%), repeated ear infections (17.9%), and tonsillitis or tonsil enlargement (10.1%).

How do the levels of morbidity observed in the sample of poor single mothers from Michigan and Georgia compare with the general population of women and children in the United States? The closest set of comparable data was collected in the 1979 National Health Interview survey. The data indicate that this sample of former AFDC recipients has higher rates of asthma/hayfever/allergies, arthritis, diabetes, epilepsy, gynecology problems, hypertension, kidney problems, and liver problems. In fact, in many instances the magnitude of the difference is very large. Comparing children in the OBRA sample with the national sample

TABLE 11.5
Morbidity: Comparison of Michigan AFDC and
National Health Interview Survey

Health Measures	% Women		% Children	
	AFDC[a]	NHIS	AFDC[a]	NHIS
Arthritis/Rheumatism	12.7	5.81	1.1	.74[b]
Asthma/Hay Fever/Allergies	26.6	2.65	21.9	7.61
Blood circulation problem	4.4		0.4	
Cancer	1.9		0.2	
Diabetes	5.7	.90	0.8	.23[b]
Epilepsy	2.7	.32[b]	1.7	.73[b]
Gynecology problem	15.6	3.50	.8	.27[b]
Heart problem/Angina	5.9	4.12	2.3	3.55
Hypertension/High blood pressure	13.3	5.71	0.8	.38[b]
Kidney problem	13.3	4.24	4.2	1.64[b]
Liver problem	1.1	.13	0.2	
Repeated chest colds/Strep throat	35.0		28.1	
Repeated ear infections	20.0		17.9	
Sickle Cell Anemia	2.1		1.7	
Tonsillitis/Tonsil enlargement	13.3		10.1	
Ulcers/Frequent stomach pains	12.9		1.9	

SOURCE: L. Verbrugge. 1982. *National Health Interview Survey Analysis.* Washington, DC: U.S. Department of HHS, National Center for Health Statistics, 1979 Survey.
a. The AFDC sample reported here were all single mothers at the time of the interview.
b. Unreliable rate (high sampling error).

reveals a pattern similar to those of their mothers. Children in the OBRA sample had higher rates of all illnesses except heart problems.

Despite the levels of poor health, 37% had no health insurance for their children and 27% had none for themselves. Even those with insurance often had such poor benefits that their coverage was almost meaningless for the types of care that they required.

Poor health and illness was associated with inability to remain employed. Those families with higher incidence of illness, with more bed and hospital days, and who received more prescription drugs were less likely to be employed. When they were not employed, they were forced back on AFDC at higher costs and for more extended periods. Many respondents reported that the loss of Medicaid insurance was their most serious problem because they themselves or their children had chronic health needs.

TABLE 11.6
Crises Following Termination (N = 316)

	Michigan % Responding One or More Times	Georgia % Responding
Run out of money	88.6	82.3
Run out of food	49.1	33
Became seriously ill at least once	39.9	N.A.
Borrowed over $300	36.8	N.A.
Had someone important die	34.6	N.A.
Had problems with partner	37.1	N.A.
Had furnace or major appliance break	32.6	N.A.
Had something bad happen to child	29.4	N.A.
Been a victim of crime	11.1	N.A.
Been to court or was arrested	12.9	N.A.
Had utilities turned off	15.9	14.5
Had something repossessed	3.1	N.A.
Had some other crisis	24.4	N.A.

NOTE: Since January, 1982, how many times, if at all, have you ——? The time interval covered 12–18 months from the month of termination.

Crises. Having to cope with serious crises, having no money, having no food, a serious illness, death, job loss, family violence, and problems of their children was almost routine for these families, as Table 11.6 indicates. Nearly nine out of ten ran out of money at least once and 62% reported that they were without money seven or more times. Half were without food at least once and a quarter ran out of food more than seven times. Several interviewers visited households in which there was no food available and where respondents were extremely anxious because of their children. Many reported that they always ran out of food at the end of the month when wages were gone and emergency food was unavailable.

Michigan respondents replied that the following were the most serious problems experienced in 1982: lack of money (28%), lack of food (10%), having something bad happen to their children (14%), having someone close die (9%), and own illness (7%). Women with lower incomes experienced somewhat more crises, particularly those involving crime and lack of money, but the correlation was not strong—probably because the income range for the entire sample was limited relative to overall need and because nearly all experienced several serious crises during the year.

Several reported suicides within the family, serious fires, rape, and other crises.

The mean number of crises per respondent was 12.59 for the twelve- to fifteen-month time period. Only 3% reported not having one or more of the crises that we asked them about. In a similar survey of low-income women in Boston, Belle (1982) reported that in a two-year period they experienced an average of 14 serious crises that required change and adjustment by the women. The Boston study reported that the lack of money took the greatest toll on mental and physical health; that one-third did not have enough money for food; 48% had at least one child with a serious school problem; and 23% rated their own health as poor. These results then are quite similar to the crises observed in the Michigan survey, again pointing to the fact that low-income women disproportionately experience serious crises and stress. The General Mills survey of a random sample of all U.S. families in 1979 reported that, in coping with inflation, 75% of the single-parent families showed similar responses to crises associated with reduced income (General Mills, 1979).

One might expect that families with a large number of crises, especially frequent crises associated with lack of money or food, with illness, or with housing problems, would reapply for AFDC and would be relatively successful in being reinstated. Of the Michigan sample, 60% did not receive AFDC or Food Stamps after their initial termination in the period 1981-1982. That group had the smallest mean number of crises (11.90). Those who subsequently received only Food Stamps had a mean of 12.06 crises while those who returned to AFDC had 15.17 and the highest mean number (15.67) occurred for those who were back on both AFDC and Food Stamps.

Indebtedness

Debts and overdue bills were constant problems for these women; some spontaneously stated that it was the most difficult to manage. As was noted above, 82% ran out of money within the year with the mean number of times that this occurred at 5.3. Often they simply could not pay all of their monthly bills, and as a result they were evicted, had their utilities turned off, and then got even further behind.

Nearly half of the families had accumulated bills of substantial amounts, but there was little likelihood that these would be paid off soon. Slightly more than half of the Michigan sample had installment debt averaging $1,616 that was unpaid. Most of this debt was for autos and household repair. Women in Michigan often had no choice about having an auto if they wished to work because public transportation was often nonexistent. Maintenance of the auto was also extremely expensive.

Women with very low incomes were more likely to have only overdue bills, not installment debt because they lacked sufficient collateral to obtain credit. Most women observed that obtaining credit was difficult and often a degrading experience. They also observed that they experienced a continual downward cycle after termination as far as their overall economic well-being.

Social Support and Networks

Many studies show that people with spouses, friends, and family who provide material, social, and psychological support are in better health than those with fewer supportive contacts (Leavy, 1983; Gore, 1978; House, Robbins, and Metzner, 1982). More recently, investigators have advocated a multifactor/multidimensional approach to social support because they have observed that it has complex and multiple effects, some of which are positive and some of which are negative (Fiore, Becker, and Coppel, 1984; House, 1981; Thoits, 1985). Social supports have positive benefits in that they reduce the negative effects of strain and provide assistance in times of crises by acting as buffers to ameliorate the effects of stressful changes such as those experienced by women and children surveyed in this study.

Social relations may have negative effects, as Belle (1982) has noted, because many individuals involved in social relationships provide as much social support as they receive. When these relationships involve greater obligations by one person rather than the other or when the interaction is conflictual, the outcome may well be negative (Sandler and Barrera, 1984). There are costs associated with receiving support, especially when these are asked for and when the receiver feels obligated to give as a result of the transaction.

This research provided the opportunity to assess the form and frequency of assistance provided through formal and informal social networks following a serious economic crisis. It also provided the opportunity to determine the sources, nature, and relative effectiveness of social supports for poor single-parent women and children. Information was obtained about informal social support provided by family and friends and also that provided by formal help-giving agencies as well as

TABLE 11.7
Coping Behavior: Help Received from Social Network
at Time of Most Serious Problem, Michigan Data Set
(N = 279) (in percentages)

| | | Type of Help Received | | |
| | | Counsel/ Reassurance/ | Money/ Material | |
Helper	*% Contacted*	*Referral*	*Goods*	*Services*
Partner	50	73	31	12
Children	52	83	6	3
Other Relatives	75	78	35	10
Friends	56	91	14	7
Minister	9	96	8	4
Social Worker	13	64	—	23
Medical Personnel	23	68	—	65
Community Agency	7	37	63	10
Lawyer	8	70	—	35
Police	10	53	—	53
Other	13	46	23	29

that which is available through the welfare structures (emergency food assistance, social insurance, and so on).

A family can cope with crises more successfully if it is embedded in social networks that can provide social support when such is needed. The data in Table 11.7 indicate that both relatives and friends were contacted and utilized extensively by these families when they were terminated from AFDC and also when they dealt with serious problems throughout 1982—the year after their termination. Size of their friendship network was considerable—only 4% reported not having close friends with whom they could visit and nearly three-fourths had between one and ten close friends. Because the size of the friendship network is more under the control of the woman than that of her relative network, these findings suggest that the large majority were not socially isolated. However, many reported that their friends were in similar circumstances to their own and could provide only short-term or limited help.

Only 5% report that they never visit relatives, but 15% responded that they had no relatives with whom they felt free to talk about problems or whom they could count on for advice or help. A similar percentage (4%) reported that they never visited friends, but 9% reported having no friends with whom they could talk about problems of concern to them.

Nonetheless, it is clear that kin and children provided the greatest amount of social support of all types and that formal caregivers assisted only in specialized areas. In turn, most of these women also reported providing social support for families and friends when they encountered crises. Some of these women, in fact, suffered because of the amount of support that they had to provide, particularly to elderly parents with whom they resided. These women became caregivers in return for having a place to live.

Coping Behavior

How else did women cope when they were terminated from AFDC? Most sought immediately to improve their employment situation; 38% asked employers for increased hours or a better job; 31% searched for a new or better job; 18% sought help from their children's father; 12% returned to school in Michigan, 7% in Georgia. Unfortunately, most were unable to effect any real changes. In total, 69% reported no job change except that 10%-14% were able to increase the number of hours that they worked. In contrast to the myth that welfare recipients give up jobs to remain on welfare, only .7% voluntarily reduced their hours or quit working. When asked why they continued working rather than attempt to receive a full AFDC benefit, more than one-third said that they had no choice except to work. Equal numbers (about one in five) reported they did not like being on AFDC, and 18% said they felt women should work. Only 22% reported that they continued working because they enjoyed their jobs, but given the types of jobs most held and the level of their remuneration, their responses were not surprising.

Because these respondents were employed mothers, child care was a serious problem, particularly after they were terminated from AFDC. They lost child-care allowances, and they found that public child-care programs were terminated in 1981 and 1982 because of cutbacks in Title XX and Title IV-A. More than half of the respondents had children under 12; 87% of these women reported that they needed child care in order to work. The child-care providers that they were able to obtain included relatives (48%), private sitters (32%), and other siblings (10%). Nonwhite mothers were more likely to use relatives while white mothers more often used private sitters and older children, sometimes keeping them out of school for that purpose. The average monthly child-care expenditure of $106 in Michigan and $60 in Georgia was a substantial proportion of the family's budget.

Women with older children appear to have encountered at least as serious problems as those with young children. More than one-third were called to school for special conferences. In total, 22% reported that their children were suspended at least once. A small number had been expelled, referred to juvenile court, sent to special schools, committed to institutions, or victimized by a crime. The numbers, although small, were disproportionately greater than would be expected in a random sample of families with children of these ages.

These women also coped by "stretching" their income through a variety of survival tactics. In Michigan 49% and 26% in Georgia obtained old produce; 3 out of 4 obtained used clothes, one in five traded items and/or obtained emergency goods; and 21% sold bottles and cans that were redeemable in Michigan. Working with neighbors and barter were also frequently employed. Few women reported illegal behavior other than paying by check without funds in the bank. Other forms of credit were typically denied to these families because of their low and precarious incomes.

Despite their financial difficulties, most of these women were unaware of benefits for which they might have been eligible, and apparently welfare staff did not inform them of their entitlements. While 93% in Michigan and 84% in Georgia filed income tax returns, only 56% applied for an earned income tax credit, and less than 20% claimed child care as tax credit. In most instances, lack of information about eligibility appeared to have been the deterrent against their taking action because those who did appeal were usually successful. Although it is not commonly recognized, the average working AFDC family of four in 1982 paid $956 in income and payroll taxes, but only received $900 in Food Stamps—the principal nonincome transfer available to these families. The net effects of taxes and Food Stamps were to reduce the average family of four's income by $46 (Smeeding, 1983). Clearly, this nonincome transfer does not have the results suggested by some federal policy makers, namely, that the poor are better off than is realized because of the nonincome transfers. These data thus refute another myth about AFDC recipients as noncontributing members of society.

DISCUSSION AND IMPLICATIONS

Overall, both subjective and objective indicators point to greater hardship for these families in the post-OBRA period. The findings correspond to those observed in several other state surveys. These

women, all of whom had been terminated from AFDC at least once, perceived that their economic and social situation had declined substantially since 1982, and many reported being in almost continual crisis. They
felt themselves to be worse off than similar women in prior years in terms
of their increased indebtedness, problems of child care, and health. Their
lives were negatively affected by the OBRA cuts despite their whole-
hearted and continuing work effort. Clearly, this population is at high
risk for extended periods of income below the poverty level, and the problem will be exacerbated as the number of mother-only families below the
poverty level increases. Thus mobility and even homelessness is a high
risk for a substantial proportion (Kamerman, 1985).

Poverty is a painful reality for millions of American women and children—just as it is for millions throughout the world. The United States
stands apart from other industrialized countries of the world in that it
has only reluctantly extended income supports to its needy citizens—
even when those in need are children, disabled, or ill—unable to care for
themselves (Goldberg and Kremen, 1987; Cass, 1986; Kahn and Kamerman, 1983). Rather than the "Great Society," it might be more appropriate to refer to us as the "Mean Society" because we have the resources to
eliminate poverty, but not the will to do so. Many income support programs are gender-marked in that they are far more punitive toward
women than toward men. They have explicit and implicit requirements
controlling the roles and behavior of women who are recipients of income support. On the other hand, women are assigned primary responsibility for socialization of the children, but they are expected to fulfill
these responsibilities with insufficient resources and few means to effect
a change. It is no wonder then that the results have been so disruptive for
families (APWA, 1985).

In the mid-1980s a new welfare priority was implemented in the
majority of states and by the federal government: workfare. These are required work and training programs for low-income women and are
said to be the most desirable solutions because women become "independent" of the welfare system. The most successful of these programs is
the Massachusetts Employment and Training Program (ET) (Savner,
Williams, and Halas, 1986). That program is promoted as a national
model, but Massachusetts has a low rate of unemployment that cannot
be discounted as a major factor in the program's success. Moreover, the
program provides child-care vouchers and transportation as well as
higher wages than were found in West Virginia, Arkansas, and Virginia
where the evaluation indicated less successful outcomes. Nonetheless,

this approach is now the main priority, despite the fact that it does little to resolve the desperate financial situation of many of the women.

The recovery of 1984-1985, while beneficial to the middle and upper classes, has not relieved the poverty of female-headed single-parent families or that of minorities. In fact, the gap between rich and poor increased in 1984 (U.S. Committee on Ways and Means, 1986). The 1978-1983 recession pushed eleven million Americans into poverty, but the economic recovery of 1984-1985 was only able to help two million move above the poverty level. Additionally, the ecological and social limits of growth and the bureaucratization of the human services are aggravated by more rather than fewer problems.

The most serious victims of impoverishment are children—at least in long-term costs to the society—and, they are innocent victims of the conservative policy initiatives. Increasing numbers of children are being reared in families with scarce resources. Resources available to families do determine to a considerable extent the opportunities and life chances of youth, especially with respect to health and education (APWA, 1986). If present trends continue whereby mother-only families have less than half of the income of their male counterparts, despite working full time, the number of women and children in poverty and homeless will continue to increase. Moreover, that poverty will not be relieved by AFDC programs unless present policies are changed. The levels of AFDC benefits in 1985 in all of the states are below those of 1965 in constant dollars (U.S. Committee on Ways and Means, 1986).

It is impossible to design a new welfare state by slight modification of selected features of social policy and not produce disastrous results. What is now required is a thoroughgoing analysis of the basic elements of the social structure, of societal ideologies regarding family policy, and of the traditions that led to the development of the modern welfare state. Such information will then enable us to discuss alternative solutions for preservation of the structures deemed necessary and desirable for the entire society, while avoiding the emergence of new problems and inequalities.

12

The Changing Distribution of Income and Wealth in the United States, 1960-1985: An Examination of the Movement Toward Two Societies, "Separate and Unequal"

Andrew J. Winnick

The period of the Reagan administration has seen an acceleration of major changes in the distribution of income that have significant effects upon the nature of American society and upon the well-being of individuals and families. However, in many respects, these changes had begun even before Reagan took office. This chapter examines the current distribution of income and also of wealth and identifies the direction and pattern of changes that have occurred over the last quarter of a century, that is, during the period 1960 to 1985. A primary focus is upon the significant changes in the direction in which the distribution of income has moved since the mid-1970s. Evidence from both the distribution of income and of wealth will be presented to support the contention that the middle class in America is shrinking as a proportion of the population and that there is an increasing degree of bipolarization occurring with the proportion of poor and quite affluent both increasing. The primary concern is with the distribution of income and wealth among families in the United States and the effects on those families of changes in these distributions. This concern is approached in a manner that highlights the differential effects upon families and children, persons of different racial and ethnic origins, and men and women.

DEVELOPING STANDARDS OF
COMPARISON FOR INCOME LEVELS

In trying to appreciate the real meaning of the distribution of income, it is necessary to place the dollar numbers in a context that is understandable and meaningful in everyday terms. There are a variety of ways of doing this. For example, in 1985, the federal government's "official" definition of poverty for a "typical" family of four was $10,989. But most economists, especially those of a progressive nature, consider this to be an unrealistically low figure. That "official" definition of poverty was computed by multiplying by three the rough estimate by the Social Security Administration of the cash income needed in early 1964 to provide an urban family of two adults and two children with a subsistence level diet. No attempt has been made by the Social Security Administration or the Bureau of the Census to modify this official definition of poverty in any substantive way. All that has happened is that, each year, the number is adjusted to take into account the larger amount of money that would be needed to overcome the effect of inflation. [1]

However, other studies have been done. For example, the Bureau of Labor Statistics (BLS), on three different occasions since World War II, has undertaken detailed studies to try to define what they originally called the Lower, the Modest But Adequate, and the Higher Budget Levels. Unfortunately, the last such detailed study was done back in 1967. From then until the Reagan administration, these numbers, too, were annually, in some cases even quarterly, adjusted for inflation and then published in the BLS's *Monthly Labor Review*. The Reagan administration stopped this process and no longer publishes these standards.

TABLE 12.1
Three Standard Budgets for a Four-Person Family (in 1985 dollars)

Budget Category (& average/person using Low Budget)	Low or Minimum Adequacy Budget	Moderate or Modest but Adequate Budget	High or Quite Comfortable Budget
Food ($4.98/day) ($3.86/day orig)	$7,268 ($5,636)	$7,268	$9,162
Housing ($283/mo./family)	$3,401	$6,661	$10,105
Transportation ($7.02/week	$1,513	$2,670	$3,589
Clothing & Personal Care ($34.22/month)	$1,643	$2,300	$3,335
Medical Care ($35.27/month)	$1,693	$1,700	$1,773
Other Consumption ($16.22/month)	$779	$1,447	$2,385
Other Items ($15.83/month)	$760	$1,248	$2,100
Social Security & Income Taxes	$3,150	$6,793	$12,435
Total Budget	$20,207 ($18,575)	$30,177	$44,884

However, I have updated them through 1985 and report that information in Table 12.1. The BLS recognized that it outdid itself in cutting back the food budget and had to admit that it was not really adequate by its own standards, stating, "It has been estimated that only about one-fourth of those who spend amounts equivalent to the cost of the lower budget food plan actually have nutritionally adequate diets" (Meyer, 1977). Therefore, most responsible economists, when working with these standards, adjust the Lower Budget's food allowance to that of the Moderate Budget. In Table 12.1 this has been done, but the originally defined lower food budget is also shown in parentheses. It should be noted that, throughout this chapter, all dollar figures have been converted to constant 1985 dollars of purchasing power to allow for meaningful comparisons of figures between various years, that is, for comparisons between dollar figures that represent levels of purchasing power unaffected by changes in the price level, for example, due to inflation—which was quite severe during the 1970s.

To summarize this part of the discussion, in 1985, the official definition of poverty was $10,989, while the Lower adjusted BLS budget was $20,207, and the Moderate Budget was $30,177.

RECENT AND COMPARATIVE DATA ON THE DISTRIBUTION OF INCOME

The significance of these numbers becomes clearer when we look at the overall distribution of income in the United States in 1985 and compare it to that in selected years back to 1960. This is done in Tables 12.2-A and 12.2-B. The A table reports the data for all families, while the B table reports that for white, black, and Hispanic families, respectively. [2]

The data for 1973 and 1983 are reported, in addition to that for each fifth year in the period, because those years have special significance. The year 1973 was when the incidence of poverty, using the Social Security Administration's "official" definition reached its lowest point since these records have been kept—11.1% of all persons and 9.7% of all persons living in families; whereas 1983 saw the highest incidence of poverty since the mid-1960s, largely due to the Reagan recession, with 15.2% of all persons and 12.3% of all persons in families living below the "official" poverty level. Moreover, as will become clear, 1973, or more generally the early 1970s, represents a major turning point in the distribution of income in many different respects.

In 1985, 13.3% of all families, and fully 30.6% of black and 25.3% of Hispanic families, had to make do with $10,000 or less (compared to the official poverty level of $10,989). Keeping in mind that the percentages in every year reported are presented with regard to income levels for 1985 to allow for meaningful comparisons as to the actual purchasing power in 1985 dollars, one sees that whether one looks at all families or at white and black families separately (data were not reported for Hispanics until 1972), there was a consistent pattern from 1960 to 1973—to wit: the percentage of families in each of the three lowest income categories fell, while that in the upper three categories rose. However, from 1973 to 1983, the percentage of families, whether one considers all, white, black, or Hispanic, living at the three lowest levels of income turned around and

TABLE 12.2-A

Distribution of Income Among All Families, 1960 to 1985 (in constant 1985 dollars of value) (in percentages)

	All Families									
	1960	1965	1970	1973	1975	1980	1983	1985	Cum in '85
Less than $5,000 "The Truly Destitute"	8.0	5.5	3.8	3.1	3.3	3.9	5.2	4.8	4.8
$5,000 to $10,000 Below the "Official" Poverty Line[a]	11.8	10.1	8.2	7.8	8.9	8.9	9.2	8.5	13.3
$10,000 to $20,000 Above "Poverty," but Below "Minimum Adequacy"[a]	33.4	28.1	20.7	19.7	21.5	21.5	21.8	20.7	34.0
$20,000 to $35,000 "Minimum Adequacy" to 14% Above "Modest-but Adequate"	30.3	33.8	35.1	31.8	32.3	31.1	29.9	28.9	62.9
$35,000 to $50,000 Up to 9% above the BLS "High Budget" Line[a]	11.3	14.7	19.3	20.8	20.0	19.5	18.3	18.8	81.7
$50,000 and above From the Lower-Upper Class to the Super Rich	5.2	7.8	13.0	16.5	13.9	15.1	15.6	18.3	100.0

a. So-called Social Security official "Poverty" level for a family of four in 1985 was $10,989. The adjusted Bureau of Labor Statistics "Minimum Adequacy" or "Low Budget" was $20,207, while the adjusted "Moderate" or "Modest but Adequate" budget was $30,177 and the "High" budget was $44,884.

TABLE 12.2-B

Income in 1985 Dollars	ALL FAMILIES			Percentage Change		WHITE FAMILIES			Percentage Change		BLACK FAMILIES			Percentage Change		HISPANIC FAMILIES		Percentage Change
	1960	1973	1985	'60-'73	'73-'85	1960	1973	1985	'60-'73	'73-'85	1960	1973	1985	'60-'73	'73-'85	1973	1985	'73-'85
0 to $10,000	19.8	10.9	13.3	-44.9	22.0	17.2	9.1	11.2	-47.1	23.1	43.4	26.9	30.6	-38.0	13.8	16.6	25.3	52.4
$10 to 20,000	33.4	19.7	20.7	-41.0	5.1	33.3	18.4	20.0	-44.7	8.7	34.7	30.4	27.3	-12.4	-18.2	30.4	27.0	-12.6
$20 to 50,000	41.6	52.8	47.7	26.9	-9.7	43.7	54.7	49.3	25.2	-9.9	21.4	36.7	35.1	71.5	-4.4	46.1	39.8	-13.7
$50,000 and up	5.2	16.5	18.3	217.3	10.9	5.8	17.6	19.6	203.4	11.4	0.9	6.0	7.0	566.7	16.7	6.3	8.1	28.6

rose, reaching levels higher than those in 1970 and, in the case of black families at the lowest income level, higher even than in 1965. In the last two years, from 1983 to 1985, there was some significant improvement with the percentage of families in these lowest categories again falling, but that improvement looks good only in comparison to the even worse percentages in the earlier Reagan years.

This picture is confirmed by the official poverty figures that show that for almost all categories the percentage levels of poverty in 1985 were higher than those in 1980, and in many cases higher than in 1975, 1970, or even 1965. These numbers are presented in Table 12.7, which will be examined in more detail at a later point.

Returning to Table 12.2-B, one finds that more than one-third of all American families (34%) lived, in 1985, on less than $20,000 at a time when the Lower BLS Budget, with the lower inadequate food allowance, was $18,575 and the more reasonable adjusted Lower Budget was $20,207. Moreover, while this was the condition for 31.2% of white families, some 52.3% of Hispanic and 57.9% of black families suffered a similar fate. Thus more than one-third of all families and more than half of all black and Hispanic families lived below the adjusted BLS Minimum Adequacy level. Moreover, all of these percentages were worse in 1985 than they had been in 1970.

However, talking in percentage terms is a bit deceptive, for it clouds the true picture as to the total number of persons affected. After all, not only was there a higher percentage of poor people in the United States in 1985 than in 1980 or 1970, but the population had been increasing over this whole period. Table 12.3 makes this point clear. Thus one must go back almost 25 years to find times when more Americans suffered the burden of poverty than has occurred during Reagan's administration. It was the conditions prevailing in those years of 1960 to 1965 that finally led this country to declare a "War on Poverty." Now, under conditions as bad or worse, this president has cut back and severely weakened many of those hard won and much needed programs.

Moving to Table 12.4, an attempt has been made to try to develop more precise estimates of the number of families in the various conceptual categories developed earlier by interpolating between the detailed income categories that the Bureau of the Census uses in reporting its data. Since this was not feasible for Hispanic families, the data are reported for "All Families" and for "Black Families." One finds that more than a third of America's families (34.5%) and more than half of its black families (58.3%) live at incomes below the Minimum Adequacy level, while

TABLE 12.3
Poverty Rate and Number of Persons in Poverty, 1960-1985

Year	Official Poverty Rate (%)	Number of Persons Living Below Poverty Level
1985	14.0	33.1 million
1984	14.4	33.7
1983	15.3	35.5
1982	15.0	34.4
1981	14.0	31.8
1980	13.0	29.3
1975	12.3	25.9
1970	12.6	25.4
1965	17.3	33.2
1960	22.2	39.9

more than half of all families (54.4%) and three-fourths of black families (75.1%) live below the Moderate level. Indeed, only 23.3% of all families and only 9.9% of black families live at or above what might be referred to as the Comfortable level; hardly a picture of an affluent America with a vast middle class living in material comfort.

THE SHRINKING MIDDLE CLASS

Aside from the issue of the current size of the middle class, there is perhaps the even more interesting and important matter of whether this portion of our population has been shrinking in recent years. If it has, and there is compelling evidence to support this contention, then serious issues are raised about the bipolarization that is implied. Indeed, to the extent this is occurring, we must question whether our society has begun to move away from the popular image of it as being predominately made up of a vast middle class, with a small lower or underclass and a small upper class, and is, instead, moving toward a form of American Apartheid with a large, relatively permanent, and relatively powerless lower class and a large, rather permanent and powerful upper class—with a shrinking middle group of increasingly less importance. Tragically, this does seem to be occurring, and on some fronts the debate has turned from whether this is happening to why has this been occurring. But before taking up this question, let us look at some of the evidence concerning the changing relative size of the middle class.

Referring back to Table 12.2-B, and using even a very broad definition of middle class, that is, the $20,000 to $50,000 bracket, it is quite

TABLE 12.4
Distribution of Families by Designated Income Categories, 1985

	All Families			Black Families		
	At Each Level			At Each Level		
	Number of Families[a]	% of Families	Cumulative Percentage	Number of Families[a]	% of Families	Cumulative Percentage
(A) Below the Poverty or Physical Subsistence Level of $10,989	9,791	15.4	15.4	2,337	33.7	33.7
(B) From "A" to the BLS Lower or Minimum Adequacy Level of $20,207	12,153	19.1	34.5	1,697	24.5	58.3
(C) From "B" to the BLS Moderate or Socially Necessary Level of $30,177	12,668	19.9	54.4	1,160	16.8	75.1
(D) From "C" to the BLS Higher or Comfortable Level of $44,884	14,132	22.3	76.7	1,036	15.0	90.1
(E) From "D" to the Upper or Affluent Level of $60,000	7,766	12.2	88.9	464	6.7	96.8
(F) Above Mere Affluence[b]	7,048	11.1	100.0	226	3.3	100.0

a. Number of families in 1,000's.
b. The top 5% bracket for All Families starts at $77,706.

instructive to compare the changes here to those that have occurred at the lower and at the highest categories. Table 12.2-B makes this picture quite clear. Here, for clarity of presentation, the income categories have been collapsed to four. What one finds is that from 1960 to 1973, the proportion of the families in the lowest two categories decreased while that at the middle and upper levels increased. However, from 1973 to 1985, among white families, the percentages at the lowest two levels—which one might refer to as the poverty and low-income levels—turned around and increased, while the highest level also continued to increase, though at a much slower rate. On the other hand, the percentage receiving a middle income decreased. For black and Hispanic families, the picture since 1973 is even more vivid with the percentages in the lowest (poverty) and highest levels increasing while the percentage in both the low-income and middle-income groups decreased. Thus the proportion of both rich and poor has been increasing since about 1973, while the proportion of middle-class families has been decreasing.

Other studies have found the same result. After a detailed examination, Bradbury (1986), in an article entitled "The Shrinking Middle Class," found that whether she defined the middle class as those families within the $20,000 to $50,000 range, or alternatively as those in the $15,000 to $40,000 range, between 1973 and 1984 there was a 5.1% or a 4%, respectively, drop in the proportion of families within that income category, while the proportion of families at the higher and lower levels increased. Moreover, she found that most of those who left the middle-class category, however defined, fell into the lower-income brackets, rather than moving up to the higher brackets.

Much of the analysis as to why the middle class has been shrinking has built upon the seminal work by Bluestone and Harrison (1982) in their *Deindustrialization of America*. This perspective argues that there has been a decline in the relative proportion, and, in some areas, in the absolute number of reasonably well-paid, typical unionized jobs in the so-called smokestack and goods-producing industries, while simultaneously there has been a significant increase in the low-paying and typically ununionized service industry on one hand and in the often high-paying, but also ununionized, high-tech area. Bluestone and Harrison argue that from 1969 to 1982, 63% of the millions of new jobs created were in those industries that paid, on average, the lowest wages. They also indicate that from 1973 to 1980, while the number of production workers in the manufacturing industries declined by 5%, there was a slight increase in overall employment in these same industries due to increases in the number of supervisory and managerial positions. [3] Moreover, McMahon and Tschetter (1986) found "that within occupational earnings groups, the earnings distributions had shifted downward, that is, each group included more lower-paying positions."

Bradbury (1986) examined the many demographic factors that some have hypothesized may be responsible for the shrinking middle class and concluded that all of those factors, even in combination, could explain only 8% (.4% out of 5.1%) of the decline in the percentage of families receiving a middle-class income and only 10% (.7% out of 7.3%) of the decrease in median family income. She concluded "that demographic changes are not responsible for the bulk of the 1973-84 decline in the size of the middle class or in median family income . . . [and that] it seems that the dwindling of the middle class is real and probably not transitory."

Given Bradbury's negative findings, and given the results of McMahon and Tschetter and of Bluestone and Harrison, it would seem that shifts within industries and occupations, as well as between them, are indeed essential causal factors for the increasing degree of inequality within American society. Another factor that can be cited is the increasing importance of part-time work—work that is often low paying and carries few benefits. For example, in October 1986, the unemployment rate remained steady at 7% and some 350,000 new jobs were created, which absorbed many new entrants to the labor force. But 228,000 of those jobs were part time ("The Economy," 1986). Moreover, while various macroeconomic factors, such as recession and inflation, may have contributed to this problem, the fact that the trend has continued for over a decade and under varying macroeconomic conditions suggests that a broad, underlying structural change, rather than a cyclical one, is occurring within the American economy.

THE POOR ARE GETTING POORER

Aside from the problems of the bipolarization implied in the shrinking proportion of the middle class are the problems inherent in the falling absolute standard of living of the poorer portions of our society. One way to view this effect of growing polarization, or growing inequality, is to look at the data in Table 12.5. As is summarized in the comments along the right hand side of that table, we see that in 1985 the poorest (in terms of income) 20%, 40%, and even 60% of our families shared among themselves the smallest proportions of our nation's income ever recorded (except in the case of the very lowest 20% for which in three years—1949,

TABLE 12.5

Percentage Share of America's Total Family Income Received
by Families Reported by Quintiles, 1947-1985

Quintile	1947	1960	1965	1970	1975	1980	1985	Comparison of 1985 to Earlier Figures
The Poorest 20%	5.0	5.0	5.2	5.4	5.4	5.1	4.6	Lowest since 1954
The Second 20%	11.8	12.1	12.2	12.2	11.8	11.6	10.9	Lowest on Record
The Third 20%	17.0	17.7	17.8	17.6	17.6	17.5	16.9	Lowest on Record
The Fourth 20%	23.1	23.7	23.9	23.8	24.1	24.3	24.2	Highest except for 1980-84 period[a]
The Richest 20%	43.0	41.4	40.9	40.9	41.1	41.6	43.5	Highest on Record
The Richest 5%	17.2	16.3	15.5	15.6	15.5	15.3	16.7	Highest on Record
The Poorest 40%	16.8	17.1	17.4	16.6	17.2	16.7	15.5	Lowest on Record
The Richest 40%	66.1	65.1	64.8	64.7	65.2	65.9	67.7	Highest on Record

a. When it fluctuated between 24.3% and 24.4%.

1950, and 1954—a figure of 4.5% was recorded, compared to the 4.6% in 1985). On the other hand, the proportion of income received by the upper 40% expanded, with the richest 20% and the richest 5% receiving the largest proportions of family income ever recorded. At the bottom of this table, one sees that the poorest 40% of America's families received, in 1985, only 15.5% of family income, while the richest 40% received 67.7%, or more than four times as much. The figures for both of these groups are, respectively, the lowest and the highest on record. [4]

To view these same statistics in slightly different terms, over the course of the first five years of the Reagan administration, the median income of the poorest 40% of the American population fell by $283 in real, inflation-adjusted, 1985 dollars, from $13,475 to $13,192, while the median income of the richest 40% of the population *increased* by $2,760, going from $45,240 to $48,000 in that same five-year period. Thus the gap between these groups widened during these Reagan years from $31,765 to $34,808, a 9.6% wider gap in only 5 years. This has truly been a time of the poor getting poorer and the rich getting richer.

One summary measure of the dramatically different pattern of changes in income since 1973 is shown in Table 12.6. Here one finds that median family income increased substantially from 1960 to 1973. However, from 1973 to 1982, despite some minor ups and downs during the late 1970s, it decreased for all families taken as a whole (one of the issues that Bradbury addressed), as well as for white, black, and Hispanic

TABLE 12.6

The Changes in Median Family Income: 1960-1985
(in constant 1985 dollars)

					Percentage Changes		
	1960[a]	1973	1983	1985	'60-'73	'73-'82	'82-'85
All Families	$20,421	$29,172	$26,124	$27,735	42.9	−10.4	6.2
White Families	$21,202	$30,484	$27,428	$29,152	43.8	−10.0	6.3
Black Families	$11,737	$17,596	$15,160	$16,786	49.9	−13.8	10.7
Hispanic Families	n/a	$21,097	$18,091	$19,027	n/a	−14.2	5.2

a. In 1960, the figure for black families is actually for "black and other races." 1967 is the first year separate data is reported for blacks alone. In 1967, blacks were 91% of the "blacks and other races" category.

families considered separately. Since 1982, there has again been some substantial improvement. Nevertheless, as of 1985, the median family income for all categories of families remained almost 5% below that which was achieved in 1973.

If one recalls the oft-quoted remark of Franklin Delano Roosevelt in the early 1930s that he looked out over a nation where one-third of its people went to bed every night either ill-fed, ill-clothed, or ill-housed, the truth is that, in 1985, by the reasonable standards defined by the Bureau of Labor Statistics, that is still the case in America. Moreover, among the minorities of our nation, the situation is far worse even than that. In addition, all of this is further worsened by the fact that the gap between rich and poor has been steadily widening, that the relative size of the middle class has been shrinking, that median family income has, until very recently, been falling and that the proportion of the nation's income available to the lower 60% of our families has been decreasing. Faced with these economic pressures, is it any wonder that we hear so much about the distress of the American family?

A FURTHER LOOK AT THE SITUATION FOR THE MINORITIES, FOR FEMALE-HEADED HOUSEHOLDS, AND FOR CHILDREN

Beyond the issue of the overall amount of poverty in 1985 is the matter of how that level has been changing over the period in question and how the burden of poverty effects different groups such as racial/ethnic groups, female-headed households, and children. Before analyzing the data in Table 12.7, it is important to note that the definition of poverty used there is the official Social Security Administration/Bureau of the Census standard, which, it should be recalled, is more than 50% lower than the far more appropriate BLS Low-Income standard. Hence what follows may be viewed as a far more positive and conservative description than that which indeed faces the American people. Table 12.7 presents data for every five years from 1960 to 1985, with an added column for the peak year since 1980 for that particular category. The data presented along the right hand side of the table all relate to families, while that along the left hand side relate to all persons in that group, whether or not they lived in families.

Racial Minorities

Looking at Table 12.7, the first thing that one should note is that it is clear that, consistently, the rate of poverty within the black community is about two to three times higher than that among whites, and the poverty rate for Hispanics is generally at about the same level as that for blacks, sometimes a bit higher, sometimes a bit lower, depending on the particular category under investigation. On the other hand, it is important to note that of the 33.1 million persons living in poverty in the United States in 1985, 22.9 million, or 69%, were white; that is, more than two out of every three poor people were white. The simple fact is that while the *rate* of poverty is far higher within the minority communities, the far larger number of whites living in America, combined with the significant degree of poverty in that community (11.4% in 1985), means that about two-thirds of the poor in the United States are and have been white. The media image of the poor as being predominately people of color is not and never has been true.

Moreover, it also should be pointed out that a similar picture emerges when one looks at the welfare figures. In 1985, 2.1 million white families received welfare benefits compared to 1.4 million black families. Moreover, while about 31% of blacks lived below the poverty line in 1985, only 21% received public assistance. More than 2 million black people living below the poverty line were *not* "on welfare" (Helmore and Laing, 1986).

Among families, the incidence of poverty is more than three times higher for blacks and Hispanics than for whites, while among unrelated individuals the differential is about 1.7 to 1, reflecting the high level of poverty (19.6%) even among white unrelated individuals. Before one leaps to any conclusions as to the cause of this, it is important to note that the poverty rate among our senior citizens, regardless of

TABLE 12.7

Comparative Data on Persons and Children in Households, Families and Female-Headed Families
Living Below the "Official" Poverty Level, 1960-1985 (in percentages)

All Persons

	1960	1965	1970	1975	1980	Peak Year[a]	1985
All Persons	22.2	17.3	12.6	12.3	13.0	15.2 ('83)	14.0
Whites	17.8	13.3	9.9	9.7	10.2	12.1 ('83)	11.4
Blacks[c]	55.1	41.8	33.5	31.3	32.5	35.7 ('83)	31.3
Hispanics[b]	n/a	n/a	21.9	26.9	25.7	29.9 ('82)	29.0

All Persons Living in Families

	1960	1965	1970	1975	1980	Peak Year[a]	1985
All Persons	20.7	15.8	10.9	10.9	11.5	13.9 ('83)	12.6
Whites	16.2	11.7	8.1	8.3	8.6	10.7 ('83)	9.9
Blacks[c]	54.9	40.9	32.2	30.1	31.1	34.7 ('82)	30.5
Hispanics[b]	n/a	n/a	21.5	26.3	25.1	29.2 ('82)	28.3

Unrelated Individuals

	1960	1965	1970	1975	1980	Peak Year[a]	1985
All Persons	45.2	39.8	32.9	25.1	22.9	23.4 ('81)	21.5
Whites	43.0	38.1	30.8	22.7	22.4	21.2 ('81)	19.6
Blacks[c]	57.0	54.4	48.3	42.1	41.0	41.0 ('80)	34.7
Hispanics[b]	n/a	n/a	29.9	36.6	32.2	36.8 ('84)	33.2

All Related Children under 18 Living in Families

	1960	1965	1970	1975	1980	Peak Year[a]	1985
All Persons	26.5	20.7	14.9	16.8	17.9	21.8 ('83)	20.1
Whites	20.0	14.4	10.5	12.5	13.4	17.0 ('83)	15.6
Blacks[c]	65.5	50.6	41.5	41.4	42.1	47.3 ('82)	43.1
Hispanics[b]	n/a	n/a	27.8	33.1	33.0	39.6 ('85)	39.6

	All Persons Age 65 and Older[d]							All Persons in Female-Headed Families						
All Persons	35.2	28.5	24.6	15.3	15.7	15.3 ('81)	12.6	48.9	46.0	38.1	37.5	36.7	40.6 ('82)	37.6
Whites[c]	33.1	26.4	22.6	13.4	13.6	13.1 ('81)	11.0	39.0	35.4	28.4	29.4	28.0	31.2 ('83)	29.8
Blacks[c]	62.5	55.1	48.0	36.3	38.1	39.0 ('81)	31.5	70.6	65.3	58.7	54.3	53.4	58.8 ('82)	53.2
Hispanics[b]	n/a	n/a	24.9	32.6	30.8	26.6 ('82)	23.9	n/a	n/a	57.4	57.2	54.5	60.1 ('82)	55.7

	All Persons in Female-Headed Households (incl. unrel. indiv.)							Related Children under 18 in Female-Headed Families						
All Persons	49.5	46.0	38.2	34.6	33.8	36.2 ('82)	33.5	68.4	64.2	53.0	52.7	50.8	56.0 ('82)	53.6
Whites[c]	42.3	38.5	31.4	28.1	27.1	28.7 ('82)	27.3	59.9	52.9	43.1	44.2	41.6	47.1 ('83)	45.2
Blacks[c]	70.0	65.1	58.8	53.6	53.1	54.7 ('82)	51.8	81.6	76.6	67.7	66.0	64.8	70.7 ('82)	66.9
Hispanics[b]	n/a	n/a	55.5	55.6	52.5	57.4 ('82)	54.2	n/a	n/a	68.7	68.4	65.0	72.4 ('85)	72.4

a. Peak Year refers to highest year in 1981-1985 period.
b. Data for "1970" are actually for 1973, the earliest year for which these data are available.
c. Data for "1960" are actually for 1959 and data for "1965" are actually for 1966 due to anomalies in the way such data are published.
d. As in the case of blacks, "1960" data are actually for 1959 and "1965" are actually for 1966.

race/ethnic origin, is significantly lower than that for unrelated in-dividuals. That is, the high rate of poverty among unrelated individuals is *not* primarily due to single older persons, quite the contrary. In fact, one striking fact is that for all racial/ethnic groups, the incidence of pov-erty among the elderly has consistently fallen and this has contributed to a similar fall in the rate for unrelated individuals.

It might be mentioned at this juncture that while the fact that the un-employment rate among blacks tends to run more than twice that for whites—throughout the latter part of 1986, for example, about 7% for whites and 15% for blacks—this is only one part of the poverty problem. One interesting facet of the recent recession period, which might broad-ly be viewed as the period 1979-1983, is that 62% of the white workers who were laid off were rehired by the same firm, while this was true for only 42% of the black workers. Moreover, of those not rehired, 17% of the blacks as compared to 14% of the whites were unable to find another job (Helmore and Laing, 1986).

Children

The poverty situation for children in America is truly hor-rible. Again referring to Table 12.7, we see that, in 1985, more than one out of every five children in the United States (20.1%) who are living in families, live in poverty. We see that more than one-third (39.6%) of all Hispanic and almost half (43.1%) of all black children under 18 in fami-lies are forced to live in those conditions. Moreover, the situation in 1985, while a bit better than during the 1981 through 1985 peak, is consider-ably worse than it was for any year back to the late 1960s. In fact, for whites, one has to go back to the early 1960s to find conditions as bad. Turning to Table 12.8, one sees that the plight of very young chil-dren, those under the age of 6, is even worse. Here, in 1985, almost one-fourth (23%) of all such young children and very close to half (47.7%) of black children lived in poverty. For such young children as a whole and for whites and Hispanics separately, these are the worst figures since these records have been kept. For blacks, the 1985 figures are only marginally below their all time peak and are at the highest levels in more than fifteen years. According to Edward Zigler, Director of the Bush Center in Child Development and Social Policy at Yale University, "Children are in the absolute worst status they have been in during my 30 years of monitoring child and family life in this country. . . . [More-over] every day more and more children are slipping into poverty, which immediately puts them at a very high risk. . ." (Gardner, 1986).

TABLE 12.8
Children Living Below the Poverty Level
(as a percentage of all children of that age)
1966-1985

	1966	*1970*	*1975*	*1980*	*1985*
Under Age 6					
All	18.1	16.6	18.2	20.7	23.0
White	12.4	11.8	14.0	16.0	18.3
Black	50.3	42.2	40.8	45.8	47.7
Hispanic	n/a	n/a	n/a	34.6	41.4
Age 6 to 15					
All	17.6	14.9	16.8	17.8	20.0
White	12.3	10.5	12.4	13.4	15.5
Black	51.9	41.5	33.6	41.2	42.4
Hispanic	n/a	n/a	n/a	33.0	39.7

NOTE: 1966 is the earliest year for which these detailed data are available.

Some important symptoms of this "high risk" are that 16% of white 17-year-olds and 47% of black 17-year-olds are functionally illiterate. In 1984, 27% of black high school graduates enrolled in college, down from a high of 32% in 1975. Black children drop out of college at almost twice the rate of white children. "Black students are placed in classes for the mildly mentally handicapped more than three times as often as white students. But they are placed in classes for the gifted and talented only half as often as white students" (Helmore and Laing, 1986).

Given the poverty under which increasing numbers of our children must live and the consequences of such conditions, it is particularly disturbing to find that the welfare programs designed to help such children have been reduced significantly in their reach and effectiveness under the Reagan administration. According to a study released in October 1986 by the House Select Committee on Children, Youth, and Families, between 1979 and 1984, while there was a 30% increase in the number of poor children (from 9.9 to 12.9 million), there was a 20% decrease in the rate of participation in the Head Start and the Aid to Families with Dependent Children (AFDC) programs. The study did find a 22% increase in the rate of participation in the Supplemental Food Program for Women, Infants and Children (WIC), but that even so, this program reached only one-third of the eligible children in 1984. Moreover, the study found that 332 counties in 19 states did not have any WIC or other feeding program at all. Amazingly, the Committee reported that the number of children receiving AFDC benefits in the "high-poverty counties" actually dropped 10% from 1979 to 1984 and that in 30 states the number of children receiving AFDC benefits dropped, despite increases in the number of poor children. The Committee concluded that "funding had not kept pace with increased demand" and that "the record growth in poverty among children has not been accompanied by increased availability of key safety net programs" ("Safety Net Programs," 1986).

If it can be said of any nation that a crucial basis upon which to judge it is the way it treats its children, then America is damned by its perpetration of a distribution of income that forces such a large proportion of its children to grow up under circumstances of absolute poverty and then does so little to alleviate those conditions.

Female-Headed Households

In recent years, there has been a good deal of concern expressed about the situation facing households headed by women. The concern is fully warranted. Looking yet again at Table 12.7, one sees that there has been little or no improvement over the course of the last fifteen years and the situation remains at a crisis level, especially for nonwhites. In 1985, more than one-third (33.5%) of the persons living in female-headed households and 37.6% of persons living in female-headed families, lived at or below the official poverty level of income, while for both black and Hispanic female-headed households the figure remained over 50%. Even among white female-headed households, the figure stood at over one-fourth (27.3%) who lived in poverty. To look at the issue from a slightly different perspective, more than half of all poor (by the official definition) households in the United States in 1985 were headed by a woman and just under half of all poor people lived in female-headed households. For comparison, "only" 15% of black and 8% of white "husband-wife families" lived below the poverty level in 1985.

When one looks at the children in female-headed families, not unexpectedly, given what has already been shown, the situation can only be described as a disaster. More than half (53.6%) of all such children live in poverty and more than two-thirds (66.9%) of black children and almost three-fourths (72.4%) of Hispanic children in female-headed families live in poverty.

To consider another aspect of this problem, between 1970 and 1985, the proportion of black children living with a never-married parent in-

creased from 5% to 24%, while the proportion of white children also increased, but only to 2.1% (Helmore and Laing, 1986).

However, while it is true that the number of female-headed households has increased in recent years, there is little evidence, especially in
the case of black and Hispanic households, to support the contention
that this is a *cause* of poverty. Many of the people who newly create these
households would have been poor even if they had stayed in their previous situations, that is, with parents or husbands. Mary Jo Bane (1984)
of Harvard University, concluded in a recent paper that

> though there has been a dramatic, and shocking, increase in female-headed
> households among blacks, and an equally dramatic "feminization" of
> black poverty, one cannot conclude that much of the poverty could have
> been avoided had families only stayed together.

Thus she found that more than two-thirds of the black women who
created new households were already poor before they made the transition. Among white women the pattern was somewhat different. Most of
them were not poor either before or after the transition into a newly
created female-headed household. However, of those white women who
were poor during their first year in the new household, three-quarters of
them were coming from nonpoverty situations. On the other hand, given
the problems encountered by any single-parent/single-earner family in
securing a high enough income to avoid poverty, and given the sexual
and racial discrimination in wage and earnings even among full-time,
full-year workers in similar industries and occupations, it is easy to
understand why female-headed families, especially where the women are
black or Hispanic, have a very high vulnerability to being poor.

Teenage Motherhood and Poverty

A closely related problem is that of teenage motherhood.
However, there are many misperceptions about their problem. One can
legitimately argue that teenage motherhood (which is not to say teenage
pregnancy) is closely tied to the incidence of poverty and that this is true
regardless of race. For example, the number of births per 100 poor white
teenage girls is 21.2 and for poor black girls, it is 22.6—very similar
figures. On the other hand, in 1985, black teenage births amounted to
25% of all black births and the black poverty rate was about 31%, while
white teenage births accounted for 12% of white births and the white poverty rate was 11% (Helmore and Laing, 1986). As for the myths concern-

ing sexuality in the black community, the U.S. Department of Health and Human Services found that between the years 1970-1985, the birth-rate among black teenage girls dropped by 10.1%, while it increased by 74.3% among white teenage girls (Helmore and Laing, 1986). Moreover, a study at Johns Hopkins University showed

> low-income black teenage girls generally have their first sexual experience about six months earlier than their white counterparts. However, low-income black teenage girls have fewer partners and engage in sexual inter-course less often than low-income white teenage girls [Helmore and Laing, 1986].

THE DISTRIBUTION OF WEALTH IN THE UNITED STATES

Throughout this chapter, the focus has been on the current earnings of individuals and families. Rich and poor have been defined in terms of income. However, in many ways, it is more appropriate to recognize that it is wealth, more than income, that is the hallmark of the rich. For with great wealth, a stream of income is assured, regardless of the current work effort. Only wealth protects one from a prolonged interruption in income generation. Moreover, while a temporarily large stream of income will gain a certain measure of status and power, real social status and political power typically depend upon the influence guaranteed only by substantial wealth. Conversely, a lack of wealth can make even a temporary period of low income an economic disaster for a family.

In July 1986, the Bureau of the Census released a study, entitled *Household Wealth and Asset Ownership: 1984,* that provided current, detailed, and reliable data on wealth holdings. This study was based on data from the Survey of Income and Program Participation (SIPP). In order to render this work on the distribution of wealth as comparable as possible to the data presented earlier in the distribution of income, wherever feasible the dollar figures have been converted into 1985 constant dollars of value.

Table 12.9 shows that wealth is far less equally distributed than income. What is particularly striking about this table is the differences in the distribution of wealth along racial/ethnic origin lines. Thus while only 8.4% of white families have zero or negative amounts of net wealth, that is, they owe more than they own, a dramatically high 30.5% of black families and 23.9% of Hispanic families share that fate. Overall, this study shows 11% of all families with negative or zero net worth. When one adds the proportion of families in the lowest positive net worth bracket ($1 to $5,180), one finds that some 22.4% of white families are accounted for, but 54.4% of black and 40.2% of Hispanic families. Again, one sees in very vivid terms how vulnerable a large proportion of families, especially among blacks and Hispanics, are to any interruption in income.

Table 12.9 also reveals some important information about the relative wealth positions of different types of families, in particular those characterized by having a married couple, those headed by a single female, and those headed by a single male. One finds that female-headed households are more than three times as likely (19.3% compared to 6%) to have a zero or negative net worth position than are married-couple families. Even single male-headed households (15.5%) are more than two and a half times more likely to be in this vulnerable situation. By the time one takes into account those in the lowest positive net worth position, one finds a total of 39.6% of female-headed and 40.6% of male-headed (one adult) families. It would appear that families with a single primary breadwinner, whether female or male, are far less likely to be able to accumulate any significant amount of wealth—not a very surprising result given the statistics on wages and earnings.

The portion on the far right in Table 12.9 provides some interesting data on the distribution of net worth within various income brackets.[5] As one would expect, there is a strong correlation between income and wealth, with a larger proportion of those families having low incomes also having little, if any, wealth as compared to those families with more income and, not surprising, more wealth. Thus, for example, 49.8% of the families in the lowest income bracket have less than $5,180 in net worth, while only 4% of those in the highest income bracket are in that situation. At the other extreme, the proportion of families with large wealth holdings increases as income increases. However, it is interesting to note that there are some low-income families who do have substantial wealth.

Overall, looking at the upper right section of Table 12.10, one finds that the 25.7% of the families that are designated as poor in terms of income share among themselves only 9.75% of the total net worth of American families, while the 12.4% with the highest income share among themselves 38% of the net worth. Thus the median net worth of the richest (in terms of income) families ($127,919) is more than 24 times that of the poorest. There is little doubt that wealth in America is far more unequally distributed than is income.

TABLE 12.9

Distribution of Household Net Worth by Race/Ethnic Group, Income, and Type of Household Using Bureau of the Census SIPP Data for 1984 (in 1985 dollars; in percentages)

Net Worth in 1985 dollars	Race/Ethnic Origin of Household				Type of Household			Equivalent Annual Income[a]			
	White	Black	Hispanic	All	Married	Female-Head	Male-Head	Less than $11,200	$11,200 to $24,900	$24,900 to $49,700	$49,700 and more
Negative or Zero	8.4	30.5	23.9	11.0	6.0	19.3	15.5	24.5	9.7	4.6	2.2
$1 to 5,180	14.0	23.9	26.3	15.3	10.5	20.3	25.1	25.3	18.9	8.8	1.8
$5,180 to 10,360	6.3	6.8	7.6	6.4	5.6	6.4	9.7	6.9	8.1	6.2	1.5
$10,360 to 25,900	12.2	14.0	11.4	12.4	12.2	12.2	13.3	11.5	13.5	14.6	5.9
$25,900 to 51,800	5.0	11.7	9.5	14.5	15.6	13.5	11.6	12.5	14.5	17.7	10.3
$51,800 to 103,600	20.7	9.3	13.1	19.3	22.7	15.3	13.0	11.8	19.1	23.9	23.5
$103,600 to 259,000	16.9	3.3	5.1	15.3	19.5	10.3	8.0	6.2	13.6	18.3	31.0
$259,000 to 518,000	4.4	.5	2.1	4.0	5.3	2.0	2.6	1.0	2.1	4.6	13.4
$518,000 or more	2.1	.1	1.0	1.9	2.7	.6	1.4	.3	.5	1.3	10.4
Totals	100.0	100.0	100.0	100.0	100.0	100.0	100.0	100.0	100.0	100.0	100.0

a. Average monthly income over four sample months multiplied by twelve.

TABLE 12.10

Median and Mean Net Worth by Income, Race/Ethnic Origin, and Type of Household
Using Bureau of the Census SIPP Data for 1984 (in 1985 dollars)

	Median Net Worth				Mean Net Worth	Distribution of:	
	White	Black	Hispanic	All	All	Net Worth	Number of Households
Equivalent Annual Income[a]							
Less than $11,200—"The Poor"	$8,747	$91	$453	$5,263	$30,727	9.7%	25.7%
$11,200 to $24,900—"Low Income"	$31,820	$4,370	$3,809	$25,534	$54,617	20.5%	30.6%
$24,900 to $49,700—"Middle Class"	$52,348	$16,552	$25,698	$48,427	$82,957	31.8%	31.3%
$49,700 and more—"High Income"	$132,854	$60,873	$103,074	$127,919	$250,769	38.0%	12.4%
						Median Net Worth without Home Equity	
Type of Household:							
Married-couple	$56,135	$13,531	$11,213	$51,920	$105,587	$12,767	
Female-Headed	$23,310	$695	$495	$14,385	$46,555	$3,084	
Male-Headed	$12,252	$3,131	$2,800	$10,239	$50,654	$4,693	

	White	Black	Hispanic	All	Relative Net Worth & Income	
					Black/White	Hispanic/White
All Households:						
Median Income	$21,876	$13,524	$16,716	$20,844	61.8%	76.4%
Median Net Worth	$40,544	$3,519	$5,090	$33,843	6.2%	12.6%
Mean Net Worth	$89,440	$20,970	$37,327	$81,568	23.4%	41.7%
Distribution of:						
Net Worth by Race/Ethnic Group	95.2%	3.0%	2.0%	b		
Households by Race/Ethnic Group	86.8%	11.0%	4.8%	b		

a. Average monthly income over four sample months multiplied by twelve.
b. Can not add three groups since Hispanics can be of any race.

Table 12.10 reports some summary statistics from Table 12.9, including the median net worth by income brackets for families in the different racial/ethnic origin groups. The phenomenon noted above of some families having low income combined with substantial wealth is limited almost entirely to white families. Thus the median net worth of white families in the lowest income bracket is $8,747, while that of black families is a mere $91 (a ratio of almost 100 to 1) and that of Hispanic families is not much more substantial at $453 (a ratio of almost 20 to 1). When one sees a reference to the median net wealth for all families in this low-income bracket ($5,263), it is essential to understand that due to the differences between the racial/ethnic origin groups, this overall figure is truly meaningless. The overall figure is a full 40% below the actual amount for white families and is almost 60 times higher than that for black families and almost 12 times higher than that for Hispanic families.

Table 12.10 also reveals that, when discussing the relative positions of different types of families, it is again essential to disaggregate by racial/ethnic origin of the families. Thus while it is true that all female-headed families have a median net worth position considerably poorer than that for married-couple families, something that was revealed initially in Table 12.9, the differences between the position of whites, on one hand, and blacks and Hispanics on the other, is vast. Thus while it is true that white female-headed families have a net worth that is only 42% of that of white married-couple families, it is nevertheless more than 33 times higher than enjoyed by black female-headed families and more than 47 times higher than that of Hispanic female-headed families. Even among male-headed families, the differences between the racial/ethnic origin groups is quite significant with white families having a net worth almost 4 times that of blacks and more than 4.3 times that of Hispanics.

As the summary statistics in the lower portion of the table indicate, the distribution of wealth across the racial/ethnic groups is far less equal than the distribution of income, using this survey's statistics for both income and wealth. Thus while black median family income is only 61.8% of that for white families, black median family net worth is an astoundingly small 6.1% of that of whites. That is, wealth, on average, is 10 times less equally distributed. For Hispanic families the differential is about 6 times (12.6% of white net worth compared to 76.4% of income).

With this distribution of wealth, the distribution of income that was described in the earlier portions of this chapter becomes not very surprising at all. Moreover, these wealth figures raise very serious questions as to whether any significant progress can be made in redistributing income on a more equitable basis, if something is not first done to break up these centers of wealth and power.

CONCLUSION

There are a number of interesting conclusions that can be drawn from the evidence cited in this study. While I would not pretend that this descriptive overview of the distribution of income and wealth in the United States is sufficient to prove these points, I do propose them as viable hypotheses that warrant serious consideration and future study.

(1) *The United States is in the midst of a serious polarization in the distribution of income.* The standard of living of the poorer sections of our population is getting worse, not better, while that of the richer sections moves ahead rapidly. The gap between the rich and the poor is growing wider, both in relative terms and in terms of the actual number of dollars involved. The poor are receiving an even smaller portion of the nation's income to share among themselves, while the rich are getting an increasing share. Meanwhile, the image of a vast, expanding, relatively affluent American middle class is seen to be a myth.

(2) *This polarization is taking on increasingly racial overtones.* Thus while the majority of the poor are now and have always been white, the incidence of poverty among the black and Hispanic portions of our population remains at levels many times that experienced by the white community. On top of this, the distribution of wealth between white families, on one hand, and black and Hispanic families, on the other, is vastly more inequitable than the distribution of income and greatly increases the vulnerability of these latter families to economic disaster whenever there is any pressure on the family's current income position.

(3) *The distribution of income also severely discriminates against women.* Thus while there has been some narrowing of the gap between white women and white men, that gap remains far wider even than that between blacks and whites. Moreover, the increasing presence of female-headed households and the remarkably high incidence of poverty and very low net worth among them suggest an increasing degree of polarization between these households and the rest of society.

(4) *By consigning one-fourth to one-half of our youngest children and one-fifth to one-third of all of our nation's children to poverty, we are laying the seeds for a degree of social degeneration and deterioration perhaps never before experienced in a modern industrialized nation.*

(5) *The view that poverty is primarily a function of unemployment and part-time employment is simply false.* Hence attempts to solve the poverty problem simply through job training and employment services will not suffice. This is not to say that these efforts are not needed. Efforts to expand employment, just as efforts to bring immediate relief to those in poverty via public assistance of one form or another, of course, are needed and crucially so. But, the primary cause of poverty and low income in the United States is the structure of wages. The point that comes across time and time again is that even when one takes the most conservatively optimistic point of view by looking at only those people who are able to work full time, full year—one still finds real poverty and unacceptably low income. [6]

One realizes that if an individual works 40 hours a week, 52 weeks a year, at a wage of $5 per hour (which is well over the minimum wage of $3.35), [7] the individual would earn only $10,000, when the official poverty level is set at $10,989 (in 1985) and when the adjusted Minimum Adequacy BLS budget requires $20,207 (again in 1985). Even if a family has two wage earners, both working full time at $5, the family has an income of only $20,000, still more than $200 below the BLS Minimum Adequacy level. Furthermore, even at the average gross hourly earnings rate for all nonsupervisory and production workers, which in 1985 was running just under $8.60, such a full-time worker would receive only $17,200, a figure well above the official poverty level, but still more than $3,000 below the Minimum Adequacy standard. The BLS Moderate standard (for 1985) of $30,177 was clearly beyond the reach of any family earning even considerably above such average wages, unless two persons in the family were employed at such wages.

When the majority of the American labor force finds itself living at these unacceptably low levels of income, despite working full-time, and when this majority has to watch an affluent minority consume the output of the majority, something is sorely wrong. This is not a new observation, but it is one that many of us had begun to lose sight of as we were told that the War on Poverty had largely been won and the time of affluence for the majority was upon us. Well, that war was not won, affluence by any real criteria remains a distant goal for the vast majority of Americans, and the problems go far beyond unemployment and job training. The entire structure of the economy and the manner in which wages are determined need to be examined and overhauled.

Tragically, this occurs at the same time as it has become quite clear to even the most uninformed that the historical period of American economic dominance over the rest of the world is long past—having ended during the early 1970s. The United States is now forced to compete more with the modern industrial nations of Europe and Asia than at any point in the last 100 years, as well as with such "newly industrializing nations" as Korea and Singapore. Many writers have analyzed this nation's economic problems and have concluded that the competitive problem is not one of American workers who are too highly paid, but of low productivity due to inadequate modernization of facilities, primitive conditions in labor relations and work organization, and an almost total lack of long-term, integrated, strategic economic planning.

Perhaps if America began to face these problems it would be able to pay reasonably livable wages to more of its workers, reduce the inequalities in income, take care of *all* of its children and begin again to address the tragic discrimination against black, Hispanic and female workers.

(6) *The distribution of wealth in the United States is far more unequal than that of income and vastly worsens the negative impact upon families of periods of either low income or of an interruption in the stream of income.* Moreover, the concentration of wealth in the hands of a very small portion of the population undermines the very foundation of American's aspirations to be a truly democratic society and lies at the root of why this nation has been unable to address some of its most severe economic problems. It must be very clear that there is no way that wealthy individuals and families are going to tolerate the reconstructing of the economy along the lines needed to gain a more equitable distribution of income. Until their control over the wealth of this nation is broken, we are highly unlikely to see any significant progress on questions pertaining to the distribution of income.

(7) *The total effect of these conclusions is to paint a picture of a nation in deep trouble.* While it may seem trite and old fashioned, the only possible way I see to solve these problems is if the people most affected— the minorities and women and poor, the people who work so hard and yet earn so relatively little, in combination with those who have been given the tools to explain and clarify what is happening and why, come together and begin to build a serious political movement. This movement must aim not just at finding immediate relief in the form of welfare reforms and the like (though those efforts are also needed), but rather this movement must begin to come to grips with the need for a fundamental restructuring of the American economy. While, sadly, I see little evidence that this is happening, I see even less hope if it does not.

NOTES

1. These facts are regularly cited in Appendix A of Bureau of the Census, U.S. Department of Commerce, *Current Population Reports: Money Income and Poverty Status of Families and Persons in the United States.*

2. Unless otherwise noted, all figures in Table 12.2 and later tables are either directly taken, or developed, from Bureau of the Census, U.S. Department of Commerce, Current Population Reports, Series P-60, in particular, those numbers that carry either the title *Money Income and Poverty Status of Families and Persons in the United States* or *Money Income of Households, Families, and Persons in the United States.*

3. These data are from an unpublished paper presented at the August 1984 Annual URPE Summer Conference.

4. Bradbury (1986, p. 54) in a footnote commented that: "Readers may be surprised that income was more unequally distributed in 1984 than in 1973, since the amounts of social security, welfare, and other transfers have grown considerably. . . . This distribution has become more unequal in spite of increases in 'pro-poor' transfers because the distribution of pre-transfer income has become even more unequal."

5. The SIPP study, upon which this table is based, obtained information from each family via four interviews taken in consecutive months. Each month the family was asked about its income, and then the average income over the four months was included in the published statistics. I merely multiplied this by three to get an annual equivalent estimated income, to render the tables reported here for wealth compatible with those reported earlier for income.

6. For a more detailed analysis of recent changes in the patterns of employment and unemployment, investment and wage structures, taxes and social assistance programs, see Winnick (1985).

7. The minimum hourly wage has failed badly, especially since the early 1970s, to keep up with inflation, let alone improve the real wage position of the lowest paid workers. In 1960, it stood at $1.00, which in 1985 dollars would be $3.63. By 1974, it had increased to $2.00, which in 1985 dollars would amount to $4.36, a significant improvement in real terms. However, in 1985, it stood at only $3.35, which in real terms is 8% below the 1960 level and more than 23% below the 1974 level. If one assumes that a person worked 40 hours per week, 52 weeks per year at the minimum wage, and expressed the earnings in constant 1985 dollars, this would result in annual earnings of $7,550 in 1960, $9,069 in 1974 and only $6,968 in 1985.

13

Poverty, the Family, and Public Policy: Historical Interpretations and a Reflection on the Future

Robert F. Kelly

The 1980s witnessed efforts to reduce the size and scope of welfare programs targeted to low-income families. These efforts engendered both resistance and widespread reflection on the history and the future of the welfare system and the poor (Moynihan, 1986). Two illustrations of this reflective mood include the popularity of Charles Murray's (1984) *Losing Ground: American Social Policy, 1950-1980*, and the deliberations of the National Conference of Catholic Bishops on the Pastoral Letter on Catholic Social Teaching and the U.S. Economy (U.S. Bishops, 1986). The premise of this chapter is that opportunities for collective reflection are rare and should be seized and used to scrutinize the models that structure the issues of family, poverty, and social policy. The chapter seeks to contribute to this task by identifying three

AUTHOR'S NOTE: This chapter was written while the author was a Visiting Scholar at the Syracuse University College of Law. J. Ross Eshleman, Theo Majka, Sandra Moore, and Sarah H. Ramsey provided valuable comments.

ideal typical models that characterize the variety of policy responses to poverty and the family in this century, developing an historical analysis of each model, and using the models to explore the future of social policy toward poor families.

The three models of public policy toward poor families are the *laissez-faire model*, the *clinical model*, and the *family support model*. Each is described in the second section. Their historical origins, political development, and contemporary manifestations are discussed in the third section. Finally, lessons from the analysis of the models are used to develop an illustration of the need to move beyond each of the models.

THE THREE MODELS

The Laissez-Faire Model

Proponents of laissez-faire economics and politics contend that government brings dependency to the poor and intrusion and alienation to the family (Murray, 1984; Berger and Berger, 1983). They assert that private charity should address the needs of the deserving poor and that public welfare spawns a class of dependent, undeserving poor. Until 1981, the laissez-faire model had had little explicit influence on federal policy since the nineteenth century. This lack of influence should not be overstated. The laissez-faire model maintained significant strength throughout the twentieth century in state and local government, especially in southern and far western states.

The distinction between the deserving and undeserving poor is pivotal to the laissez-faire model and reflects its reliance on individualism. If poverty results from weak will, it follows that such individuals are undeserving and should be treated accordingly. If a person in poverty is truly unable to control his or her fate, then the label of deserving poor is applicable. Because the laissez-faire model sees the division between the deserving and undeserving poor as natural and because of fear that government aid will distort the distinction, proponents of laissez-faire oppose governmental involvement with the issue of poverty. Consistent with the Poor Law of 1834, the laissez-faire model accepts the concept of "less eligibility," that is, that life on relief should be less attractive than life with a job. The principle of less eligibility is for the labor market what the principle of restricting government regulation is for the economy as a whole. It allows market forces to produce efficient production and allocation decisions.

TABLE 13.1
Defining Characteristics of the Laissez-Faire, Clinical, and
Family Support Models of Public Policy Toward Poor Families

Laissez-Faire Model

Emphasizes *individual achievement* and *free markets*.
Believes in the adequacy of *private charity* as a response to poverty.
Emphasizes the need to distinguish between the *deserving and the undeserving poor*.
Fears that state welfare programs will create a *dependent class*.

The Clinical Model

Uses the *medical model* to analyze and treat poor families.
Focuses on *individual* rather than *structural* sources of poverty and family problems.
Places the poor in a *patient relationship* with service providing professionals.
Relies on an *optimistic view* of the ability of *science* to provide remedies for social ills.
Emphasizes *in-kind transfers and services* over cash transfers.
Gives rise to a *fragmented* social welfare system.
Engenders high *stigma* costs.

The Family Support Model

Emphasizes the *family* as a *group* over the *individual*.
Bases its analysis on an *institutional/structural critique* of the economy and the state vis-à-vis the family
Stresses cash transfers that are universal in coverage and unobtrusive in administration.

The strength of the laissez-faire model is not confined to conservative political and economic elites. According to most public opinion research, the distinction between the deserving and the undeserving poor is deeply embedded in the political ideology of the American public (Heclo, 1985) (see the first panel of Table 13.1 for the defining characteristics of the laissez-faire model).

The Clinical Model

Since the 1930s, the clinical model has exercised the greatest influence of the three models on social welfare policy. The clinical model maintains that individuals in poor families are to some degree ill, deviant, or underdeveloped in those characteristics associated with successful economic and social functioning. It follows that the illness requires professional attention to identify the problem and to pursue a course of treatment. For the clinical model, numerous generic pathologies exist, but the focus of treatment is the individual. The clinical model is an imposition of the medical model of physical pathology on the phenomena of the family and poverty. This model, with its origins in the progressive era, provided the impetus for the professionalization of social work and family services in the twentieth century.

The clinical model powerfully influenced the War on Poverty and, in spite of recent attacks upon Great Society programs, the clinical model remains pervasive in social welfare policy. For this reason, it is instructive to discern its manifestations in current welfare policy. In the social welfare system of the 1980s, one finds at least forty different income and in-kind transfer systems directly or indirectly intended to reduce poverty. Scores of other programs treat the poor with a plethora of sociomedical services (MacDonald, 1983). With few exceptions, cash, in-kind, and remedial service programs are targeted to specific groups who are defined by the common problems that the clinical model sees as engendering poverty. In a commentary on MacDonald's study of participation in these programs, the editors of *Focus* note the following:

> Each program has its own set of criteria for determining eligibility. Among the criteria are "the age and sex of the household head, the type of family, the presence of children and whether or not they are in school, the amount and source of the household members' income, the amount and type of their assets, their employment history and current employment status, their veterans status, their health, their location, their housing. . . [MacDonald, 1983, p. 5].

The clinical model has several notable characteristics, the *first* of which is its definition of poverty in individualistic rather than structural terms. This tendency deflects attention from systemic issues such as labor market structure and income distribution.

A *second* characteristic of the clinical approach is that it is costly because it spins off new programs, professions, and bureaucracies as new problems are identified. This feature of the clinical model, combined with the fact that states have discretion over the administration and funding of most federal poverty programs, results in hundreds of different types of programs across the nation. There is no doubt that these programs address real needs, but the point to emphasize is that the clinical model represents a unique, but not inevitable, way of structuring policy responses to poverty. One consequence of this approach is stigmatization. Because the poor are singled out as ill, they are stigmatized and placed in dependent relationships with professional service providers. Like any patient, they must take what is prescribed. Indeed, the notion of prescription helps to explain the American welfare system's attraction to *in-kind* programs. Food Stamps, Medicaid, and public housing tie consumption to prescribed remedial objectives. The model's assumption that the capacity of the poor is diminished implicitly dovetails with the laissez-faire concept of the undeserving poor. That is, neither an ill or an incompetent patient, nor a person who lives off the "dole" is trustworthy. The clinical model's structuring of the issue of poverty in these terms has two important consequences: (1) it facilitates the construction of regulatory bureaucracies that define the poor as deviant and exercise substantial social control over their lives, and (2) because it has encouraged the development of administrative systems that preserve the distinction between the deserving and undeserving poor, the clinical model is insensitive to the working poor whose only problem is an income deficit (Kelly, 1985; Donzelot, 1979).

Clearly income programs such as Aid to Families with Dependent Children (AFDC) are important parts of the public welfare system. As such, there are elements in the present system that are consistent with what is described as the family support model. It is not being argued that the American system fails to provide any form of family support, but rather that the way in which even cash programs are formulated is strongly influenced by the clinical model (see the second panel of Table 13.1 for the major tenets of the clinical model).

The Family Support Model

The family support model is the least prominent of the three models. Relative to the laissez-faire and clinical models, its historical manifestations have been brief. The family support model maintains that when the economy fails to provide sufficiently for the nation's families, these families, as units, are worthy of governmental support in the form of minimum family wages, family or child allowances, income support, or state sponsored employment (Dumon and Aldous, 1979; Ryan, 1906). It holds that when support is provided, it should be as universal as possible and that the administration of the programs should be unobtrusive. The model differs from the clinical model in several respects, but perhaps most important is its emphasis on the *family*, rather than the *individual*.

In this, the family support model is decidedly Catholic, European, collectivistic, and traditional, for it assumes that the family is an extremely valuable institution and that it requires protection from the modern economy and state. This proposition stands in contrast to the laissez-faire view of the poor family as morally weak and undeserving, and the clinical model's view of the poor family as ill.

The family support model employs a simple economic conception of poverty, poverty is the inability to buy goods and services at accepted social levels of consumption. It asserts that to respond to poverty, public policy should support a minimum family wage, employment programs for the jobless, and/or an income maintenance system. The model's emphasis on income and employment is based upon three beliefs: *first*, with adequate income and time most of the physical and behavioral disorders associated with poverty will heal, *second*, government regulation of the family should be limited, and *third*, income and employment support policies are the least intrusive methods of state involvement with families. Because of its agrarian and Catholic origins, the family support model profoundly mistrusts the modern economy and state (see the third panel of Table 13.1 for the basic tenets of the family support model).

THE THREE MODELS IN
HISTORICAL PERSPECTIVE

In this section an historical account of the three models is presented. Because the laissez-faire and clinical models are the most prominent, their stories are interwoven in the first part of the discussion. Because the family support model often goes unrecognized in historical accounts of social policy, and because it stands in contrast in many ways to the other models, its story is highlighted in the second part of the section.

Before discussing the history of each model it is important to consider two issues that influence the historical analysis of public policies toward poor families. *First*, the family and poverty have always been highly emotional and political issues in America. To the framers of the Constitution, the idea of family called forth suspicion because it evoked images of the privileged European aristocracy. The family was to be contained. It was for this reason that the power to make explicit family policy was retained by the states. In America, the ideals that inspired government were individualism and community based on fraternity, not family (Schorr, 1979; McWilliams, 1973; Rubin, 1986). This hostile view of the family made it difficult for Americans even to conceive of the term *family policy* (Moynihan, 1968). A similar hostility existed with respect to poverty. In a nation imbued with the work ethic and endowed with the seemingly limitless resources, poverty was viewed as a result of individual failure.

Second, it is difficult to discern a tradition of explicit family policies in the United States comparable to that in Europe (Schorr, 1979; Dumon and Aldous, 1979). As a result, it is best to describe the history of American family policy as an incremental body of implicit policies. However, in the case of public policies toward poor families this rule does not so fully obtain. For example, discourses concerning the regulation of immigrant family life and, later, fears of the so-called welfare class were explicit and policies focused openly on these concerns. Thus there is more historical material to mine when attention is focused on family policy toward the poor.

Of the three models of public policy the earliest was the laissez-faire. Its origins in the late eighteenth and nineteenth centuries may be divided into two stages. The first dates to pre-Civil War nineteenth-century America. It is epitomized in the images of the yeoman and pioneer families. This approach was more a rationale for dealing with poverty when it appeared than it was a public policy. At the time, the laissez-faire model held that if a person was poor, it was either because of laziness or because of lack of the initiative to find a better place to live in a nation so bountiful. There was a recognition that undeserved hardship could come upon families, but private charity was viewed as sufficient in such cases. At this time, it was difficult to conceive of state assistance for the poor because government was small and circumscribed. This preindustrial view of poverty was based on an image of the family as a rural, Protestant, and self-sufficient entity (Rubin, 1986, pp. 15, 17). In spite of its emphasis on the belief that one's station in life was the result of one's efforts, the charity of this time was ungrudging and based in a fraternal spirit (Cott, 1977).

In the last decades of the nineteenth century the rugged independence of the early laissez-faire model endured, but its focus changed to reflect the nation's increasing industrialization, urbanization, and the arrival of immigrants. In the new and evolving world of corporate capitalism, the solidarities of the previous era were weakened. The poverty of the immigrant slums could not be reconciled easily with the ideology of a bountiful land. Under these conditions the benign charity of the earlier stage of the model turned defensive and hostile.

As modern life became fragmented and urban, the family took on new meaning. The family became a haven in a heartless world in that it was differentiated, and eventually receded, from the public and economic spheres as state and corporate influences expanded (Lasch, 1977). In this context, the image and the reality of the nuclear family took on great importance. The nuclear family was seen as providing a sphere in which one's ascriptive identity as a family member was more important than what one did in the achievement-based public sphere.

This middle-class version of the laissez-faire model shared with the yeoman's version a faith in the individual and a distrust of government. Perhaps the best examples of this form of the laissez-faire model were the Charity Organization Societies of the 1880s and 1890s. These organizations opposed outdoor aid, aid to people in their homes, because it was feared that it would lead to dependency (Patterson, 1981, p. 21). Rather, an indoor workhouse approach was favored in which the poor could be better controlled. Control meant seeing that charity was given to the deserving and withheld from the undeserving poor.

The turn of the century decades witnessed the great migrations. It is understandable that the laissez-faire view of poverty and the nuclear family would prove inhospitable to the immigrants for they typically came from Catholic, peasant communities in which the family was held superior to the individual, the economy, and the state, if not the church.

The laissez-faire model characterized America's approach to poverty until the turn of the century, at which point the clinical model, under the influence of the Progressive Movement, increasingly exercised influence. In response to the laissez-faire tradition and the social transformations of this period, the Progressive Movement provided an alternative that stressed social reform and experimentation. Compulsory education was expanded, child labor and workers' compensation laws were enacted, and the profession of social work and the family and juvenile courts were invented (Kett, 1977).

The Progressive ideology saw reform as *prevention* and *rehabilitation*. In this, the success of the medical profession in public health provided a model for action. Lasch (1977, p. 15) notes:

> Educators, psychiatrists, social workers and penologists saw themselves as doctors to a sick society, and they demanded the broadest possible delegation of medical authority in order to heal it.

The Progressives believed that society could advance just as the human species had evolved. This notion, combined with the medical model, gave rise to both an optimistic and an individualistic ideology.

The clinical model defined poor and troubled families as individuals with specific illnesses or injuries (e.g., poor education, low motivation, poor housing and hygiene, drunkenness, promiscuity) who needed individual therapy. Because the diseases that gave rise to poverty could be communicated in the slums and within the family, it was necessary not only to treat existing illness, but also to prevent and control it through institutions such as public education and family and juvenile courts. The clinical model was also based on a vision of human nature as malleable (Lasch, 1977). Changing people for the better, or in less optimistic terms, controlling them, was the route chosen to respond to the massive changes that society was undergoing. This was a major departure from the vision of the laissez-faire model. For example, the Progressives had a positive faith in the ability of the economy to assimilate the immigrants and in the ability of the government to educate them. Further, in spite of the fact that the immigrants were viewed as ill or deviant, they were also thought to be curable through the practice of social and mental hygiene and "medical jurisprudence" (Lasch, 1977, p. 16).

This view, when combined with the optimism and individualism of the Progressives, proved overly simplistic in its virtual blindness to the structural sources of poverty. It was also *coercive*. In the name of progress, it built total institutions whose goals were to reform, reeducate, and control the immigrants (Kett, 1977; Lasch, 1977, Donzelot, 1979).

The optimism and humanism of the Progressives were dealt serious blows by the World War I. It was difficult to maintain that rational and progressive governments could perfect society, when the same governments were unable to avert the disasters of war and the ravages of a vengeful peace. With the economic expansion of the postwar 1920s, the Progressives and their ideology were in decline. However, the institutional foundations built by the Progressives, in the incipient social and family service professions, the therapeutic family and juvenile court systems, and the precedent that government had an ameliorative role to play, remained.

Some historians have suggested that the Progressive Movement did have a structural focus with the Settlement Houses given as the primary example (Axinn and Levin, 1975). To a degree, this is true. The movement certainly was not monolithic in nature. However, the point to be emphasized in an analysis of the issues of family and poverty policy is that the individualistic tendencies within the movement were strong and became dominant following the Russian Revolution—a period in which fear of institutional reform ran high and personal change was considered safe by comparison. These individualistic predispositions were further reinforced by the reception of Freudian psychoanalytic theory and practice in the 1920s and 1930s (Rieff, 1966).

During the Progressive Era, the laissez-faire model remained influential and the booming and optimistic period of the 1920s witnessed a minor resurgence of the model corresponding to the decline of the Progressive Movement. The Depression marked a major realignment of the influence of the three models of social policy. In the early days of the Depression the laissez-faire model, as professed by the Hoover administration, lost credibility under the weight of the stark reality of economic hardship. Large numbers of Americans, many of whom adhered to the laissez-faire view, were destitute through no apparent fault of their own. The laissez-faire model had no way to explain or respond to the Depression.

The clinical model expanded again during the Depression. In the early Depression years, the problems faced by government were so massive that the first response was to supply relief and public work—an approach consistent with the family support model. However, as the crisis abated, laissez-faire proponents criticized what they saw as the excesses of big government and the loss of privacy resulting from governmental intervention in the affairs of towns, states, and individuals. Hence they fought what was seen as the slow growth of state socialism. These criticisms had the effect of moving the New Deal away from family support policies and in the direction of the clinical model. Such influences can be seen in the Social Security Act that emphasized social insurance and categorical programs for the needy rather than income support.

During the late 1940s and 1950s the clinical model shaped policies concerning poor families, but the level of concern within government about poverty was minimal. The 1950s were prosperous years strikingly similar to the pre-Depression twenties. Indeed, in the late 1950s, there was a resurgence of the laissez-faire model's hostility to the poor and to public welfare (Patterson, 1981).

The 1960s brought the War on Poverty. As in the early days of the Depression, the first reaction to the perceived problems of poverty in the early 1960s was a structural analysis suggesting the need for income support and job creation programs—in short the family support model (Wilson and Neckerman, 1985; Patterson, 1981). This initial reaction gave way under criticism from proponents of both the laissez-faire and clinical models, the result being a rapid and massive expansion of programs guided by the clinical model.

The actual impact of the War on Poverty on the poor is a matter of substantial debate (Murray, 1984). However, the interpretation supported by the best available data is extremely revealing with respect to the clinical model. This view suggests that in the period 1965-1980, increases in the demand for labor were the best predictors of decreases in pretransfer poverty and that cash transfers did improve the condition of the poor, especially during periods of weak demand for labor (Danziger and Gottschalk, 1986). That is, cash transfer made a difference. Ironically, the thrust of the War on Poverty was ideologically and programatically on people changing rather than job creation or income support (Hamilton and Hamilton, 1985). Under the banner of providing opportunity, the Office of Economic Opportunity (OEO) engaged in community organization, personal rehabilitation, education, and other service programs. With the possible exception of legal services and Headstart, research suggests that the poor were not significantly better off because of these programs.

This evaluation of the War on Poverty should be tempered in certain respects. The optimism of the economic growth of the 1950s and the 1960s obscured the fact that the War on Poverty was a first attempt made by relatively young professions. Since the War on Poverty and because of it, policy analysts have learned that the poor are more rational than they are sick and that this rationality is expressed in self-interested responses to structural constraints in the social environment. The programs of the War on Poverty failed to have significant impacts, not because human nature is immutable, but because the opportunity structure that defined the lives of the poor remained largely unaltered by the programs.

The laissez-faire model experienced a resurgence during the Reagan administration. The Jepsen-Smith Family Protection Act, introduced in various forms in the Congress since 1981, is a laissez-faire document that seeks to deregulate the family. So also were the welfare provisions of the Omnibus Budget Reconciliation Act of 1981. The administration's strategy has been to reduce the federal government's power by decentralizing it into the hands of the states. This states' rights strategy is based on the belief that states are more responsible in their social spending than the Congress because they are more accountable to the electorate. In fact some research does indicate that the states are less generous to poor families than the federal government (Plotnick and Skidmore, 1975).[1] The emphasis on decentralization, in combination with the laissez-faire belief that competition should be introduced in federal programs, explains the Reagan administration's attraction to voucher programs in housing, health, and education programs.

Attention is next focused on the family support model. The ideal of the family's primacy over the economy and the state constantly appears in late nineteenth- and early twentieth-century papal thought (Leo XIII, 1891; Pius XI, 1931). The church of the eighteenth and nineteenth centuries was still a church of peasants, albeit peasants who were increasingly industrialized and urbanized. These transformations were viewed by Catholic social thinkers as a threat to the fabric of peasant family life, an institution that had provided for the intergenerational transmission of Catholicism for centuries. Because urban industrial life provided neither wage security nor alternatives to wage labor, it was argued that some form of *minimum living wage* was necessary (Baum, 1982; Ryan, 1906). Although Leo XIII did not mention the term *family living wage* in the 1891 encyclical *On the Condition of Labor*, the concept of a family living wage was inferred from the thrust of the statement and accepted by most contemporary European Catholic thinkers (Ryan, 1906, p. 110). It should also be noted that a Catholic socialist movement existed in the late nineteenth century and that its moderate thinkers influenced Leo (Ryan, 1906, p. 34). The family support model flourished in Europe because of the great needs resulting from the destruction of World War I and the Depression. In the late 1920s and 1930s family wages and income supplements for workers who headed households were won by family unions in Belgium and France. In the post-World War II period the family support model was championed by Christian Democrats, Social Democrats, and moderate socialists throughout Western Europe in the form of family and child allowances, income support, and job creation policies. The family support model has continued to characterize European social policy. Clinically oriented poverty and family service programs have only recently been introduced in Europe (Dumon and Aldous, 1979, p. 45).

In the early twentieth century the family support model did not fare well in the United States. For those few Americans who considered Catholic social thought, the family support model was sullied by its connection with the often conservative political stances taken by the church and the image of compliant peasants manipulated by a European ecclesiastical hierarchy (Dolan, 1985). Immigrants aware of the family support model were careful not to invoke it because they recognized that the collectivist aspects of Catholic social thought were antithetical both to the laissez-faire and the clinical models' approaches to the family and economy. While some Catholic socialists invoked the family support model and Catholic bishops periodically alluded to it in pastoral letters during the Depression, the family support model was seldom voiced by Catholics or their hierarchy in the first half of the century. An exception is John A. Ryan's book, *A Living Wage*, that built on the European tradition of family support and applied it to the American scene. Ryan (1906, p. viii), a priest and economist, described his book as an attempt to show

> that religion, as represented by the oldest and largest of the Christian denominations, professes, nay, urges, a definite and considerable measure of industrial justice.

It is understandable that the family support model did not gain support in the first decades of the century. With some exceptions the immigrant church was assimilationist in nature. Many influential bishops (e.g., Wood and Corrigan) strongly identified with business and provided only grudging support for the labor movement (Dolan, 1985). Further, the "red scare" often singled out and punished immigrant Catholics espousing the family support model either in Christian Democratic or socialist terms.

For all of its conservative heritage, the family support model was supportive of an institutional and critical analysis of family and poverty in relation to the capitalist economic order and the liberal state. Hence it carried a potentially radical message. Yet, with the exception of Ryan's book and the founding of the Catholic Worker Movement in 1933, it is difficult to document critical analyses of the American political economy produced by Catholic proponents of the family support approach until the 1960s. In spite of this, it is important to emphasize that this minority perspective contributed to an evolving perspective that families should be a focus of public policy and that the state and the capitalist economic order often harmed family life. This influence can be found throughout the twentieth century in the leadership and support that Catholic legislators provided for minimum wage and other employment legislation.

While the family support model never deeply penetrated American policy discourse, there were three short episodes in the twentieth century in which the model was considered seriously. In each, the early New Deal years, the early days of the War on Poverty, and the period of experimentation with negative income tax programs in the early 1970s, the family support model was supplanted by the clinical model, the laissez-faire model, or some combination of the two.

The family support model changed over time with respect to its goals. At the turn of the century what was first spoken of as a minimum living wage by Leo XIII was expanded in the concept of a minimum family living wage and later simply a family wage. With the Depression, this concept was adapted to the fact that many workers could not find employment. The result was another expansion of what the model meant by support, one that included direct income support and job supply programs.

The early days of the New Deal witnessed a strong but temporary reliance on the family support model. Because the laissez-faire model resisted the notion that state action should be taken in response to the Depression and because the clinical model was not yet sufficiently consolidated to provide direction in the face of such problems a policy vacuum existed. Hence a job and income support approach to the crisis consistent with the family support model was taken, and, to a large extent, it worked (Patterson, 1981, pp. 57-60). As the immediate crisis subsided and the administration considered institutionalizing its response, the laissez-faire and clinical models reasserted themselves in an oddly cooperative manner. Because the family support model implied a structural critique of American society, a laissez-faire backlash was to be expected. The backlash was based in the fear that the work ethic would be damaged by flirtations with socialism. These fears were coupled with criticism of the costs of the work and relief programs and disdain for the bureaucracies they engendered. Under these circumstances a compromise between the feared socialism of the family support model and the individualism of the laissez-faire approach was found in the clinical model. The clinical model emphasized the development of opportunities for recovery, rather than income support through redistributive methods. Hence it appeared responsive, cost-effective, and supportive of the work ethic. As such, the clinical model effectively supplanted the structural critique made by the family support model and explicitly recognized the undeniably devastating effects of poverty.

A process similar to that occurring during the New Deal took place in the early 1960s. It is beyond the scope of this discussion to examine the reasons that a poverty crisis was perceived to exist in the early 1960s. However, convincing evidence suggests that such a crisis did exist and that the first response to it was a "structural" one consistent with the family support model (Wilson and Neckerman, 1985; Patterson, 1981, pp. 94-96). The best example of the structuralist critique and its relationship to the family support model was Harrington's (1962) book, *The Other America*, and the manner in which it was received by the Kennedy administration. It is not coincidental that Harrington, a democratic socialist, had experienced the Catholic Worker Movement as a young man. After a brief period of discussion and experimentation with programs consistent with the family support model, the entrenched clinical model reasserted itself and gave direction to the War on Poverty (Hamilton and Hamilton, 1985).

In the late 1960s, owing to frustration with the welfare system, policymakers again considered the family support approach in the form of a negative income tax (NIT). The reasons for this concern are instructive. The categorical nature of the programs that derived from the clinical model's conception of poverty had excluded many families from support—namely, the working poor and two-parent families. Policy analysts such as Moynihan were also concerned about the suspected marriage disincentive of the AFDC system's eligibility rules favoring single-parent over two-parent families. Moynihan was a Catholic, but more important he was a member of the first generation of a native-born Catholic intelligencia and he had returned to Catholic social theory as a point of departure for his own social policy analysis. It is not coincidental that he was attracted to the idea of a NIT.

There was also a laissez-faire interest in the NIT. Neoclassical economist Milton Friedman (1962) argued that the costs of running a categorical welfare system were excessive. He suggested that a NIT fully integrated with the income tax system would reduce these costs and eliminate the irrational cumulative tax rates among welfare programs.

Two events shaped the fate of this encounter with the family support model, the Nixon administration's Family Assistance Plan (FAP) in the early 1970s and the income maintenance experiments of the late 1960s and 1970s. FAP was presented as a solution to "the welfare mess," that is, the expanding size and cost of the welfare system and its costly bureaucracy. FAP was a radical departure from past welfare policies because one- and two-parent families and the working poor were to be covered. It was unique in defining participation not simply in terms of social illness or poverty, but also in terms of a family role—that of parent. Hence FAP was a direct assault upon the clinical model. FAP was also a conservative program in that it carried a small price and contained strict work requirements. But FAP was also traditional as most family support programs are traditional in that it sought to enhance family integrity against the intrusiveness of the state and the unpredictability of the economy. As such, FAP was a plan consistent with the European and Catholic family support models.

FAP failed because, while it contained provisions intended to gain the support of most interest groups, it contained at least one provision that alienated each important interest group. Conservatives could not abide providing an income floor for the poor. Family support activists found the support levels low and the work requirements unacceptable. Finally, the clinical model's proponents, because they saw FAP as a challenge to their professional control of the poverty business, attacked the program (Patterson, 1981).

The negative income tax experiments were initiated because of concern that reforms in the income maintenance system such as a NIT would reduce work effort. This question was important because, unlike any existing categorical programs, a NIT would cover males during prime working years. Hence it was felt that there was a need to assess the program's labor supply impact and the degree to which it could be administered effectively. Because it seemed clear that a NIT would enhance family stability, the experiments were also concerned with measuring the extent of the expected improvements.

By the time the experiments ended in the late 1970s, political interest in a NIT had passed due to FAP's failure, inflation, and a weak economy. The results of the experiments further sealed this fate. On the work disincentive issue, the first set of experiments (New Jersey) found a rather low labor supply reduction rate, 6%-12% depending on the generosity of the programs, for men and higher levels for women. The corresponding figures were higher in the second set of experiments (Seattle/Denver Income Maintenance Experiments, SIME/DIME), but not by a large amount. These findings alone were not sufficient to damage the concept of a NIT. However, the marital instability findings from SIME/DIME were a public policy bombshell. After two and a half years, marital instability increased 80% for whites and 42% for blacks in the experimental groups in the SIME/DIME study (Bishop, 1980). The NIT was expected to stabilize families rather than disrupt them! While the interpretation of the marital instability findings have been criticized on methodological and ideological grounds, they are well established in the minds of policymakers. A NIT is dead for the foreseeable future because in addition to its costs and labor supply effects, it is considered to be destructive of family bonds.

CONCLUSION

The Welfare Dilemma and Future Demands on Family Policy

It has been argued that the laissez-faire, clinical, and family support models serve as useful ideal types of the modes of policy analysis brought to bear on the issues of poverty and family in the United States. In this section the limitations of each model and the prospects for moving beyond them are discussed. To evaluate the models it is important to understand what is expected of welfare and family policies. This is done in two ways, *first* through a discussion of how each model responds to the issues that constitute the so-called welfare dilemma and *second* by describing two socioeconomic trends that will powerfully effect the demands made on social policy in the next two decades.

Debates concerning the meaning and resolution of the welfare dilemma revolve around a number of related issues upon which the models take distinct positions. The most important of these issues include (1) the meaning of *economic justice*, (2) the long- and short-term *costs* of the social welfare system, (3) the issue of *work disincentives*, (4) the degree to which the welfare system includes the *working poor*, (5) the *categorical* nature of programs, (6) the impact of welfare programs on *family formation* and *dissolution*, (7) the *stigma* effect of the system, and (8) the *multiple-program/tax rate* structure of the system.

It is possible to show how each of the models handles each of these issues in a manner that leads to conflict. For the present discussion, it will suffice to give two such examples.

Considering the *categorical* nature of the welfare system, one finds that the laissez-faire proponents, when faced with clinically oriented categorical programs, either oppose them on the basis of cost and intrusiveness or use them to enhance social control by reinforcing the distinction between the deserving and undeserving poor through income reporting, work requirements, and stigma-laden programs such as Food Stamps. The clinical model is supportive of categorical programs because it is thought that they facilitate treatment. Many clinical proponents recognize that categorical programs engender stigma and they support initiatives to minimize these effects. The family support model strongly opposes categorical programs and favors universal or unobtrusive income-tested transfer and work programs.

There is also the issue of the welfare system's *stigma effect*, namely, that the work involved in participating in the welfare system frequently is degrading. For the clinical model, stigma is a cost of doing business implicit in the medical model. For the family support proponents, stigma is an unnecessary and harmful element in the welfare system. They seek to eliminate it by integrating income support with the tax system and cashing out service and in-kind programs (Moynihan, 1986; U.S. Bishops, 1986). They also note that stigma discounts the value of transfers and, that when internalized, it contributes to a host of stress-related problems. It is precisely because of the discounting effect of stigma that such procedures are attractive to laissez-faire proponents. Stigma raises the transaction costs of welfare and makes low-wage employment more attractive because it reduces the opportunity cost of employment. Laissez-faire supporters view stigma, *first*, as a deterrent to any unjustified use of public funds, and, *second*, as a symbolic reward for those who choose work over the dole, in short, stigma enhances social control.

The antagonistic positions of the three models on the question of the categorical structure of welfare and stigma are repeated for each of the other major issues constituting the welfare dilemma. It is because of these antagonisms that all recent efforts to reform welfare have failed. Of course, the welfare dilemma has existed for some time—and history has the disquieting capacity to add new and urgent problems to those that have not yet been resolved. Two such problems will have an important impact on welfare and family policy in the near future.

The *first* trend is the result of the structural transformation of the American economy from one with a large and relatively well-paid industrial working class to one that is technologically sophisticated, service oriented, and increasingly weak in terms of its international trade position. While the service sector has generated significant employment opportunities, new jobs tend to be of two types, those requiring high degrees of technical training and those that are relatively unskilled, unorganized, and low paid. Unemployed industrial workers generally cannot compete for the first type of job and are dissatisfied with the second because such jobs result in a lowered standard of living, that is skidding. How former-skilled and semiskilled industrial workers and their children respond to diminished status in a progressively dualized labor market will have a great impact on the future demands placed upon the social welfare system (Bluestone and Harrison, 1982).

The *second* trend is the development and entrenchment of an urban underclass. It is clear that the configuration of poverty in America has changed markedly in the last two decades. Poverty has been dualized in two senses, first certain sectors of the population have made significant strides toward income independence while others have become more deeply entrenched in poverty, and second the income differential between the poor and the well off has widened and the position of the middle class has eroded. One group that has made substantial progress is the elderly. In 1969, 28.5% of the elderly lived below the official poverty level; by 1983 the comparable figure, including adjustments for in-kind transfers, was 3.3%, nearly a 90% decrease (Danziger, Haveman, and Plotnick, 1985). On the other hand, the position of single women with children, black women in particular, children, and young black men has deteriorated precipitously and certain sectors of these groups now constitute an underclass (Kelly, 1985). In this context, it is important to recognize that among employed black men, occupational status has improved significantly in the last four decades (Wilson and Neckerman, 1985). What has occurred is that jobs in the middle sectors of the labor market are less plentiful in general and this has had a disproportionately large negative effect on young, black workers, who previously would have entered these sectors. These developments leave black women with an increasingly small pool of economically "marriageable" men and, as a result, there is increased poverty and dependence on welfare.

Given how each model deals with the major issues that constitute the welfare dilemma and given the two socioeconomic trends that are transforming American social structure, what are the major strengths and weaknesses of each model?

The major strength of the laissez-faire model is its emphasis on enhancing economic independence. In this it shares common ground with the family support model. However, economic independence for the laissez-faire model is defined in negative terms—specifically as freedom from the intrusiveness that laissez-faire supporters see as characteristic of the clinical model. Because of the laissez-faire model's emphasis on the individual, it lacks an appreciation of the institutional factors influencing family life. It fails to recognize that family independence is not a matter of simply protecting families from the state, but also involves active support of the family when it is endangered by economic change. Hence the laissez-faire model has little to contribute with respect to macro-institutional trends such as deindustrialization or the development of an underclass.

In terms of future social policies, it is likely the laissez-faire model will exercise a veto over the expansion of programs based on the clinical model regardless of the political party in power. More important for fashioning future policy is the fact that political and public sentiment has settled upon the conviction that family independence from governmental intrusiveness is a virtue (Heclo, 1985).

The major strengths of the clinical model are its emphasis on the ill-nesses—social, psychological, and physical—that result from poverty and its realization that this relationship is stress related (Syme and Berkman, 1976). However, the understanding of the stress-related nature of pathologies among the poor is not fully utilized by the clinical model because of its adherence to a disease-specific therapeutic, rather than epidemiological/structural, approach. The broader structural approach suggests that higher degrees of stress are found among the poor because of income deficits that have their source in the political economy and re-sult in increased levels of stress that have the generalized effect of reduc-ing the host organism's resistance (Kelly, 1985). It follows that illness and injury can be reduced among the poor on a wide scale only if stress levels are reduced and that this is likely to occur only if income levels rise. In-come support through transfers or employment should be viewed as a necessary but not a sufficient strategy for dealing with poverty. That is, there will be a continuing need for clinical strategies, but clinical pro-grams without income support are nearly certain to be ineffective. This conclusion is supported by epidemiological stress research and by the failures of service programs that lacked a strong income support component.

While it is true that targeted remedial services have a poor record, the targeting of income support to specific categories of the poor has been successful (Danziger and Gottschalk, 1985). The best example of this suc-cess is the vast improvement in the income position of the elderly in the last two decades. Thus in evaluating categorical programs based on the clinical model, it is crucial to distinguish between categorical income pro-grams and categorical service programs. The former have a relatively suc-cessful record, while the latter do not. This distinction is important because although categorical programs increase the risk of stigma, the risk has a greater payoff with income rather than service programs.

There are two other weaknesses inherent in the clinical model. The first is the bureaucratic costliness of the large number of programs that the model engenders. The second is the development of professional groups whose interests often do not foster realistic assessments of the typically ineffectual outcomes of clinical programs for the poor.

The major strengths of the family support model have been discussed implicitly in relation to the other two models. Because of the family support model's emphasis on income support, it is compatible with stress theories of the pathologies of economic hardship. Similarly, its reliance on an institutional analysis of the economy and family better prepares it to deal with the welfare dilemma and transformations in American society previously discussed. These features of the family support model explain its attraction to some liberals and even some neo-Marxians. The model also possesses some appeal for conservatives because of its emphasis on preserving family independence against excessive state intervention.

The major weakness of the family support model is cost. A universal family/child support system is currently out of the question for budgetary reasons. The same is true with respect to a negative income tax, which has the added difficulty of fears about work disincentives and marital instability.

The Future of Public Policy Toward Poor Families

In the late 1970s, the Manpower Development Research Corporation (MDRC) conducted the National Supported Work Demonstration (NSWD). The program was targeted at four underclass groups: long-term welfare women, ex-drug addicts, nonviolent felon parolees, and troubled youth who had not completed high school. Supported work's goals were to improve employment and employability, reduce welfare dependency, criminal behavior and drug use, and enhance family stability by providing counseling and job training in a supervised work situation where expectations were gradually increased and positive reinforcement and group/peer support were readily available (Hollister, Kemper, and Maynard, 1984).

Supported work is crucial to the present analysis for three reasons. *First*, supported work was successful in achieving its goals for dependent welfare mothers and to lesser degrees ex-addicts and ex-convicts. It had virtually no impact on troubled youth. Successful work programs are rare in the American experience. *Second*, the thinking behind the program's development was extremely eclectic. Supported work drew upon behaviorism, human capital theory, dual labor market theory, and sociological stress theory (Kelly, 1985). Eclecticism is not itself virtue, but the eclecticism of the supported work program was focused on a clear goal, getting something to work for the poor. *Third*, supported work provides a clear example of the benefits of going beyond each of the three models and formulating new ones. Just as supported work was based on a synthesis of many social scientific approaches to poverty, so also its success may be attributed to the fact that it moved beyond each of the three models.

Supported work's responsiveness to the concerns of the family support model may be seen in the primacy it placed on providing paid employment to participants. It also recognized that its participants had been harmed by long histories of poverty. Thus consistent with the clinical model, supported work possessed a remedial component. Above all else, the program recognized paid employment was a necessary condition for the remedial component to be effective. Supported work was based firmly both in an understanding of the effects of stress on the individual and the institutional sources of stress. Finally, the program was responsive to the laissez-faire model in its concern for the development of independent living and its emphasis on the integration of participants with the formal labor market. Two editorial comments in the *New York Times* (1980, p. 20E) capture the degree to which supported work bridged the three models:

> Liberals have long contended that even the most dependent welfare recipients possess the work ethic. Conservatives have long contended that welfare funds can be used to encourage work. This experiment shows that both are right.

> For taxpayers, it [supported work] can mean spending fewer dollars for welfare. For welfare recipients, it can mean earning more dollars, and pride, from work.

It is not being suggested that supported work is a panacea for all of the problems of poor families, but rather that it represents a unique and valuable lesson. Hence attention is next focused on pushing the concept of supported work beyond each of the models and in doing so exploring the future of welfare and family policy.

An expanded national supported work program would be responsive to the needs of poor families and the nation. Research has demonstrated that supported work is effective in integrating certain sectors of the underclass with the labor market—in particular dependent welfare mothers and ex-addicts. While supported work had little impact on parolees and troubled youth, it is likely this resulted from supported work's lack of an employment guarantee and the program's low-wage levels relative to those available in the underground economy. If the base wage and wage rates of supported work could be made more competitive with those in the informal economy, that is, if the opportunity costs of employment in the formal economy were reduced, two valuable objectives might be achieved: (1) the size of the underclass could be reduced and productive labor added to the economy, and (2) tax revenues lost to the informal economy could be recaptured and these benefits might in themselves offset the cost of increased wage rates and job guarantees.

An expanded supported work system could be fully integrated with the AFDC system. Indeed, such a provision was included in the proposed Family Economic Security Act of 1985 (Moynihan, 1985). AFDC is a well-targeted program and over half of all first-time AFDC recipients leave the welfare rolls after two years (Ellwood and Bane, 1984). These are women with dependent children who because of divorce, separation, abandonment, death of a spouse, or unemployment need short-term financial support and who, on their own, will successfully enter the labor market. For these reasons, participation in a supported work program should not be required until a first-time recipient has received AFDC benefits for 18 to 24 months. Such an approach would have the effect of building on AFDC's strength as a source of short-term financial support, while delaying the intrusiveness that supported work would necessarily involve until absolutely necessary. By keeping supported work targeted to those who most need it, cost-effectiveness would be enhanced.

The expansion of supported work into a national program along these lines would require political compromise among adherents of the three models of poverty policy. As noted, the idea of a guaranteed income in the form of a NIT system is dead for the foreseeable future. However, there is substantial support for providing some type of income floor for Americans, albeit with a heavy reliance on in-kind transfers. At the same time there is strong sentiment for work requirements as conditions for receiving welfare. Much of the difficulty with past work requirements resulted from the fact that an insufficient supply of jobs existed, and that of those jobs available, few were of the type that led to a better future. The compromise proposed here is that the supported work program would be both *required* and *guaranteed*. The requirement that AFDC recipients enter the program after 18 months presumably would be politically attractive to laissez-faire proponents. While work requirements have generally been objectionable to proponents of the family support model, the guarantee of a supported work job should elicit support because income support would be provided through a program with a proven record for enhancing independent living. It should also be noted that results from recent research on job guarantee programs for poor young workers support the suggestion that guarantees significantly increase the benefits of employment programs (Gueron, 1984). It is also important to emphasize that the states are currently under pressure to initiate or enhance workfare-type programs. Supported work is clearly the best available model for such programs and it is encouraging that states such as Michigan and New York are using it in just this manner.

Job guarantees, improved base wages, and wage scales are important for three reasons: (1) they will increase the attractiveness of supported work relative to the informal economy for groups such as male criminals and troubled youth, (2) they will further the goal of providing an income floor, and (3) the more attractive the program, the more likely it is that it would provide a useful vehicle for retraining long-term displaced industrial workers.

Clearly, supported work cannot be all things to all people. For example, the proposals outlined here only indirectly touch on the problems of the working poor. More important than the proposal itself, however, is the fact supported work represents the type of cross-model thinking that places the interests of poor families above that of ideological purity. The proposal dares to use the terms *work guarantee* and *work requirement* simultaneously, both as a demand for a quality employment program and as a compromise in order to achieve the goal of basic income security. Is this heresy? It is argued that it is not, especially when the proposal is embedded in a program such as supported work—a program that rigorous evaluation research indicates can make a difference in the lives of poor families.

NOTE

1. There is evidence that the Reagan administration has forced the states into a less laissez-faire approach to poverty policy. Examples include states cooperating in suits against the administration's policy of cutting Social Security disability benefits, expanding health care for the poor, and increased educational spending.

References

Acosta, Frank Xavier, Ralph A. Catalano, Jeanne P. Gordus, and Paula Rayman. 1985. *Unemployment and Mental Health: A Report on Research Resources for Technical Assistance.* Prepared for the National Institute of Mental Health.

Aiken, Michael, Louis A. Ferman, and Harold L. Sheppard. 1966. *Economic Failure, Alienation and Extremism.* Ann Arbor: University of Michigan.

Alexander, T. 1982. "Practical Uses for a Useless Science." *Fortune* (May):138-145.

American Public Welfare Association. 1985. *A Matter of Choice: Investing in Low-Income Families and Their Children.* Washington, DC: American Public Welfare Association.

———1986. *One in Four: Report on Children and Poverty.* Washington DC: American Public Welfare Association.

Anderson, E. 1978. *A Place on the Corner.* Chicago: University of Chicago Press.

Anderson, M. 1978. *Welfare.* Stanford, CA: Hoover Institute Press.

Angell, Robert C. 1936. *The Family Encounters the Depression.* New York: Scribner.

Apple, Michael. 1982. *Power and Education.* Boston: Routledge & Kegan Paul.

Atkinson, Thomas, Ramsay Liem, and Joan H. Liem. 1986. "The Social Costs of Unemployment: Implications for Social Support." *Journal of Health and Social Behavior* 27:317-331.

Atleson, James B. 1983. *Values and Assumptions in American Labor Law.* Amherst: University of Massachusetts Press.

Auletta, K. 1982. *The Underclass.* New York: Random House.

Axinn, June and Hermann Levin. 1975. *Social Welfare: A History of the American Response Need.* New York: Dodd, Mead.

Ayres, R. and S. Miller. 1981-1982. "Robotics, CAM, and Industrial Productivity." *National Productivity Review* 1:42-66.

———1982. "Industrial Robots on the Line." *Technology Review* (May/June):35-46.

Bagshaw, Michael and Robert H. Schnorbus. 1980. "The Local Market Response to a Plant Shutdown." *Economic Review* (Federal Reserve Bank of Cleveland) (January):16-24.

Bailey, Stephen K. 1950. *Congress Makes a Law.* New York: Columbia.

Bakke, E. Wight. 1933. *The Unemployed Man.* London: Nisbet.

———1940. *Citizens Without Work: A Study of the Effects of Unemployment upon the Worker's Social Relations and Practices.* New Haven, CT: Yale University Press.

Bane, Mary Jo. 1984. "Household Composition and Poverty: Which Comes First?" Williamsburg Conference, Institute for Research on Poverty, University of Wisconsin—Madison.

———1986. "Household Composition and Poverty." In *Fighting Poverty: What Works and What Doesn't,* edited by Sheldon Danziger and D. Weinberg. Cambridge, MA: Harvard University Press.

———and David T. Ellwood. 1983. *Dynamics of Dependency and Routes of Self-Sufficiency.* Cambridge, MA: Harvard University (Final Report to U.S. Department of Health and Human Services).

Barnett, Rosalind and Grace K. Baruch. 1985. "Women's Involvement in Multiple Roles, Role Strain, and Psychological Distress." *Journal of Personality and Social Psychology* 49:135-145.

Baruch, Grace K. and Rosalind Barnett. 1986. "Role Quality, Multiple Role Involvement, and Psychological Well-Being of Midlife Women." *Journal of Personality and Social Psychology* 51:578-585.

Baum, Gregory. 1982. *The Priority of Labor: A Commentary on Laborem Exercens.* New York: Paulist Press.

Beale, R. L. 1986. "Multiple Work-Family Role Strain and Psychological Well- *Being* among Black Americans." *Dissertation, University of Michigan.*

Beauregard, Robert A., Carl E. Van Horn, and David Ford. 1983. "Governmental Assistance to Displaced Workers: A Historical Perspective." *Journal of Health and Human Resources Administration* 6:166-184.

Bell, W. 1965. *Aid to Dependent Children.* New York: Columbia University Press.

Bellah, Robert N., R. Madsen, W. M. Sullivan, A. Swidler, and S. M. Tipton. 1985. *Habits of the Heart: Individualism and Commitment in American Life.* Berkeley: University of California Press.

Belle, D. ed. 1982. *Lives in Stress.* Beverly Hills, CA: Sage.

Bendick, Marc. 1983a. "The Swedish 'Active Labor Market' Approach to Reemploying Workers Dislocated by Economic Change." *Journal of Health and Human Resources Administration* 6:209-225.

————1983b. "The Role of Public Programs and Private Markets in Reemploying Displaced Workers." *Policy Studies Review* 2:715-733.

————and Terry F. Buss. n.d. "Workers Displaced by Plant Closings in the Youngstown/Warren Area." (unpublished)

Berger, Brigitte. 1979. "The Family and Mediating Structures as Agents for Child Care." Pp. 1-16 in *Child Care and Mediating Structures,* edited by Brigitte Berger and Sidney Callahan. Washington, DC: American Enterprise Institute.

————1980. "The Family as a Mediating Structure." Pp. 144-169 in *Democracy and Mediating Structures,* edited by Michael Novak. Washington, DC: American Enterprise Institute.

————and Peter L. Berger. 1983. *The War Over the Family: Capturing the Middle Ground.* Garden City, NY: Doubleday.

Bishop, John. 1980. "Jobs, Cash Transfers, and Marital Instability: A Review and a Synthesis of the Evidence." *Journal of Human Resources* 15:301-334.

Block, Fred. 1977. "The Ruling Class Does Not Rule." *Socialist Revolution* 33:6-28.

————1984a. "The Myth of Reindustrialization." *Socialist Review* 14(73):59-76.

————1984b. "The Political Perils of Full Employment." *Socialist Review* 14(75/76): 24-29.

————1984c. "Technological Change and Employment: New Perspectives on an Old Controversy." *Economia & Lavoro* 18:3-21.

————1985. "Postindustrial Development and the Obsolescence of Economic Categories." *Politics & Society* 14:71-104.

————Richard A. Cloward, Barbara Ehrenreich, and Frances Fox Piven. 1986. "The Trouble With Full Employment." *The Nation* (May):694-697.

Bluestone, Barry and Bennett Harrison. 1982. *The Deindustrialization of America: Plant Closings, Community Abandonment and the Dismantling of Basic Industry.* New York: Basic Books.

Bould, Sally. 1980. "Unemployment as a Factor in Early Retirement." *American Journal of Economics and Sociology* 39:123-136.

Bowles, Roy and Eli Newberger. 1982. "Violence Experienced by Children: Issues of Etiology for Different Manifestations." Paper presented at the annual meeting of the American Public Health Association.

Bowles, Samuel and Herbert Gintis. 1976. *Schooling in Capitalist America.* New York: Basic Books.

Bowles, Samuel, David M. Gordon, and Thomas E. Weisskopf. 1983. *Beyond the Wasteland.* Garden City, NY: Doubleday.

Bowman, Phillip J. 1980. "Toward a Dual Labor Market Approach to Black-on-Black Homicide." *Public Health Reports* 95:555-556.

———1983a. "Significant Involvement and Functional Relevance: A Challenge to Survey Research." *Social Work Research* 19:21-26.

———1983b. "Quality of Family Life Among Black Husband-Fathers: Impact of Economic Marginality and Cultural Resources." Paper presented at Groves Conference on Marriage and the Family.

———1984. "A Discouragement-Centered Approach to Studying Unemployment among Black Youth: Hopelessness, Attributions and Psychological Distress." *International Journal of Mental Health* 13:68-91.

———1985. "Black Fathers and the Provider Role: Strain, Informal Coping Resources and Life Happiness." Pp. 9-19 in *Empirical Research in Black Psychology,* edited by A. W. Boykin. Washington, DC: National Institute for Mental Health.

———G. Gurin, and C. Howard. 1984. *Motivation and Economic Mobility of the Poor: A Longitudinal Study of Black Youth.* Ann Arbor, MI: Institute for Social Research (Final Report to U.S. Department of Health and Human Services).

Bowman, Phillip J. and C. Howard. 1985. "Race-related Socialization, Motivation and Academic Achievement: A Study of Black Youth in Three Generation Families." *Journal of the American Academy of Child Psychiatry* 24:134-141.

Bowman, Phillip J., J. S. Jackson, S. J. Hatchett, and G. Gurin. 1982. "Joblessness and Discouragement among Black Americans." *Economic Outlook U.S.A.* (Autumn):85-88.

Bradbury, Katharine L. 1986. "The Shrinking Middle Class." *New England Economic Review* (September/October):41-55.

Bramel, Dana and Ron Friend. 1981. "Hawthorne, the Myth of the Docile Worker, and Class Bias in Psychology." *American Psychologist* 36:867-878.

Brenner, M. Harvey. 1973. *Mental Illness and the Economy.* Cambridge, MA: Harvard University Press.

———1976. *Estimating the Social Costs of National Economic Policy: Implications for Mental and Physical Health and Criminal Aggression.* Testimony before Joint Economic Committee 94th Congress, October 26. Washington, DC: Government Printing Office.

———1979. "Influence of the Social Environment on Psychopathology: The Historic Perspective." Pp. 161-175 in *Stress and Mental Disorder,* edited by J. E. Barrett. New York: Raven.

Briggs, V. M. 1970. "The Negro in American Industry: A Review of Seven Studies." *Journal of Human Resources* 5:371-381.

Brimmer, A. 1973. *Employment and Income in the Black Community: Trends and Outlook.* Los Angeles, CA: UCLA Institute of Government Affairs.

———1974. "Economic Developments in the Black Community." *Public Interest* (Winter):48.

———1976. "Economic Growth, Employment and Income Trends among Black Americans." Pp. 142-163 in *Jobs for Americans,* edited by Eli Ginzberg. Englewood Cliffs, NJ: Prentice-Hall.

Brody, David. 1980. *Workers in Industrial America.* New York: Oxford.

Bryant, Barbara E. 1975. "Respondent Selection in a Time of Changing Household Composition." *Journal of Marketing Research* 12:129-135.

Buckingham, W. 1961. *Automation: Its Impact on Business and People.* New York: Harper.

Bureau of National Affairs. 1986. *Work and Family: A Changing Dynamic.* Washington, DC: author.

Burr, Wesley R. 1973. "Families Under Stress." *Theory Construction and Sociology of the Family,* edited by Wesley R. Burr. New York: John Wiley.

Buss, Terry F. 1956. "Assessing the Accuracy of BLS Local Unemployment Rates: A Case Study." *Labor and Industrial Relations Review* 39:241- 250.

———1984. *A Labor Market Study of the Youngstown/Warren SMSA.* Columbus: Ohio Bureau of Employment Services.

———and F. Stevens Redburn. 1980. "Evaluating Human Service Delivery During a Plant Shutdown." *Journal of Health and Human Resources Administration* 3:229-250.

———1983a. *Shutdown at Youngstown: Public Policy for Mass Unemployment.* Albany: State University of New York Press.

———1983b. *Mass Unemployment: Plant Closings and Community Mental Health.* Beverly Hills, CA: Sage.

Cass, Bettina. 1986. "Income Support for Families." *Social Security Review Issue Paper No. 1.* Canberra, ACT, Australia: Department of Social Security.

Catalano, Ralph. 1982. Reported in Michael Waldholz "Child Abuse Seems to be Increasing in Areas with High Unemployment." *Wall Street* Journal (August 6).

———and David Dooley. 1980. "Economic Change in Primary Prevention." Pp. 21-40 in *Prevention in Mental Health: Research, Policy, and Practice,* edited by R. H. Price, R. F. Ketterer, B. C. Bader, and J. Monahan. Beverly Hills, CA: Sage.

Cavan, Ruth S. and Katharine H. Ranck. 1938. *The Family and the Depression: A Study of One Hundred Chicago Families.* Chicago: University of Chicago Press.

Cazenave, Noel A. 1981. "Black Men in America: The Quest for Manhood." Pp. 176-185 in *Black Families,* edited by Harriette P. McAdoo. Beverly Hills, CA: Sage.

Cetron, M. and T. O'Toole. 1982. *Encounters with the Future: A Forecast of Life into the 21st Century.* New York: McGraw-Hill.

Cherlin, Andrew. 1979. "Work Life and Marital Dissolution." In *Divorce and Separation,* edited by George Levinger and Oliver C. Moles. New York: Basic Books.

———1981. *Marriages Divorce, Remarriage.* Cambridge, MA: Harvard University Press.

Choates, P. 1982. *Retooling the American Work Force.* Washington, DC: Northwest-Midwest Institute.

Ciancanelli, Penelope. 1983. "Women's Transition to Wage Labor: A Critique of Labor Force Statistics and Reestimation of Labor Force Participation of Married Women in the United States from 1900 to 1930." Unpublished Ph.D. thesis, New School for Social Research.

Cobb, Sidney. 1974. "A Model for Life Events and Their Consequences." *Stressful Life Events,* edited by B. Dohrenwend and B. P. Dohrenwend. New York: John Wiley.

———and Stanislav V. Kasl. 1977. *Termination: The Consequences of Job Loss.* Cincinnati, OH: National Institute for Occupational Safety and Health.

Cohn, Richard M. 1978. "The Effects of Employment Status Change on Self Attitudes." *Social Psychology* 41:51-93.

Coles, Robert. 1967. *Children of Crisis.* Boston: Little, Brown.

Collins, Glen. 1983. "Children and Stress: A Search for Causes." *New York Times* (October 3).

Coser, Lewis A. and Irving Howe. 1974. *The New Conservatives.* New York: Quadrangle.

Cott, Nancy F. 1977. *The Bonds of Womanhood: "Woman's Sphere" in New England, 1780-1835.* New Haven, CT: Yale University Press.

Cronkite, Ruth C. and Rudolf H. Moos. 1984. "The Role of Predisposing and Moderating Factors in the Stress-Illness Relationship." *Journal of Health and Social Behavior* 25:372-393.

Croog, S. H. 1970. "The Family as a Source of Stress." Pp. 19-53 in *Social Stress,* edited by S. Levine and N. A. Scoth. Chicago: Aldine.

Cross, T. 1985. *The Black Power Imperative: Racial Inequality and the Politics of Nonviolence.* New York: Faulkner.

Curran, Charles E. 1977. "American and Catholic: American Catholic Social Ethics 1880-1965." *Thought* 52:50-74.

Curtin, Richard T., Christopher J. Gordon, and Michael Ponza. 1981. "Coping with Unemployment among American Households." *Economic Outlook U.S.A.* 8:39-41.

Danziger, Sheldon. 1985. *The Impact of the Reagan Budget Cuts on Working Welfare Women in Wisconsin.* Madison: University of Wisconsin, Institute for Research in Poverty.

―――and Peter Gottschalk. 1985. "The Poverty of Losing Ground." *Challenge* 28:32-38.

―――1986. "Families with Children Have Fared Worst." *Challenge* 29:40-47.

Danziger, Sheldon, Robert Haveman, and Robert Plotnick. 1985. "Transfers, Market Income and the Trend in Poverty." Paper presented at the Conference, Poverty and Policy: Retrospect and Prospects, Williamsburg, Virginia, Institute for Research on Poverty, University of Wisconsin.

Deitch, Cynthia. 1984. "Collective Action and Unemployment: The Response to Job Loss by Workers and Community Groups." *International Journal of Mental Health* 13:139-153.

Department of Health and Social Security. 1985. *For Richer for Poorer? DHSS Cohort Study of Unemployed Men.* London: Her Majesty's Stationery Office.

Dill, D., E. Feld, J. Martin, S. Burkemarr, and D. Belle. 1980. "The Impact of the Environment on the Coping Efforts of Low-Income Mothers." *Family Relations* 3:503-509.

Dingle, D. T. 1985. "Black Enterprise Annual Economic Outlook: Seeking a Foundation for Stability." *Black Enterprise* (January):46-60.

Doeringer, Peter B. and Michael J. Piore. 1971. *Internal Labor Markets and Manpower Analysis.* Lexington, MA: D. C. Heath.

Dolan, Jay. 1985. *The American Catholic Experience.* New York: Doubleday. Donzelot, Jacques. 1979. *The Policing of Families.* New York: Pantheon.

Douglas, Paul H. 1925. *Wages and the Family.* Chicago: University of Chicago Press.

Drucker, Peter F. 1981. "The Next American Work Force: Demographics and U.S. Economic Policy." *Commentary* (October):3-10.

Dumon, Wilfried and Joan Aldous. 1979. "European and United States Political Contexts for Family Policy Research." Pp. 425-50 in *Family Policy,* edited by Gerald McDonald and F. Ivan Nye. Minneapolis: National Council on Family Relations.

Duncan, Greg. 1984. *Years of Poverty, Years of Plenty.* Ann Arbor, MI: Institute for Social Research.

Eagleson, J. and P. Scharper. eds. 1979. *Puebla and Beyond.* Maryknoll, NY: Orbis.

"The Economy." 1986. *Christian Science Monitor* (November 10):21.

Edsall, Thomas Byrne. 1984. *The New Politics of Inequality.* New York: W. W. Norton.

Ehrenreich, Barbara. 1983. *The Hearts of Men.* New York: Anchor.

―――1986. "The Decline of the Middle Class." *New York Times Magazine* (September):57 ff.

Eisenberg, Philip and Paul Lazarsfeld. 1938. "The Psychological Effects of Unemployment." *Psychological Bulletin* 35:355-390.

Elder, Glen H., Jr. 1974. *Children of the Great Depression.* Chicago: University of Chicago Press.

Ellwood, David T. and Mary Jo Bane. 1983. *The Dynamics of Dependence: The Routes to Self Sufficiency.* Cambridge, MA: Harvard University (Report prepared for the U.S. Department of Health and Human Services.)

————1984. *The Impact of AFDC on Family Structure and Living Arrangements.* Cambridge, MA: Harvard University (Report to U.S. Department of Health and Human Services).

Ernst, R. T. and L. Hugg. 1976. *Black America: Geographical Perspectives.* Garden City, NY: Anchor/Doubleday.

Esping-Andersen, Gosta. 1986. *Politics Against Markets.* Princeton: Princeton University Press.

Etzioni, Amitai. 1983. *An Immodest Agenda: Rebuilding America Before the Twenty-first Century.* New York: McGraw-Hill.

Farley, Reynolds, H. Schuman, S. Bianchi, D. Colosanto, and S. Hatchett. 1978. "Chocolate City, Vanilla Suburbs: Will the Trend Toward Racially Separated Communities Continue?" *Social Science Research* 7:319-344.

Feather, N. T. and P. R. Davenport. 1981. "Unemployment and Depressive Affect: A Motivational and Attributional Analysis." *Journal of Personality and Social Psychology* 41:422-436.

Ferman, Louis A. 1971. "Regional Unemployment, Poverty, and Relocation." *Poverty* and *Human Resources Abstracts* 6:499-517.

————1984. "The Political Economy of Human Services: The Michigan Case." *International Journal of Mental Health* 13:125-138.

————and John Gardner. 1979. "Economic Deprivation, Social Mobility, and Mental Health." Pp. 193-224 in *Mental Health and Economy,* edited by Louis A. Ferman and Jeanne P. Gordus. Kalamazoo, MI: Upjohn Institute for Employment Research.

Ferman, Louis A. and Jeanne P. Gordus. eds. 1979. *Mental Health and the Economy.* Kalamazoo, MI: Upjohn Institute for Employment Research.

Fiore, J., J. Becker, and D. Coppel. 1984. "Social Network Intersections: A Buffer or a Stress." *American Journal of Community Psychology* 11(4):432-439.

Fisher, Kathleen. 1983. "A Review of the Literature on Plant Closing." *Monitor* (American Psychological Association) (January):2-18.

Flaim, Paul and Ellen Sehgal. 1985. "Displaced Workers of 1979-83: How Well Have They Fared?" *Monthly Labor Review* (June):3-16.

Foltman, Felician F. 1968. *White and Blue Collars in a Mill Shutdown.* Ithaca: Cornell University Press.

Frazier, E. Franklin. 1939. *The Negro Family in the United States.* Chicago: University of Chicago Press. (reprinted in 1966)

Freedman, Jonathon, David Sears, and J. Merrill Carlsmith. 1981. *Social Psychology.* Englewood Cliffs, NJ: Prentice-Hall.

Freeman, R. B. and D. A. Wise. 1982. *The Youth Unemployment Problem: Its Nature, Causes and Consequences.* Chicago: University of Chicago Press.

Fried, Marc. 1979. "Role Adaptation and the Appraisal of Work-Related Stress." Pp. 139-192 in *Mental Health and the Economy,* edited by L. A. Ferman and J. P. Gordus. Kalamazoo, MI: W.E. Upjohn Institute for Employment Research.

Friedman, Milton. 1962. *Capitalism and Freedom.* Chicago: University of Chicago Press.

Frisch, Michael and Dorothy Watts. 1980. "Oral History and the Presentation of Class Consciousness: The New York Times Vs. the Buffalo Unemployed." *International Journal of Oral History* 1:89-110.

Fryer, David and Roy Payne. 1984. "Proactive Behavior in Unemployment: Findings and Implications." *Leisure Studies* 3:273-295.

Furstenberg, Frank F., Jr. 1974. "Work Experience and Family Life." Pp. 341-360 in *Work and the Quality of Life: Resource Papers for Work in America,* edited by James O'Toole. Cambridge: MIT Press.

Garber, J., and M.E.P. Seligman. 1980. *Human Helplessness: Theory* and *Applications.* New York: Academic Press.

Gardner, Marilyn. 1986. "Children of the 1980s: Our Choices, Their Futures." *Christian Science Monitor* (September 16).

Garrity, John. 1978. *Unemployment in History.* New York: Harper & Row.

Gary, L. E. 1981. *Black Men.* Beverly Hills, CA: Sage.

General Accounting Office. 1985. *Evaluation of the Impact of OBRA on AFDC Recipients in Twelve Cities.* Washington, DC: Government Printing Office.

General Mills. 1979. *The American Family Report: Family Health in an Era of Stress.* Minneapolis, MN: author.

Gervarter, W. B. 1982. *An Overview of Artificial Intelligence and Robotics.* Washington, DC: U.S. Department of Commerce, Bureau of Standards.

Giddens, Anthony. 1979. *Central Problems in Social Theory: Action, Structure, and Contradiction in Social Analysis.* Berkeley: University of California Press.

Gil, David. 1971. "Violence Against Children." *Journal of Marriage and the Family* 33:637-648.

———1973. *Violence Against Children: Physical Child Abuse in the United States.* Cambridge, MA: Harvard University Press.

Gilder, George. 1981. *Wealth and Poverty.* New York: Basic Books.

Ginsberg, Eli. 1977. "The Job Problem." *Scientific American* (November):43-51.

Ginsburg, Helen. 1983. *Full Employment and Public Policy: The United States and Sweden.* Lexington, MA: D. C. Heath.

Glasgow, D. G. 1980. *The Black Underclass.* San Francisco: Jossey-Bass.

Glazer, Nona, Linda Majka, Joan Acker, and Christine Bose. 1977. "The Homemaker, the Family, and Employment." Pp. 155-169 in *American Women Workers in a Full Employment Economy, A Compendium.* Joint Economic Committee of Congress, Subcommittee on Economic Growth and Stabilization. Washington, DC: Government Printing Office.

Goldberg, Gertrude and Eleanor Kremen. 1987. "The Feminization of Poverty: Only in America?" *Social Policy* 17:3-15.

Goode, William J. 1960. "A Theory of Role Strain." *American Sociological Review* 11: 483-496.

Gordon, David, Richard Edwards, and Michael Reich. 1982. *Segmented Work, Divided Workers.* Cambridge: Cambridge University.

Gordus, Jeanne P., P. Jarley, and L. A. Ferman. 1981. *Plant Closings and Economic Dislocation.* Kalamazoo, MI: W.E. Upjohn Institute for Employment Research.

Gordus, Jeanne P. and Sean P. McAlinden. 1984. *Economic Change, Physical Illness, Mental Illness, and Social Deviance: A Study for the Joint Economic Committee.* Washington, DC: Government Printing Office.

———and Karen Yamakawa. 1984. *Labor Force Status, Program Participation and Economic Adjustment of Displaced Auto Workers.* Report to the United States Department of Commerce.

Gordus, Jeanne P., Karen Yamakawa, Pramila Hemrajani, and Christopher Gohrband. 1986. *An Analysis of Program Participation in the Employment Transition Program (ETP).* Ann Arbor: University of Michigan Institute of Science and Technology.

Gore, Susan. 1978. "The Effect of Social Support in Moderating the Health Consequences of Unemployment." *Journal of Health and Social Behavior* 19:157-165.

Grayson, Paul J. 1985. "The Closure of a Factory and Its Impact on Health." *International Journal of Health Services* 15:69-93.

Green, L. 1982. "A Learned Helplessness Analysis of Problems Confronting the Black Community." Pp. 73-93 in *Behavioral Modification in Black Populations*, edited by S. Turner and R. Jones. New York: Plenum.

Green, Philip. 1981. *The Pursuit of Inequality*.

Green, W. J. 1980. "Generations Without Work." *RF Illustrated: The Rockefeller Foundation* 4:14-15.

Greenberger, E. and L. Steinberg. 1986. *When Teenagers Work: The Psychological and Social Cost of Adolescent Employment*. New York: Basic Books.

Grossman, Richard. 1985. "Environmentalists and Labor." *Socialist Review* 82(83):63-87.

Gueron, Judith. 1984. *Lessons from a Job Guarantee: The Youth Incentive Entitlement Pilot Projects*. New York: Manpower Demonstration Research Corporation.

Gurin, Patricia and Edgar Epps. 1974. *Black Consciousness, Identity and Achievement*. New York: John Wiley.

Guzda, H. P. 1982. "Labor Department's First Program to Assist Black Workers." *Monthly Labor Review* 6:39-44.

Haans, N. 1977. *Coping and Defending: Processes of Self-Environment Organization*. New York: Academic Press.

Haber, William, L. A. Ferman, and J. R. Hudson. 1963. *The Impact of Technological Change*. Kalamazoo, MI: W.E. Upjohn Institute for Employment Research.

Hamilton, C. V. 1986. "Social Policy and the Welfare of Black Americans: From Rights to Resources." *Political Science Quarterly* 101:239-257.

Hamilton, Charles and Donna Hamilton. 1985. "Social Policies, Civil Rights and Poverty." Paper presented at the conference, Poverty and Policy: Retrospect and Prospects, Williamsburg, VA, Institute for Research on Poverty, University of Wisconsin.

Hansen, Gary B. et al. 1980. *Hardrock Miners in a Shutdown*. Logan: Utah State University.

Harrington, Michael. 1962. *The Other America*. New York: Macmillan.

————1984. *The New American Poverty*. New York: Penguin.

Harrison, A. O., P. J. Bowman, and R. L. Beal. 1985. "Role Strain, Coping Resources, and Psychological Well-Being among Black Working Mothers." Pp. 21-28 in *Empirical Research in Black Psychology*, edited by A. W. Boykin. Washington, DC: National Institute for Mental Health.

Harrison, Bennett. 1974. "The Theory of the Dual Economy." In *The Worker in Postindustrial Capitalism: Liberal and Radical Responses*, edited by B. Silverman and M. Yanowich. New York: Free Press.

————1984. "Plant Closures: Efforts to Cushion the Blow." *Monthly Labor Review* 107:41-43.

Heckler, Margorie M. et al. 1985. "Report of the Secretary's Task Force on Black and Minority Health." Washington, DC: U.S. Dept. of Health and Human Services (also see related subcommittee reports and commissioned papers).

Heclo, Hugh. 1985. "The Political Foundation of Antipoverty Policy." Paper presented at the conference, Poverty and Policy: Retrospect and Prospects, Williamsburg, VA, Institute for Research on Poverty, University of Wisconsin.

Helmore, Kristin and Karen Laing. 1986. "Exiles Among Us: Poor and Black in America." *Christian Science Monitor* (November 13, 18, 19, 20).

Hill, Martha S. and Mary Corcoran. 1979. "Unemployment Among Family Men: A Ten Year Longitudinal Study." *Monthly Labor Review* (November):19-23.

Hill, Reuben, 1958. "Generic Features of Families Under Stress." *Social Casework* 39:139-150.

————1974. *Families Under Stress*. New York: Harper.

Hill, Robert. 1971. *The Strengths of Black Families*. New York: Emerson Hall.

Hollister, Robinson G., Peter Kemper, and Rebecca A. Maynard. eds. 1984. *The National Supported Work Demonstration.* Madison: University of Wisconsin.

Holmes, Thomas H. and Richard H. Rahe. 1967. "The Social Readjustment Rating Scale." *Journal of Psychosomatic Research* 11:213-218.

Horkheimer, Max. 1972. "Authority and the Family." Pp. 47-125 in *Critical Theory,* by Max Horkheimer, translated by Herder and Herder. New York: Seabury.

Horowitz, Alan. 1984. "The Economy and Social Pathology." *Annual Review of Sociology* 10:95-119.

House, James S. 1981. *Work Stress and Social Support.* Reading, MA: Addison-Wesley.

House, James S., C. Robbins, and H. Metzner. 1982. "The Association of Social Relationships and Activities with Mortality: Prospective Evidence from the Tecumseh Community Health Study." *American Journal of Epidemiology* 16:123-140.

Hudson, Ray and David Sadler. 1985. "Communities in Crisis: The Social and Political Effects of Steel Closures in Prance, West Germany, and the United Kingdom." *Urban Affairs Quarterly* 21:171-186.

Hunt, H. A. and T. L. Hunt. 1983. *Human Resource Implications of Robotics.* Kalamazoo, MI: W. E. Upjohn Institute for Employment Reserach.

Jackson, James S. and S. J. Hatchett. 1986. "Intergenerational Research: Methodological Considerations." Pp. 51-76 in *Intergenerational Relations,* edited by N. Datun, A. L. Green, and H. W. Reese. Hillsdale, NJ: Erlbaum.

Jackson, James S., M. E. Tucker, and P. J. Bowman. 1982. "Conceptual and Methodological Problems in Survey Research on Black Populations." Pp. 11-39 in *Methodological Problems in Minority Research,* edited by William Liu. Chicago: Pacific/Asian American Mental Health Research Center.

Jahoda, Marie. 1979. "The Impact of Unemployment in the 1970s." *Bulletin of the British Psychological Society* 32:309-314.

———1982. *Employment and Unemployment: A Sociopsychological Analysis.* New York: Cambridge University Press.

———Paul P. Lazarsfeld, and Hans Zeisel. 1971. *Marienthal: The Sociography of an Unemployed Community.* London: Tavistock.

Joe, T. and F. Farrow. 1982. *Profiles of Families in Poverty: Effects of the FY 1983 Budget Proposal on the Poor.* Washington, DC: Center for the Study of Social Policy.

Jones, K. M., N. Riley, N. Hara, and D. Hatchett. 1986. "The Black Male in Jeopardy." *Crisis* 93:19-46.

Justice, Blair and D. P. Duncan. 1977. "Child Abuse as a Work-Related Problem." *Corrective and Social Psychiatry* 23:53-55.

Kahn, Alfred and Sheila Kamerman. 1983. *Income Transfers for Families with Children: An Eight-Country Study.* Philadelphia: Temple University Press.

Kamerman, Sheila. 1985. "Young, Poor and a Mother Alone: Problems and Possible Solutions." In *Services to Young Families,* edited by H. McAdoo and J. Parkman. Washington, DC: American Public Welfare Association.

Kaplan, Howard B. 1983. *Psychosocial Stress: Trends in Theory and Research.* New York: Academic Press.

Katz, Arnold and Joseph E. Hight. 1977. "The Economics of Unemployment Insurance: A Symposium." *Industrial and Labor Relations Review* 30:431- 526.

Kaufman, H. G. 1982. *Professionals in Search of Work.* New York: John Wiley.

Kelly, Robert F. 1985. "The Family and the Urban Underclass: An Integrative Framework." *Journal of Family Issues* 6:159-184.

———Ann Workman Sheldon, and Greer Litton Fox. 1985. "The Impact of Economic Dislocation on the Health of Children." Pp. 94-111 in *Understanding the Economic*

Crisis, edited by J. Boulet, A. M. DeBritto, and S. A. Ray. Ann Arbor: University of Michigan.

Kelvin, P. and J. E. Jarrett. 1985. *Unemployment: Its Social Psychological Effects.* New-York: Cambridge University Press.

Kerkhofs, J., A. Mendoza, and L. Hartsens. 1976. "The Quest for Truly Human Communities." *Pro Mundi Vita Bulletin* 62:6-14.

Kessler, Ronald C. 1979. "Stress, Social Status, and Psychological Distress." *Journal of Health and Social Behavior* 20:259-272.

Kessler, Ronald C. and Jane D. McLeod. 1984. "Sex Differences in Vulnerability to Undesirable Life Events." *American Sociological Review* 49:620-631.

Kett, Joseph F. 1977. *Rites of Passage: Adolescence in America, 1790 to the Present.* New York: Basic Books.

King, Craig. 1982. "The Social Impacts of Mass Layoff." Ann Arbor: University of Michigan, Center for Research on Social Organization.

Komarovsky, Mirra. 1940. *The Unemployed Man and His Family.* New York: Columbia University Press.

Kristol, Irving. 1978. *Two Cheers for Capitalism.* New York: Basic Books.

———1983. *Reflections of a Neoconservative.* New York: Basic Books.

Kuttner, Robert. 1984. *The Economic Illusion.* Boston: Houghton Mifflin.

Kuznets, Simon. 1971. *Economic Growth of Nations.* Cambridge, MA: Harvard University Press.

Larson, Jeffry H. 1984. "The Effect of Husband's Unemployment on Marital and Family Relations in Blue-Collar Families." *Family Relations* 33:503-511.

Lasch, Christopher. 1977. *Haven in a Heartless World: The Family Besieged.* New York: Basic Books.

———1978. *The Culture of Narcissism.* New York: W. W. Norton.

———1983. *The Minimal Self.* New York: W. W. Norton.

Lazarus, Richard S. and S. Folkman. 1980. *Stress, Appraisal and Coping.* New York: Springer.

Leavy, P. 1983. "Social Support and Psychological Disorder." *Journal of Community Psychology* 11:3-21.

Leo XIII. 1891. "On the Condition of Labor" (Rerum Novarum) in *Seven Great Encyclicals,* edited by W. J. Gibbons. New York: Paulist Press (1963).

Leon, C. B. 1982. "Occupational Winners and Losers: Who They Were During 1972-1980." *Monthly Labor Review* (June):18-28.

Leontief, Wassily W. 1982. "The Distribution of Work and Income. *Scientific American* (September):188-204.

———and Faye Duchin. 1986. *The Future Impact of Automation on Workers.* New York: Oxford University Press.

Leventman, Paula. 1981. *Professionals Out of Work.* New York: Free Press.

Lewis, Robert A. and Graham B. Spanier. 1979. "Theorizing about the Quality and Stability of Marriage." Pp. 268-294 in *Contemporary Theories about the Family.* Vol. 2, edited by Wesley R. Burr, Reuben Hill, F. Ivan Nye, and Ira L. Reiss. New York: Free Press.

Lieberman, Morton A. and L. Borman. 1979. *Self-Help Groups for Coping with Crisis.* San Francisco: Jossey-Bass.

Liebow, Elliot. 1967. *Tally's Corner: A Study of Street Corner Men.* Boston: Little, Brown.

Liem, Ramsay. 1983a. "Reconsidering the Concept of Social Victim: The Case of the Unemployed." Paper presented at the annual meeting of the American Psychological Association.

————1983b. "Unemployment: Personal and Family Effects." Paper presented at the Conference on Unemployment During Economic Recession: Its Effect on the Family, Bunker Hill Community College.

————and Paula Rayman. 1982. "Health and Social Costs of Unemployment: Research and Policy Considerations." *American Psychologist* 37:1116-1123.

Liker, Jeffrey K. and Glen H. Elder, Jr. 1983. "Economic Hardship and Marital Relations in the 1930s." *American Sociological Review* 48:343-359.

Lipsky, D. E. 1970. "Interplant Transfer and Terminated Workers: A Case Study." *Industrial and Labor Relations Review* 23:191-206.

Liu, Yih Wu and Anthony H. Stocks. 1983. "A Labor-Oriented Quarterly Econometric Forecasting Model of the Youngstown-Warren SMSA." *Regional Science and Urban Economics* 13:317-340.

Lonergan, B.J.P. 1974. "Theology in Its New Context." In *A Second Collection,* edited by W.F.J. Ryan and B. J. Tyrrell. Philadelphia: Westminster.

Luria, D. 1981. *Technology's Employment and the Factory of the Future.* Detroit: Autofact III Conference.

MacDonald, Maurice. 1983. *Multiple Benefits and Income Adequacy for Food Stamps Participant and Nonparticipant Households* (with highlights and executive summary by the United States Department of Agriculture, Food and Nutrition Service, Office of Analysis and Evaluation). Washington, DC: U.S. Department of Agriculture.

Majka, Linda C. 1984. "The Impact of Recent Economic Change on Families and the Role of Women." Pp. 99-108 in *The Changing Family,* edited by S. Saxton, P. Voydanoff, and A. Zukowski. Chicago: Loyola.

————1988. "Gender and the Economy: Women in 'the Free-Market Family.'" In *With Both Eyes Open: Seeing Beyond Gender,* edited by Patricia Johnson and Janet Kalven. New York: Pilgrim.

Mandle, Jay R. and Louis Ferleger. 1985. "Achieving Full Employment." *Socialist Review* (November-December):77-91.

Mangum, Garth L. and S. P. Seninger. 1978. *Coming of Age in the Ghetto: A Dilemma of Youth Unemployment.* Baltimore: Johns Hopkins University.

Mansfield, E. 1971. *Technological Change.* New York: Norton.

Margolis, Lewis E. 1982a. *Helping the Families of Unemployed Workers.* Chapel Hill: University of North Carolina, Bush Institute for Child and Family Policy.

————1982b. "Help Wanted." *Pediatrics* 69.

————and Dale C. Farran. 1981. "Unemployment: The Health Consequences for Children." *North Carolina Medical Journal* 42:849-850.

————1984. "Unemployment and Children." *International Journal of Mental Health* 13:107-124.

Marshall, Gordon. 1984. "On the Sociology of Women's Unemployment, Its Neglect and Significance." *Sociology Review* 32:234-259.

Martin, G. M. 1982a. "Industrial Robots Join the Workforce." *Occupational Outlook Quarterly* (Fall):2-11.

————1982b. "Manufacturing Engineering." *Occupational Outlook Quarterly* (Fall):22-26.

McAdoo, Harriette. 1981. *Black Families.* Beverly Hills, CA: Sage.

————1984. "Poverty Equals Women and Their Children." *Point of View* (Spring):8-9.

McCubbin, Hamilton I. 1979. "Integrating Coping Behavior in Family Stress Theory." *Journal of Marriage and the Family* 41:234-244.

————Constance B. Joy, A. Elizabeth Cauble, Joan K. Comeau, Joan M. Patterson, and Richard H. Needle. 1980. "Family Stress and Coping: A Decade Review." *Journal of Marriage and the Family* 42:855-871.

McCubbin, Hamilton I., Andrea S. Larsen, and David H. Olson. 1982. "F-COPES: Family Coping Strategies." Pp. 101-119 in *Family Inventories: Inventories Used in a National Survey of Families Across the Life Cycle,* edited by David H. Olson, Hamilton I. McCubbin, Howard Barnes, Andrea Larsen, Marla Muxen, and Marc Wilson. St. Paul: University of Minnesota, Family Social Science.

McCubbin, Hamilton I. and Joan M. Patterson. 1983. "The Family Stress Process: The Double ABCX Model of Adjustment and Adaptation." *Marriage and Family Review* 6:7-37.

McElvaine, Robert. ed. 1983. *Down and Out in the Great Depression.* Chapel Hill: University of North Carolina Press.

McFarlane, Allan H., Geoffrey R. Norman, David L. Streiner, and Ranjan G. Roy. 1983. "The Process of Social Stress: Stable, Reciprocal and Mediating Relationships." *Journal of Health and Social Behavior* 24:160-173.

McMahon, Patrick J. and John H. Tschetter. 1986. "The Declining Middle Class: A Further Analysis." *Monthly Labor Review* (September):22-27.

McWilliams, Wilson Carey. 1973. *The Idea of Fraternity in America.* Berkeley: University of California Press.

Menaghan, Elizabeth. 1983a. "Marital Stress and Family Transitions: A Panel Analysis." *Journal of Marriage and the Family* 45:371-386.

———1983b. "Individual Coping Efforts and Family Studies: Conceptual and Methodological Issues." *Marriage and Family Review* 6:113-135.

Merton, Thomas. 1960. *Disputed Questions.* New York: Farrar, Strauss & Cudahy.

Meyer, Peter. 1977. "Notes on the Distribution of Income." *Working Papers.* Pennsylvania State University, Department of Community Development.

Mick, Stephen S. 1975. "Social and Personal Costs of a Plant Shutdown." *Industrial Relations* 14:203-208.

Miller, George. 1983. "Hello Poverty; Goodbye Economic Gains." *New York Times* (August 14).

Moen, Phyllis. 1979. "Family Impacts of the 1975 Recession: Duration of Employment." *Journal of Marriage and the Family,* 41:561-572.

———Edward Kain, and Glen H. Elder, Jr. 1983. "Economic Conditions and Family Life: Contemporary and Historical Perspectives." Pp. 213-259 in *American Families and the Economy: The High Costs of Living,* edited by Richard Nelson and Felicity Skidmore. Washington, DC: National Academy Press.

Moos, Rudolph H. 1976. *Human Adaptation: Coping with Life Stress.* Lexington: Heath.

Morris-Vann, Artie. 1984. "Testimony." Congressional Hearing, U. S. House of Representatives, Select Committee on Children, Youth and Families, March 5. Washington, DC.

Moynihan, Daniel P. 1965. *The Negro Family: The Case for National Action.* Washington, DC: Government Printing Office.

———1968. "Foreword." Pp. V-XVII in *Nation and Family* by Alva Myrdal. Cambridge: MIT Press.

———1973. *The Politics of a Guaranteed Income.* New York: Vintage.

———1986. *Family and Nation: The Godkin Lectures.* San Diego: Harcourt Brace Jovanovich.

"Multiple Benefits: Fitting the Pieces Together." 1983. *Focus* 6:5-9.

Murray, Charles. 1984. *Losing Ground: American Social Policy, 1950-1980.* New York: Basic Books.

Murray, John C. 1960. *We Hold these Truths.* New York: Sheed & Ward.

Novak, Michael. 1982. *The Spirit of Democratic Capitalism.* New York: Simon & Schuster.

———1985. "Toward the Future: Catholic Social Teaching and the U.S. Economy." Public lecture, University of Dayton.

Nowak, Thomas C. and Kay A. Snyder. 1984. "Job Loss, Marital Happiness and House-hold Tension: Do Women Fare Better than Men?" Paper presented at the annual meeting of the Society for the Study of Social Problems.

O'Connor, James. 1984. *Accumulation Crisis.* New York: Basil Blackwell.

Office of Technology Assessment. 1986. *Technology and Structural Employment: Re-employing Displaced Adults.* Washington, D.C.: Government Printing Office.

Ohio Legislature. 1980. *Proceedings of the Steel Legislative Conference.* Columbus: author.

Olson, David H., H. I. McCubbin, H. Barnes, A. Larsen, M. Muxen, and M. Wilson. 1982. *Family Inventories.* St. Paul: University of Minnesota, Family Social Sciences.

Olson, David H., Douglas H. Sprenkle, and Candyce S. Russell. 1979. "Circumplex Model of Marital and Family Systems: I. Cohesion and Adaptability Dimensions, Family Types, and Clinical Applications." *Family Process* 18:3-28.

Palmer, John and Isabel Sawhill. 1982. *The Reagan Experiment.* Washington, DC: Urban Institute.

Patterson, James J. 1981. *America's Struggle Against Poverty, 1900-1980.* Cambridge, MA: Harvard University Press.

Paulter, Katherine and John Lewko. 1983. "Children's Worries and Exposures to Un-employment: A Preliminary Investigation." Laurentian University. (unpublished)

Pearce, Diana. 1982. *The Poverty of Our Future: The Impact of Reagan's Budget Cuts on Women Minorities and Children.* Washington, DC: Center for National Policy Review.

Pearlin, Leonard I. 1983. "Role Strains and Personal Stress." Pp. 3-32 in *Psychosocial Stress: Trends in Theory and Research,* edited by Howard B. Kaplan. New York: Academic Press.

———Morton A. Lieberman, Elizabeth G. Menaghan, and Joseph T. Mullan. 1981. "The Stress Process." *Journal of Health and Social Behavior* 22:337-356.

Pearlin, Leonard I. and Carmi Schooler. 1978. "The Structure of Coping." *Journal of Health and Social Behavior* 19:2-21.

Perrucci, Carolyn C. and Robert Perrucci. 1986. "Unemployment and Mental Health: Research and Policy Implications." Paper presented at the annual meeting of the Society for the Study of Social Problems.

———Dena B. Targ, and Harry R. Targ. 1985. "The Impact of a Plant Closing on Workers and the Community." Pp. 231-260 in *Research in the Sociology of Work.* Vol. 3, edited by Richard L. Simpson and Ida Harper Simpson. Greenwich, CT: JAI.

Perrucci, Carolyn C. and Dena B. Targ. 1988. "Effects of a Plant Closing on Marriage and Family Life." Pp. 55-71 in *Families and Economic Distress: Coping Strategies and Social Policy,* edited by Patricia Voydanoff and Linda C. Majka. Newbury Park, CA: Sage.

Piliavin, Irving and Rosemary Gartner. 1979. *Assumptions and Achievements of Man-power Programs for Offenders: Implications for Supported Work.* Madison: University of Wisconsin Institute for Research on Poverty.

Piore, Michael J. 1975. "Notes for a Theory of Labor Market Stratification." Pp. 125-150 in *Labor Market Segmentation,* edited by Richard C. Edwards, Michael Reich, and David M. Gordon. Lexington, MA: D. C. Heath.

Pius XI. 1931. "On Reconstructing the Social Order." In *Seven Great Encyclicals,* edited by W. J. Gibbons. New York: Paulist Press (1963).

Piven, Frances Fox and Richard A. Cloward. 1977. *Poor People's Movements.* New York: Random House.

Plotnick, Robert and Felicity Skidmore. 1975. *Progress Against Poverty.* New York: Academic Press.

Powell, Douglas H. and Paul J. Driscoll. 1973. "Middle Class Professionals Face Unemployment." *Society* 10:18-26.
Rappaport, Julian. 1985. "The Power of Empowerment Language." *Social Policy* (Fall):15-
   21.
Rayman, Paula. 1982. "The World of Not Working: An Evaluation of Urban Social Service Response to Unemployment." *Journal of Health and Human Resources Administration* 4:319-333.
————1983. "Out of Work: The Effects of Urban Unemployment." (unpublished)
————1988. "Unemployment and Family Life: The Meaning for Children." Pp. 121-137 in
   Families and Economic Distress: Coping Strategies and Social Policy, edited by
   Patricia Voydanoff and Linda C. Majka. Newbury Park, CA: Sage.
————and Barry Bluestone. *Out of Work.* National Institute of Mental Health Final
   Report, Center for Work and Mental Health, Rockville, Maryland.
Redburn, F. Stevens and Terry F. Buss. 1984. "Religious Leaders as Policy Advocates: The
   Youngstown Steel Mill Closing." Pp. 83-94 in *Public Policy Formation,* edited by
   Robert Eyestone. Greenwich, CT: JAI.
Rees, J. 1979. Technological Change and Regional Shifts in American Manufacturing."
   Professional Geographer 31:45-54.
Rieff, Philip 1966. *The Triumph of the Therapeutic.* New York: Harper & Row.
Rogers-Rose. L. 1980. *The Black Woman.* Beverly Hills, CA: Sage.
Root, Kenneth. 1983. "Human Responses to Plant Closures." Paper presented at the
   annual meeting of the American Association for the Advancement of Science.
————1984. "The Human Response to Plant Closures." *Annals of the American Academy
   of Political and Social Science* 475:52-65.
Rosen, Ellen I. 1983. "Laid Off: Displaced Blue Collar Women in New England." Paper
   presented at the annual meeting of the Society for the Study of Social Problems.
Rosenbaum, M. and K. Ben-Ari. 1985. "Learned Helplessness and Learned Resourceful-
   ness: Effects of Noncontingent Success and Failure on the Individuals Differing in Self-
   Control Skills." *Journal of Personality and Social Psychology* 48:198-215.
Rosenthal, Sidney. 1985. "Building a Conservative Elite." *Washington Post National
   Weekly Edition* (October 14):6-10.
Rubin, Eva R. 1986. *The Supreme Court and the American Family.* New York: Green-
   wood.
Ryan, John A. 1906. *A Living Wage.* New York: Macmillan.
Ryan, William. 1971. *Blaming the Victim.* New York: Pantheon.
Sadler, David. 1984. "Works Closure at British Steel and the Nature of the State." *Politi-
   cal Geography Quarterly* 3:297-311.
"Safety Net Programs: Are They Reaching Poor Children?" 1986. *Columbus Dispatch* (Oc-
   tober 3):10.
Sahal, D. 1981. *Patterns of Technological Innovation.* Reading, MA: Addison-Wesley.
Samuelson, Robert J. 1980. "On Mobility." *National Journal* 16.
Sandberg, Carl. 1936. *The People Yes.* New York: Harcourt & Brace.
Sandler, I. and M. Barrera. 1984. "Toward a Multimethod Approach to Assessing the Ef-
   fects of Social Support." *American Journal of Community Psychology* 12(1):37-52.
Sarbin, T. R. and V. L. Allen. 1968. "Role Theory." In *Handbook of Social Psychology,*
   edited by G. Lindzey and E. Aronson. Reading, MA: Addison-Wesley.
Savner, S., L. Williams, and M. Ralas. 1986. "The Massachusetts Employment and Train-
   ing Program (ET)." *Clearinghouse Review* 20:123-131.
Schaefer, Catherine, James C. Coyne, and Richard S. Lazarus. 1981. "The Health-Related
   Functions of Social Support." *Journal of Behavioral Medicine* 4:381-406.

Schervish, Paul G. 1981. "The Structure of Employment and Unemployment." Pp. 154-186 in *Sociological Perspectives on the Labor Market,* edited by Ivar Berg. New York: Academic Press.

Scholzman, Kay L. 1979. "Women and Unemployment: Assessing the Biggest Myths." Pp. 290-312 in *Women: A Feminist Perspective,* edited by Jo Freeman. Palo Alto, CA: Mayfield.

————and Sidney Verba. 1979. *Injury to Insult: Unemployment, Class, and Political Response.* Cambridge, MA: Harvard University Press.

Schor, Juliet. 1985. "The Economics and Politics of Full Employment." *Socialist Review* 81:65-92.

Schore, Lee. 1984. "The Fremont Experience: A Counseling Program for Dislocated Workers." *International Journal of Mental Health* 13:154-168.

Schorr, Alvin L. 1979. "Views of Family Policy." Pp. 13-15 in *Family Policy,* edited by Gerald McDonald and F. Ivan Nye. Minneapolis: National Council on Family Relations.

Schultz, George P. and Arnold R. Weber. 1966. *Strategies for Displaced Workers.* New York: Harper & Row.

Sheppard, Harold A., Louis A. Ferman, and Seymour Faber. 1959. *Too Old to Work Too Young to Retire.* Washington, DC: Government Printing Office.

Siddique, C. Muhammad. 1981. "Orderly Careers and Social Integration." *Industrial Relations* 20:297-305.

Sidel, Ruth. 1986. *Women and Children Last.* New York: Viking.

Sinfield, Adrian. 1981. *What Unemployment Means.* Oxford: Martin Robertson. Sirianni, Carmen and Michele Eayrs. n.d. "Time, Work and Equality." *Theory and Society.*

Slote, Alfred. 1969. *Termination: The Closing at Baker Plant.* Indianapolis: Bobbs-Merrill.

Smeeding, T. 1983. "Recent Increases in Poverty in the U.S.: What the Official Estimates Fail to Show." Testimony before the House Ways and Means Subcommittee on Oversight, Public Assistance, and Unemployment. Washington, DC: Government Printing Office.

Smolensky, Eugene. 1985. "Is the Golden Age of Poverty Policy Right Around the Corner?" *Focus* 8:9-11, 18.

Spanier, Graham B. 1976. "Measuring Dyadic Adjustment: New Scales for Assessing the Quality of marriage and Similar Dyads." *Journal of Marriage and the Family* 38:15-28.

Sprenkle, Douglas H. and David H. Olson 1978. "Circumplex Model of Marital Systems: An Empirical Study of Clinic and Non-Clinic Couples." *Journal of Marriage and Family Counseling* 4:59-74.

Stack, Carol. 1974. *All Our Kin: Strategies for Survival in a Black Community.* New York: Harper & Row.

Steinberg, Laurence D., Ralph Catalano, and David Dooley. 1981. "Economic Antecedents of Child Abuse and Neglect." *Child Development* 52:975-985.

Steinfels, Peter. 1979. *The Neoconservatives.* New York: Simon & Schuster.

Stockman, David. 1983. *Poverty in America.* Statement before the House Ways and Means Subcommittees on Oversight, Public Assistance, and Unemployment. Washington, DC: Government Printing Office.

Strange, William, 1977. *Job Loss: A Psychosocial Study of Worker Reactions to Unemployment.* Washington, DC: Employment and Training Administration.

Syme, Leonard S. and Lisa F. Berkman. 1976. "Social Class, Susceptibility and Sickness." *American Journal of Epidemiology* 104:1-8.

Tausig, Mark. 1982. "Measuring Life Events." *Journal of Health and Social Behavior* 23:52-64.

Taylor, S. E. 1983. "Adjustment to Life Threatening Events: A Theory of Cognitive Adaptation." *American Psychologist* 37:1161-1173.

Thoits, Peggy A. 1983a. "Dimensions of Life Events that Influence Psychological Distress: An Evaluation and Synthesis of the Literature." Pp. 33-103 in *Psychosocial Stress: Trends in Theory and Research*, edited by Howard B. Kaplan. New York: Academic Press.

———1983b. "Multiple Identities and Psychological Well-Being: A Reformulation and Test of the Social Isolation Hypothesis." *American Sociological Review* 48:174-187.

———1985. "Social Support and Psychological Well-Being." Pp. 51-72 in *Social Support Theory, Research and Application*, edited by I. Sarason and B. Sarason. Boston: Martin Nijhoff.

Titmuss, Richard M. 1971. *The Gift Relationship*. New York: Random House.

Turner, R. Jay. 1983. "Direct, Indirect and Moderating Effects of Social Support on Psychological Distress and Associated Conditions." Pp. 105-155 in *Psychosocial Stress: Trends in Theory and Research*, edited by Howard B. Kaplan. New York: Academic Press.

U.S. Bishops. 1986. *Economic Justice for All: Pastoral Letter on Catholic Social Teaching and the U.S. Economy*. Washington, DC: U.S. Catholic Conference.

U.S. Bureau of the Census. 1979. *The Social and Economic Status of the Black Population in the United States: A Historical View, 1790-1978*. Washington, DC: Government Printing Office.

———1986a. "Money, Income and Poverty Status of Families and Persons in the United States: 1984 (Advance Data from the March 1986 Current Population Survey)." In *Current Population Reports, Series P-60*. No. 154. Washington, DC: Government Printing Office.

———1986b. "Money Income of Households, Families and Persons in the United States: 1984." In *Current Population Reports, Series P-60*. No. 151. Washington, DC: Government Printing Office.

———1986c. "Household Wealth and Asset Ownership: 1984." In *Current Population Reports, Series P-70*. Washington, DC: Government Printing Office.

U.S. Department of Commerce, Bureau of the Census. 1986. *Money, Income and Poverty Status of Families and Persons in the United States: 1985, Series P-60*. Washington, DC: Government Printing Office.

U.S. Department of Labor, Bureau of Labor Statistics. 1985. *Employment in Perspective: Women in the Labor Force*. Third Quarter. Washington, DC: Government Printing Office.

U.S. House of Representatives. 1984. *The Impact of the OBRA Changes on Poverty in the U.S.* Washington, DC: Government Printing Office.

U.S. House of Representatives Committee on Ways and Means. 1985. *Children in Poverty*. Washington, DC: Government Printing Office.

———1986. *Background Material and Data on Programs within the Jurisdiction of the Committee on Ways and Means*. Washington, DC: Government Printing Office.

U.S. Senate. 1986. *Congressional Record Act*.

Vatican II Document. 1965. *Guadium et Spes, The Church in the Modern World*.

Vaughan, Roger J., Robert Pollard, and Barbara Dyer. 1985. *The Wealth of the State*. Washington, DC: Council of State Planning Agencies.

Veroff, Joseph, Elizabeth Douvan, and Richard A. Kulka. 1981. *The Inner American*. New York: Basic Books.

Voydanoff, Patricia. 1983. "Unemployment: Family Strategies for Adaptation." Pp. 90-102 in *Stress and the Family, Vol. II, Coping with Catastrophe*, edited by Charles R. Figley and Hamilton I. McCubbin. New York: Brunner/Mazel.

————1984. "Economic Distress and Families: Policy Issues." *Journal of Family Issues* 5:273-288.

————and Brenda W. Donnelly. 1986. "Economic Distress and Mental Health: Coping Strategies and Social Supports." Report submitted to the Ohio Department of Mental Health.

————1987. "Economic Distress, Family Coping and Quality of Family Life." Pp. 98-116 in *Families and Economic Distress: Coping Strategies and Social Policy,* edited by Patricia Voydanoff and Linda C. Majka. Beverly Hills, CA: Sage.

Wallis, J. 1980. "Rebuilding the Church." *Sojourners* 9:11.

Warr, Peter. 1984. "Job Loss and Unemployment, and Psychological Well-Being." Pp. 263-285 in *Role Transitions Exploration, and Explanations,* edited by V. Allen and E. Van de Vleirt. New York: Plenum.

Weeks, Edward C. and Sandra Drengacz. 1982. "The Non-Economic Impacts of Community Economic Shock." *Journal of Health and Human Resources Administration* 4:303-318.

Wilcock, R. C. and W. H. Franke. 1963. *Unwanted Workers: Permanent Layoffs and Long-Term Unemployment.* New York: Free Press.

Wilkinson, Doris and R. Taylor. 1977. *The Black Male in America.* Chicago: Nelson-Nelson-Hill.

Wilson, William J. 1978. *The Declining Significance of Race.* Chicago: University of Chicago Press.

————1985. "Cycles of Deprivation and the Underclass Debate." *Social Service Review* 59:541-559.

————and Kathryn Neckerman. 1984. "The Black Underclass." *Wilson Quarterly* 8:88-99.

————1985. "Poverty and Family Structure: The Widening Gap Between Evidence and Public Policy Issues." Paper presented at the conference, Poverty and Policy: Retrospect and Prospects, Williamsburg, VA Institute for Research on Poverty, University of Wisconsin.

Winnick, Andrew J. 1985. "Reagan's Economic Program and Supply Side Economics: An Evaluation." *Insurgent Sociologist* (Spring).

Wool, H. 1978. *Discouraged Workers, Potential Workers, and National Employment Policy.* Washington, DC: National Commission for Manpower Policy.

World Synod of Bishops. 1971. *Justice in the World.*

Wuthnow, Robert. 1985. "American Democracy and the Democratization of American Religion." Paper presented at the annual meeting of the American Sociological Association.

Young, Anne McDougall. 1979. "Job Search of Recipients of Unemployment Insurance." *Monthly Labor Review* 102:49-54.

About the Authors

Fred Block is Associate Professor of Sociology at the University of Pennsylvania. He has written recently on state theory and postindustrial political economy. His most recent books include *The Mean Season: The Attack on the Welfare State*, written with Richard A. Cloward, Barbara Ehrenreich, and Frances Fox Piven, and *Revising State Theory*.

Phillip J. Bowman is currently Assistant Professor of Psychology with the University of Illinois at Urbana—Champaign. After receiving his Ph.D. in social psychology from the University of Michigan (1977), he remained at Michigan as a Research Scientist in the Survey Research Center of the Institute for Social Research. Between 1978 and 1984 he worked on three unique national surveys of the black American population. His current research focuses on expectancy-value theory with emphasis on role strain and adaptation, motivation and organizational performance, and attitudes and racial inequality. He is also interested in the implications of theory-driven survey research for designing responsive public policy and preventive intervention. He is author or coauthor of several journal articles and book chapters and frequently presents papers at national and local conferences.

Terry F. Buss is Professor of Urban Studies at the University of Akron. Taking advantage of his location in America's distressed industrial heartland, he has published books and many articles on a variety of public policy issues, including mass unemployment, human service delivery, labor markets, economic development, and human capital resources. His latest book, coauthored with F. Stevens Redburn, is *Hidden Unemployment: Discouraged Workers and Public Policy* (to be published by Praeger in 1987). He received his doctorate in political science and mathematics from Ohio State University in 1976.

Brenda W. Donnelly is Research Associate of the Center for the Study of Family Development at the University of Dayton. She received her Ph.D. degree in sociology from the University of Delaware in 1985. Her research interests include adolescent pregnancy, religion and family life, and social protest. Her forthcoming publications include articles in the *Journal of Family Issues* and the *Journal of the Scientific Study of Religion*.

Jeanne Prial Gordus is the Director of the Employment Transition Program at the Institute of Science and Technology at the University of Michigan. For more than 10 years, her research and program work has focused upon the entry and exit of individuals into the labor market, the operation of the labor market, and the relationship between education and employment. Unemployment research is a major activity of the Employment Transition Program, which includes a major intervention element in which research-based programs are developed, field-tested, evaluated, and disseminated. She has authored and coauthored four books and monographs and numerous scholarly articles. Recent books include *Plant Closing and Economic Dislocation*, published by W. E. Upjohn, and a monograph done for the Joint Economic Committee of the U.S. Congress, *Economic Change, Physical Illness, Mental Illness, and Social Deviance*.

Margaret Hohman, SCN, currently a staff member of the Cincinnati Archidiocesan Office of Social Action and World Peace in Dayton, Ohio, taught science and math in high school and college. She received a Ph.D. in physical chemistry from St. Louis University, and a Masters in theological studies from Catholic Theological Union in Chicago. One of the two original staff members of NETWORK, a religious lobby in Washington, D.C., she worked in Washington for four years. She also spent two years as a core member of a House of Prayer. Her primary responsibility in the Dayton office is working with parish peace and justice committees.

Robert F. Kelly is Associate Professor of Sociology and Chair of the Department of Sociology at Le Moyne College. Currently, he is engaged in research on the law, children, families, and public policy. His recent research has appeared in *Teaching Sociology*, *Journal of Social Services Research*, *Dickinson Law Review*, *Journal of Family Issues*, *Journal of Marriage and the Family*, *Family Relations*, and *Children and Youth Services Review*.

Ramsay Liem is Associate Professor of Psychology and current Director of Graduate Studies in Psychology at Boston College. He has long-standing interests in the relationships among social class, economic change, and mental health. He codirects the Work and Unemployment Project, a panel study of family and personal effects of involuntary job loss. He also conducts research on social stress processes. Most recently he has been reexamining the ideological and theoretical grounding of processes of social victimization and studying individual and cultural expressions of efficacy and authorship among unemployed workers. His most current publication, with T. Atkinson and J. Liem, is "The Social Costs of Unemployment: Implications for Social Support," *Journal of Health and Social Behavior*, December 1986.

Linda C. Majka is Associate Professor of Sociology at the University of Dayton. She is coauthor of a book with Theo Majka entitled *Farm Workers, Agribusiness, and the State* (Philadelphia: Temple University Press, 1982). She has also published several articles on labor movements, families, and the status of women. She received her Ph.D. from the University of California at Santa Barbara in 1978. Among her research interests are studies of the social impact of economic change. She currently teaches and writes on social inequality, women in American society, families, and social problems for sociology and women's studies.

Carolyn C. Perrucci is Professor of Sociology and Cochairperson of women's studies at Purdue University. Complementing her research on blue-collar unemployment is a longstanding research interest in professional career patterns. Recent publications concern gender equity in academia (*Sociology and Social Research*, 1986) and science-based career patterns (*Women in Scientific and Engineering Professions*, University of Michigan Press, 1984).

Paula Rayman is Research Program Director at Stone Center, Wellesley College. She is currently working on a project concerning women and unemployment and a longitudinal study of work/family life integration and stress. She is author of *The Kibbutz Community and Nation-Building* (Princeton University Press); coeditor of *Nonviolent Action and Social Change* (John Wiley); and coauthor of *Out of Work* (National Institute of Mental Health). She is currently series editor of *Labor and Social Change,* Temple University Press. She has been awarded a postdoctoral fellowship by NIMH at Children's Hospital and a Bunting Fellowship at Radcliffe College, 1985-1986.

F. Stevens Redburn is an Economist with the U.S. Office of Management and Budget. Since 1979, he has helped design and manage a series of national studies addressing current housing and community development policy problems. His most recent books are *Revitalizing the U.S. Economy* (coedited with Terry Buss and Larry Ledebur, published by Praeger) and *Responding to America's Homeless: Public Policy Alternatives* (coauthored with Terry Buss, published by Praeger). His other publications have dealt with economic development, industrial policy, housing, and a broad range of issues in urban policy and public administration. He holds a Ph.D. in political science from the University of North Carolina at Chapel Hill.

Rosemary C. Sarri is Professor of Social Work and Faculty Associate in the Center for Political Studies, Institute for Social Research, University of Michigan. Her research interests have included studies of children and youth welfare systems, deviance and criminal justice systems, women and poverty, and the effects of social policy and social administration on the delivery of human services. She has served as adviser and consultant in social welfare and social work education at national and international levels. She is the author of more than 60 books and articles on juvenile justice, female crime, women and poverty, the management of human services, school malperformance, child welfare, and social policy. Her most recent volumes include *The Impact of Federal Policy Change on AFDC Recipients and Their Families* (1984) and *The Entrapped Woman: Catch-22 Strategies on Deviance and Control* (1987).

Dena B. Targ is Associate Professor of Family Studies in the Department of Child Development and Family Studies, Purdue University. Her research concerns the intersection of social problems and family problems. Her most recently published book is *Mental Patients and Social Networks* (Auburn House, 1982). The impact of plant closings on displaced workers and their families is the current focus of her research.

Patricia Voydanoff is Director of the Center for the Study of Family Development at the University of Dayton. Books she has authored, edited, or coedited include *The Implications of Work-Family Relationships for Productivity* (Work in America Institute), *Work and Family: Changing Roles of Men and Women* (Mayfield Publishing), *The Changing Family: Reflections on Familiaris Consortio* (Loyola University Press), and *Work and Family Life* (Sage Publications, 1987). Her research on the work and family roles of men and women and the effects of economic distress on families has been published in numerous scholarly journals.

Andrew J. Winnick earned his Ph.D. in economics (with distinction) from the University of Wisconsin and his B.A. in mathematics in economics (Phi Beta Kappa) from the University of California—Berkeley. For twelve years, he held the Chair in Political Economy at Antioch College before moving to Central State University of Ohio, an "Historically Black" college where he is currently an Associate Professor in the College of Business and Economics. He has also served on the faculties of the University of California—Santa Barbara, San Francisco State

University, and the University of Maryland's European Division. He has presented invited lectures at more than thirty universities in the United States, Belgium, Holland, and Great Britain and has published many articles on such topics as the distribution of income, a critique of Reaganomics and Supply-Side Economics, and the political economy of foreign policy. He has also served on the research staff of the President's Council of Economics and of the Federal Reserve Bank of San Francisco.

Karen Yamakawa, a Research Associate at the University of Michigan's Institute of Science and Technology, has been with the Employment Transition Program since 1982. Prior to her joining the program she had extensive contacts with practitioners in employment and training and professionals in human resource development through assisting students who pursued careers in these fields. With a Master of Science degree in vocational rehabilitation counseling and additional course work in computer science, her research interests concern the impact of job loss on individuals and the effectiveness of intervention for displaced workers. She was part of a research team that conducted a study of displaced auto workers, and she has also coauthored several of the project reports of the Employment Transition Program.

NOTES

NOTES

NOTES

NOTES

NOTES